A Life on Hold

A Life on Hold

LIVING WITH SCHIZOPHRENIA

Josie Méndez-Negrete

University of New Mexico Press | Albuquerque

© 2015 by the University of New Mexico Press
All rights reserved. Published 2015
Printed in the United States of America
20 19 18 17 16 15   1 2 3 4 5 6

Library of Congress Cataloging-in-Publication Data

Méndez-Negrete, Josie.
  A life on hold : living with schizophrenia / Josie Méndez-Negrete.
      pages cm
  Includes bibliographical references.
    ISBN 978-0-8263-4056-6 (pbk. : alk. paper) — ISBN 978-0-8263-4057-3 (electronic)
  1. Méndez-Negrete, Josie. 2. Schizophrenics—Family relationships—United States.
  3. Parents of mentally ill children—United States—Biography. I. Title.
    RC514.M436 2015
    616.89'80092—dc23
    [B]
                              2014042185

Cover illustration courtesy of the author.
Author photo courtesy of Bui Thang.
All illustrations courtesy of the author.
Designed by Lila Sanchez
Composed in Janson Text and Myriad Pro

This is a work of nonfiction. Some names have been changed throughout the text to protect the privacy of those who have been a part of my son's life.

To Felisa, my younger sister and Tito's substitute mother, who is always there for both of us. To our family and social network, I extend my immense appreciation, as you stay with us in our journey. Thanks to each one of you for your compassion and the love you share with Tito and me.

Jorge, without you I would have not survived—you made it all manageable. You personify the meaning of acceptance, compassion, and love in our lives.

Jorge Andres, now I can rest assured that in my absence you will be there for your brother. You know what it's like to be responsible for one who is your flesh and soul!

Life is Hell . . .

No one believes me
No one cares
All I hear is laughter and stares
I deal with my demons
Life is hell
All I have left is
A padded room/a jail cell
If just one person would understand
Maybe I'd live the life I know I can
I am not crazy
Believe me I'm sane
I'm mentally ill and in a lot of pain
Forgive me world
For having morals, hopes, and dreams
I'm living life wanting to scream
All I believe in is lost and shot
Oh, well!
I don't want to live
I'm already in hell.

—Robert López Jr. (Tito), 2009

Contents

Preface

After more than twenty years of living inside mental illness as the mother of a son with schizophrenia, I continue to be in awe of Tito's ability to make sense of and deal with his life. Despite the countless suicide threats, he survives one day at a time.

Presently, in addition to Felisa, there are more family members and friends involved in my son's support—Ernest, Tomás, Amá, and Mitch, among others—who continue to make themselves available to Tito when he needs them, while relying on Tía Felisa as his emotional support.

Rather than live as a ward of the state, after two efforts at living independently that could have resulted in serious harm to Tito— violence and drugs or exploitation from those in whose environment he lived—he has returned to board-and-care living. No longer legally under the supervision of the County of Santa Clara in California, he has achieved and attained his individual rights after having successfully completed a program at a semiclosed facility that transitioned him into the community.

As always, Tito longs to find work and have his own family— children, intimacy, and love. He wants to have a relationship with someone who accepts him just as he is—a man who dreams of having a so-called normal life; this and more I wish for my son as I pray to the Creator and ask all the forces of the universe to protect him. Soon enough I will return to my community of upbringing, San José, California, to be there for him—to support him in whatever way I can. I will arrive with the hope that as we age together we will create a relationship that will keep us sane, for each other's sake.

Acknowledgments

I thank family members and friends who have supported Tito and our family throughout the trajectory of his life path, including my dearest sisters Felisa and Margaret; Amá; my brother Ernest and his wife, Sue, who along with other family members stepped up to give Tito a hand when he needed it; and particularly our departed *tíos*, Gabriel and Juanita. I express my appreciation to my friends Elisa, Tom, and their daughter CiCi; Lorelei and Tim; Comadre Mitch; Rudy and Maria; Belinda and Gilbert; and the countless professionals who stepped up to assist Tito when he most needed their support.

Colleagues and students who read the manuscript in its varying stages—Lilliana, Norma, Sandra, and Crystal, as well as "eagle-eyed" Rita Urquijo Ruiz, who edited the final draft by my side—inspired me to finish the manuscript. Gloria H. Cuádraz, thank you for suggesting I send the manuscript to W. Clark Whitehorn, editor-in-chief at the University of New Mexico Press. Both of you have made my dream of publishing this book a reality.

To all who crossed our path and assisted us through our journey, gracias! To my son, Tito, I am the person I have become because you are in my life.

Introduction

Living With and Inside Mental Illness

For the past twenty-four years, my son, Robert López Jr., known as Tito, and our family and those who continue to be in our lives, have endured the emotional and psychological ups and downs of living with someone who has schizophrenia. He was not yet twenty-one years old when he experienced the onset of mental illness. In this book, I write as the mother of a son for whom I had much hope and many expectations. Written in a quilt of narratives, the book weaves in and out of the disease, describing the odyssey of living within the mental health system and inside the ravages of mental illness. While there is ample clinical, medical, and research literature about the disease, a book about the personal experiences of a Mexican American dealing with schizophrenia has yet to be written.

Much research and purging of emotional hurt has gone into writing this book, as society still continues to blame mothers for their loved ones' conditions, and mothers continue to be perceived as the source of their children's mental illness (Huey 2007). Bernard Scharts and John V. Flowers (2010) make the case for this trajectory of blame as it categorizes various mental illnesses to a particular type of mother—her characteristics being what shapes the mental disorder. Yet Huey, in his writings about schizophrenia, emphasizes the importance of family support and involvement premised on a vision of hope for recovery. From other scholars, such as Vanessa Taylor (2011), we learn that when the disease appears, it does so as an outward display of negative self-care—lack of sleep and distorted eating patterns included. Ronald Pies (1999) not only documents the financial costs to families and society but also exposes the emotional and psychological costs borne by those who must deal with these types of illnesses. They must avoid trauma and conflict in their lives because of the frailty and vulnerability with which they must contend. As a society, we should create an environment framed inside an understanding of the illness and its effects on those who have been diagnosed, as well as the roles their loved ones take on, while attempting to educate those who detach as potential support so that the few relatives who stay the course may continue to provide a hand.

Tito's story is not told as a typical linear narrative. Instead, it captures his illness through memories and recollections of the life he had before schizophrenia, which more often than not takes him back to a time when he perceived himself as free of the illness. The stories he retells or recalls allow him to remain inside his humanity. We learn about the onset of his illness and the ways in which he coped, hid, or denied what was happening to him. The multiple flights into health are also evidence in the tragedy that has become his life, and through them, the reader can glean the humor and hope Tito retains.

The epigraphs that begin each of the sections in the narrative are words of wisdom that framed my learning, understanding, and coping. Whatever emerges in Tito's life, the stories he carries provide me with the means to better understand him. And while this knowledge comforts me, the storytelling, as suggested by Frank (2002), allows me understand Tito's need to tell me about his life as he has lived it, recalled it, or imagined it, even when I have lived it with him or have been the source of the story. While the voices inside his mind attempt to trap him in the illness, the storytelling provides him an alternative to accepting the limitations of the illness. It is almost as if sharing his recollections of life before the illness frees him from its grasps. Larry Davidson (1993) argues that voices function as regulatory mechanisms, helping those who are mentally ill deal with life events that matter in their fragmented lives, as is often the case with Tito's need to celebrate his birthday regardless of where I find myself.

The cultural and environmental frame of reference provides a way of dealing with mental illness apart from how it is fragmentarily presented in the literature, and sometimes it is our children who remind us about alternative ways of understanding their issues. Our view of the world, based on our own respective trajectories, gives us the tools needed to deal with institutions of mental health that have forgotten to humanize our loved ones. Medication as social control numbs those who contend with mental illness, largely because of our social preconception that they are prone to violence. But this limits and further depletes the lives of those who are compromised by mental illness (see Roy Porter's *Madness* and Peter R. Breggin's *Your Drug May Be Your Problem* to explore this issue).

Tenacity, resilience, and creativity allow Tito to cope with his life—a strategy that also has allowed me to reject the blame and shame often associated with those who must care for the mentally ill or those who fail to support loved ones who have been diagnosed with mental illness. Writing these stories, in a way that is accessible to others who may be confronting a similar situation—and not using specialized clinical or research rhetoric—is a way to show that we are not alone, that we are all impacted by mental illness. With this book, I call for alternative, more humane venues in the treatment of the mentally ill. Rather than warehousing them or keeping them in holding tanks, where their only release from their disease is the ever-present smoke from the cigarettes we have accepted as tools to ease their anxiety, it is my hope that new alternatives for their treatment will be implemented.

It's All Around Us, We Don't See It

Historically, families of persons who have schizophrenia often were blamed for the development of the condition. . . . These notions, which never had much systematic empiric support, have been abandoned.

—Leighton Y. Huey et al., "Families and Schizophrenia"

Because my son Tito lives with schizophrenia, we—family, friends, and others invested in him—also live with it. As someone with a social worker background who is now a professor of sociology in Mexican American studies, I've learned that mental illness is all around us. It's among coworkers. It's hiding in the clear of day under freeways or in homeless shelters. We just don't allow ourselves to see it. When we suspect it in our midst, we pretend it's not there. It's less painful that way, and we can rest assured in the pretense of not seeing, because it hurts too much to witness its real impact. Since we perceive them as abnormal or dysfunctional, we make the mentally ill invisible. Most of the time, we fear them. To ease the guilt and to humanize ourselves, we give them handouts—a few coins, clothing discards, or blankets at wintertime—to make ourselves feel better.

As they try to make themselves visible, we cry for their failed aspirations. We long for what they could have been—writers, lawyers, doctors, poets. The dreams lost inside the illness. Still, they carry their brilliance with them as they walk the streets, making sense only to themselves. With their internal voices sometimes audible to others, they amble in funny gaits, and sometimes, as if dancing or trying to capture something with their flailing hands, shooing away some threat to which only they are aware, they amuse us.

Distracted inside their own world and imagination, we think of *them* as unfeeling and unloving, as if the illness had stripped them of their ability to emote and care. We fail to hear their prayers for love, their desire to be normal so they can fit in, as they fend off loneliness and isolation and contend with mockery or derision in their lives.

Tito's voice resides in the everyday of our lives. His illness is our schizophrenia.

Mindful Engagement

Family involvement often is critical to the recovery process and must be engaged actively whenever possible . . . in a redesigned model of care that is explicitly collaborative in its orientation and routinely includes evidence-based treatments that are informed by a vision of recovery.

—Leighton Y. Huey et al., "Families and Schizophrenia"

Living inside the expectation of what is to come, based on what Tito and I have survived, I make every effort to repair my fragmented self and shore up my social identities in order to carry out my duties as a professor, wife, friend, and relative all the while trying to be a mindful mother. Negotiating the persona that engenders all the aspects of what it means to be my "self," I contend with the expectations the illness imposes on me. Like Tito, I sort out my mind to stay connected to the voice that gives me strength to carry on. He contends with eight fictive communities inside his mind, trudging to find his own voice, while I pay attention to keep my own voice, exercising patience and compassion for both of us.

After all these years, it's clear that schizophrenia destroys families. It kills spirits and decimates minds. Throughout Tito's journey, his main struggle has been his fear of the impending loss of family support. When loved ones have distanced themselves from him, both of us have refrained from judging their absence. Sharing in his disappointment, I try not to dwell on their abandonment. Only they know why they stay away.

Still, despite all that mental illness encompasses, I have never been more certain that the disease does not deplete our loved ones of their ability to feel and love. As Tito's mother, the most painful experience is to hear him speak about feeling alone and isolated, "left to rot like old discards or as a throwaway," as he often charges when he feels abandoned.

As trite as it may sound, I would gladly take my son's place, if only to give him the respite he desperately needs. My heart aches as I hear him talk, but all I'm able to do is listen—and not always as patiently as I should. I'm powerless to make others heed his need to make him part of their lives; their presence in it has to take place of their own volition.

Tito still lives inside the illusion that there is a cure. Even in the bleakest moments of his life, when he is thinking about ending it all, Tito longs to live. He wants his own family, although a family comes with responsibilities he is not certain he could carry out.

A Rat and a Motel

Looking for Love

During the last century, quite a few "renowned" experts concluded that mothers were to blame for a host of childhood emotional disorders: autism was allegedly caused by detached "refrigerator mothers," asthma by smothering mothers, and schizophrenia by mothers sending "double-bind" messages.

—Bernard Scharts and John V. Flowers, *How to Fail as a Therapist*

As the mother of a son who has lived with schizophrenia for over twenty years, people assume that I have all the answers. This is not the case.

Every time Tito has a break, the disease takes on unpredictable and complex qualities. He has resided in thirty-something institutions; he's lived in so many places, I've lost track. Most recently, with the cutbacks in mental health services, Tito has had to do it on his own, with less support from those who run the board-and-care facility in which he resides. There, they use a "tough love" approach: the male owner and operator of the facility plays good cop with the residents, who must also contend with a tough female caretaker who is the bad cop and sets limits for them.

Despite their support and willingness to make services available, they are unable to make this process an easy one for Tito. The conservator, the room-and-board operators, and a select group of family members, including me, are working together to guide him, but not without difficulties along the way. For example, in the past two years Tito has had several breaks. The most recent one he called an emotional break; he didn't see it as a mental break because it was an obsessive infatuation with a forty-one-year-old woman. He fell in love. This time with someone who was only two years older than he was and could still reproduce, rather than with a woman beyond childbearing years, as in the past.

He met her in a nearby open residential facility for women. Christy Heller soon controlled his everyday life. Given his desire for a family, it wasn't surprising to see him jump into yet another relationship. According to Tito, "She would tell me to jump, and I would ask, 'How high?'" She was supposed to be the one—his future wife, the fiancée he latched on to. She made it possible for Tito to have love.

Heller was a woman on General Assistance who was trying to receive Social Security benefits because of a disability. She had attached herself to Tito as a resource to meet her personal needs: he bought her cigarettes and got her bus passes so she could get herself to doctor's appointments, and he took her out to dinner as well as arranged weekend getaways for the two of them, if only to spend time in a motel watching television in a private space. "It's not the sex, it's the company," Tito often said after those weekend getaways.

Certain about her future in his life, Tito introduced Heller to various family members and then to me. She seemed nice enough, but there was something about her. She always wanted something. Whenever I visited Tito, Heller, as his fiancée, became another charge to take along on our outings. A sharp woman, she acted overly nice, gave me cards to let me know she understood my importance in Tito's life. She often complimented me as she told me about her difficulties with her only son. I didn't ask her to elaborate or tell me about it, because I didn't want to know. She was already in my life, and I had no control over it. Tito had chosen her.

A couple of months into their relationship, Tito called to tell me that Heller, whom he previously had described as a player to me, was now pregnant with his child. He was elated. He could not imagine anything better ever happening in his life. At first, I made a strong effort not to point out the negative consequences of a pregnancy and their ability to tend to a child. I thought about it but kept it to myself. Tito emphasized the pregnancy, happy over the possibility of fatherhood. All he could talk about was Heller's condition.

I was baffled. In prior conversations, Tito had made it clear that he did not intend to bring children into the world because of his illness. Now, he wanted nothing more than to have that child. The way he saw it, he would finally get his own family with Christy Heller, the woman he said he loved "most in the entire world." Tito had taken the bait. He had fallen for the trap. When I was around my son and his fiancée, I didn't see love. From Heller, dependence on and tolerance for Tito was all I witnessed—and this was not love.

"Momma, Christy is pregnant with my baby," Tito repeated once again, careful not to give me too much of a pause in which to speak, out of apprehension for my response. Chirping, he queried, "Aren't you happy for me?"

"Son," I replied, "how can I be happy? This is not right. You're not even well enough to take care of yourself. How can you take care of a child?" I didn't want to put a damper on his happiness, but I couldn't help but respond. Thinking that I had to be myself—he knows me for my honesty—I uttered how I felt without sugarcoating it.

Horrified by the hardships I imagined for them, I felt devastated, but I didn't want my son to have children. Almost at the point of suggesting an abortion, I withheld additional comments about Tito's right to reproduce. Taking time to calm down, I repressed those thoughts and asserted my point, not allowing Tito to interrupt—something he is prone to do when excited. Thus I heard myself explaining what I perceived to be the physical complications associated with her pregnancy.

"I'm sad," I said. "This is not something to celebrate. Your 'girl,' as you call her, has a bad back. She'll have a hard time carrying the baby to term. I'm concerned about her safety."

Tito didn't listen to a thing I said. He just went on about his joy. "I'm happy. Why can't you be happy for me? You always spoil things, especially when it's not your way."

For the next three weeks, Tito called incessantly, and I turned off the ringer on the telephone to give myself some respite. As was the pattern, I soon gave in and called back. He tried to convince me that

Heller's pregnancy was a good thing. "We can take care of each other," he said.

Tito spoke as if the impending offspring was the magic pill that would fix all their problems. The telephone calls continued, and every time he called, Tito made the case for his love for children, arguing that he would do right by the child. As if to bolster his argument, he reminded me that "Christy, all on her own, raised her twenty-year-old son who now lives in South Carolina. We can do it together." It was not easy to be impressed, given the information Heller had shared with me about her relationship with her son; she had not seen or talked to him for five years.

Suffice it to say, the pregnancy turned out to be false. Heller may not have been expecting or may have experienced a miscarriage; only she knows. The aftermath of the incident brought forth another separation in that rocky relationship, which had already endured six splits. Regardless, the combination of mental illness and children did not make sense to me. Tito had enough difficulties to deal with in his life.

Friends and relatives were concerned about Tito. Some brought up the idea of sterilization. "Give him a vasectomy," some argued. Others suggested Heller get a hysterectomy. In either situation, it was not my decision to make. "Children are born to mentally ill parents, and we have no control over that," I often retorted.

As for Tito and Christy, they broke up again. The most recent breakup came about during one of their mini-honeymoons, an outing made possible through the appearance of a rat in the bathroom at the board-and-care facility Heller occupied with female roommates. Because of that rat, Tito called every relative and friend who had helped him in the past, pleading with them to put her up for a few days until the facility operator brought it up to code. The responsibility he felt for her care was a burden he did not hesitate to impose on anyone in the family, either by asking to provide her housing or to put them up in a motel for the night.

"She's horrified of rats," he explained. "She needs to move. Help me pay for a motel for five days until the place is cleaned up."

"No, I will not pay for a motel, Tito. Son, you need to speak to the owner of the facility, so they clean up. Call licensing and report it."

Of course, the rat was just an excuse for another time-out. Without any help from family and friends, I later learned that Heller had pushed Tito to tap the conservator for personal money so they could spend time together, although the request was not made in time for them to spend the weekend. My son, who is extremely creative and knows how to use the system, asked for spending money—eight dollars—to be set aside by the board-and-care operator. He concocted the excuse of a trip to Great America, a theme park in the area, so he and Heller could get away from it all. With money in hand, they rented a motel for a night, resting on the hope that Tito could get someone in the family to pay for the next night.

Giving It All

Still Trying

Before experiencing a psychotic break, schizophrenic patients often experience a prodromal phase during which they have less severe symptoms of psychosis. These may include anxiety, restlessness, hallucinations, delusions, and a gradual loss of reality.

—Vanessa Taylor, "Schizophrenic Break"

It was a summer day—the third weekend of July 2009—and as had been the case with most of Tito's breaks, I was out of town at a professional conference, tending to multiple responsibilities when his request for another night at the motel came. He was desperate. He had tried to figure out a way to pay for the night so he and Heller could continue their weekend together, but no one had come through.

My husband, Jorge, because he understood Tito's needs to have physical, sexual, and intimate contact with his girlfriend, relented and paid for another night at the motel, even though he usually leaves such things to me. Jorge made a credit card transaction for one more night. The only condition was that Tito refrain from asking again—as if this were possible.

When early Monday morning came, we learned that Tito had returned to the room-and-board facility to get his medication. After that, he went to see Bob Miller to ask for more money, which Miller was unable to provide. What I later learned was that Heller had also gone with Tito, ready to make an inquest about what Miller had done with Tito's fund allocations, while also making a case for having the capacity to take care of Tito and his money. Miller did not fall for the scam. Instead, he asked Heller to leave the meeting, telling her this was a private matter between Tito and him.

Tito had no choice but to return to the board-and-care facility. This move resulted in the final breakup. It was then he told me about Heller's designs: "She was pissed, Momma. She left without even looking back and we haven't talked since—five days ago. We broke up. This is for good. I mean it. She was just using me. Dave [the program operator of the facility that housed Tito] made me see it."

Life is not easy for Tito. He is alone again and about to come undone. As he tries to gain his independence, with the help of Dave, the board-and-care operator, and Miller, the conservator who cares, my family and friends support him, helping him to learn to rely on himself as he abstains from enacting his boy-who-cried-wolf screams for help every time he confuses a want with a need. For Tito, all his wants are needs. He's yet to learn the difference.

I talked to Tito the other day. He sounded good. More to himself that to me, he said, "I don't need a woman to make me happy. I only need myself. That's what I'm gonna work on, Momma. I'll make you proud." I can't imagine things changing, only getting worse.

Most recently, Tito has been worried about budget cuts and the effect these will have on him and those who reside at his board-and-care facility. As conditions in the mental health system worsen, instead of a social worker, Tito will have to make do with social support groups. He just needs a place to find his own voice to talk about what consumes him when delusions, hallucinations, paranoia, and depression take control of his life.

As for me, I have resolved to remain healthy and to tend to myself so that I can be there for Tito when he calls, so that I am clearheaded enough to listen with an open heart and to help him when he needs it. With the recognition that the disease he deals with is slippery and complex, my aim is to act confidently and respond firmly to each request Tito makes. It's not always easy; I give in more than I refuse. For now, with the beginning of every new day, I rest assured in the confidence that Tito has a conscience and the commitment to not hurt himself or others. Praying that he does not come to harm, I keep him in my thoughts every minute of my life.

Tito's journey is never ending. When the medicine no longer works, he has setbacks that invariably involve readmission to a hospital. There, in addition to examining his physical condition, psychiatrists and mental health professionals go about adjusting the medication. Their aim is to make possible Tito's return to the community and his one-day-at-a-time life. For the rest of his life, they will continue to dispense thirty or more pills a day to treat his psychosis and the medical side effects.

Pills are not the magic solution. They do not always abate the effects of mental illness. Recently, Tito described the physical side effects of his medication as a burning or stabbing sensation, as though fire ants had taken up residency in his body and were crawling inside him, making it difficult for him to walk and freezing his muscles. He is tired most of the time and often tells me that he is not going to live beyond forty. Other times, he threatens that if he does not die from the physical turmoil of the disease, he will "end it all." Those are the times when an "I can't take it anymore" slips out of his lips, even as he continues to talk about his hopes for a future.

Voices and Lessons

Schizophrenia Shows Up Unexpectedly

Schizophrenia is a mental disorder characterized by gross distortion of reality, language disturbances, fragmentation of thought and other troubling symptoms. The cost of caring for schizophrenic patients comes to more than $17 billion per year in this country—but this figure can never capture the emotional cost borne by patients and their families.

—Ronald Pies, "How Families Can Cope with Schizophrenia"

As a social worker, I never had to deal with a schizophrenic person who was depressed. The most troubled patient I saw in my practice was an adolescent girl experiencing a brief psychotic episode due to the conflicts she confronted in school and her demanding parents. This experience did not even prepare me to imagine how to deal with the illness that would overcome Tito.

Despite professional knowledge, when it came to Tito I found myself relying on the wisdom and advice I received from a mental health professor. It was easy to help others based on the book knowledge I had amassed, along with the intuitive tools I picked up as a survivor of abuse. The problems we dealt with in that context, because they were not mine, appeared to be so simple.

"Start where they're at," the professor told me. "Let them tell you their story. No one listens to them anyway; be the first one who does." These were easy words to go by when dealing with problems confronted by other parents and their families. Her words also reassured me that Tito, a short young man who has been known to say that he is "almost five feet and five inches tall" when asked about his height, would not be scary or dangerous. Some have described Tito as cute, like a furry teddy bear with "a full beard that covers the face he wants to hide from the world." The professor's words gave comfort, and I rested on my knowledge of the person Tito was before the illness to feel safe when he was not well.

With only academic knowledge to guide me, I learned to rely on a self-help philosophy that I've used with addicts—one day at a time—to help Tito through the day. Given that I expect him to be anxious and unable to concentrate, attributes assigned to individuals with schizophrenia, I tried to keep from focusing on his behavior and the consequences of it. Instead, I focused on one issue or problem at a time, with the expectation that that approach would work. According to one of my professors, "It's best to let the person drive the interactions."

When Tito visited my commuter home near downtown San José, I could tell he felt uncomfortable outside his environment. He paced, approached me, and let out a gargantuan sigh. Then he greeted me, almost as if I were not his mother, telling me he was glad to be around me.

Despite his wrinkled clothes and gangster appearance—dressed in black and red, with baggy pants that hang to the middle of his backside, exposing a bit of his boxer shorts, and a long-sleeved shirt buttoned up to the top—Tito is more than cute; I would call him handsome. Yes, he is short of stature, but he is very well proportioned—broad shoulders and strong features—with an American Indian nose I connect to his Apache ancestry. His eyes are large, with long eyelashes, and he sports a short military-style haircut.

"Buenos días, m'ijo," I said, silently committing myself to make every effort to understand him. Then we tried to engage in conversation. But he was not ready to talk. Although he has been known to talk about everything and nothing, he remained silent, not even responding to my "Good morning, son." He gleaned my insecurities.

His silence framed our interaction, as I was at a loss for what to say beyond the salutation. I waited for him to start, and he finally began to talk about "the end of life as [he] knew it"—the time before he was struck by mental illness. Without prodding, and in an attempt to show me that he is more self-aware than some sane individuals around us, he told me about the issues he contends with. He impressed me with the knowledge he had amassed about schizophrenia. I had to admit that his insight was uncanny and unexpected. This day, he didn't fit or display the classic symptoms in the books I've read. He wasn't delusional. He was unencumbered by the paranoia associated with the disease, and he wasn't experiencing hallucinations. He was in the here and now, trying to explain the illness with which he struggles.

As if reading my mind, Tito dispelled stereotypes I had been carrying about those with schizophrenia, and I made every effort to hear him. I thought without speaking my thoughts. Tito still didn't say much. He tested me. Kept me guessing about the way the illness affects him as he spoke about various individuals he has lived with and the stage of their disease, almost as if to prepare me for what's to come.

"Do you think you'll end up like Bill?" Tito asked no one in particular after describing the gait and movement associated with the long-term use of medication.

Thinking it was a rhetorical question, I waited for him to continue without pressing him. As I was about to give up on having a conversation, Tito began speaking in a fairy-tale way that I've learned to appreciate and from which I have gleaned kernels of his truth. He likes to tell stories. Talking appears to keep schizophrenia at bay, protecting him, detaching him from the illness that limits him, when each crisis—a psychotic break—becomes one of *those times* for him. Every break is both an end and a beginning, for both of us. For him, it is another time when he has to stitch his life back together, to make sense of the times before. It's heartbreaking for all of us. Tito has had so many relapses we've lost track.

Deep in thought, I didn't even notice that Tito had begun to talk again. So I pulled myself together to listen to my son.

"It's hard for me to explain, Momma," he said. "But I can still picture myself circling around my family members in our home on the West Side of Santa Cruz, California, acting like a vulture awaiting its kill. Just like a predatory bird. Always having to call up my defenses, trying to figure out the reason for my illness. No one in the family allowed themselves to see it, even though everyone tried to figure out what was going on with me. How could they know? I was the first one. There were no recollections of anyone else being crazy, like me."

"Yeah, m'ijo," I responded. "I imagined it all as behavioral problems brought on by the difficulties of having a hard time growing up. Or just as an identity problem."

A disjointed chuckle came out of him. "As if I were trying to find myself in those around me. No one could understand my rebellion. My depression. My disappointment. My anger. My confusion. My pain. How could you? Shit, how could they? I didn't even know if I was coming or going. It must've been confusing for everyone. I was never a problem kid, never a druggie or a gangbanger, and not even a spoiled brat. I couldn't make sense of my behavior, my changes. No one had a clue. Nada! Zip! Zero! And *pa' acabarla de chingar*, I was the most lost in myself. I don't think any of you believed what you were seeing. Can't say I even realized it. It was hard enough for me not to drown in the confusion."

I didn't expect the clarity with which Tito spoke and didn't interrupt him to try to fill in the information he gave. Expressing himself as he might have with the therapists and counselors who treated him, Tito continued, "We all lived in the denial of my situation, particularly you and Dad, Momma. ¡Pobrecitos! ¿Qué más podían hacer?"

Smoking Mirrors

Fractured Realities

Schizophrenic patients' specific vulnerability and sensitivity to stress requires an accepting and uncritical environment. Their sensitivity to understimulation leads to a need for optimal stimulation and a structured psychosocial environment. . . . Deficiencies include mainly the lack of an adequate job, and poverty. . . . The most consistently express need is for money—money can buy autonomy.

—Heinz Katschnig, "Schizophrenia and Quality of Life"

Tito lived in an eight-story building, a long, thin box located at the corner of University and Emerson in Palo Alto, California. The administrative staff occupied the L-shaped portion of the bottom floor, with the two avenues merging at the base of the L. The north side was on Emerson, and the south side housed the garage, where the residents went to smoke their ever-lit cigarettes. There were a few parking spaces for staff, and once in a while one opened up for those of us who visited our loved ones.

The reception area, decorated with ochre-colored floral wallpaper, held a giant mirror that covered the side of the wall that faced the elevators. Faux wood pots housed a couple of fake fig trees, which stood next to two forever-empty chairs. Entrance to the facility was on University Avenue, and during the day, visitors could come in freely to see their friends and family. In the evening, access to the building was granted only through a security intercom system.

One morning when I went to visit Tito, I found him in the reception area speaking to no one in particular. Consumed by the words he was uttering, he paced back and forth. Rather than let him continue, I went to him and guided him to one of those two chairs. We sat, and I made an effort to engage him. When he finally saw that it was me, he let out a cry of happiness and gave me a hug as if he were not spiraling down into psychosis. I spoke to him in Spanish because it soothed him.

"*Curanderos, hierbas, limpias,*" he responded. "Nothing worked. You didn't understand my behavior. You tried to help. Tried all you knew, even consulted with your friends in the medical profession, but nothing worked."

He must have been talking about the onset of his illness, for he continued to speak to me as if I were doing an assessment. "Didn't want to go to school," he said. "I refused to study. Broke curfew. Didn't listen. Argued for the hell of it. In a nutshell I was a hellion at fifteen. Not yet old enough to have an after-school job, tried to find one—*pero nada*. I went about looking for a job like the good worker, as you would often tease." He let out a hearty laugh as if to show we had been in collusion all along.

"Couldn't get hired—wasn't sixteen or old enough to work," he continued. "So I even failed at finding a job. Couldn't do anything right. 'Member? It was then, in desperation and after exploring a number of options, that you and Dad took the tíos'—Gabriel and Juanita's—offer for me to go live in the ranch with them." Pointing at me as if to emphasize his resentment, he said, "You sent me to a *pinche* rancho. Sent me to Mexico to set me straight. Yeah! Mexico. What a bunch a crap!"

He became more agitated, on the verge of an outbreak. "Yeah, you sent me to my grandmother's hometown of Rancho de Cosalima. The place that everyone hoped would be the magic pill. Make me grow up. Get me out of my phase. Whatever it was. Didn't do the trick, though. Six months later I came back. Slowly breaking apart in front of your very eyes, but I hid it well. Don't you think? Didn't even have a clue, did you?"

Tito stopped talking. Spent from the conversation, he slumped, sitting on the chair, exhausted. Soon I walked him to the visitor's room and encouraged him to rest. He went to his room, and I drove to see Amá—what we all called my mother, Alejandrina—in East San José.

Looking Back and Beyond

[It] was not until 2004 that sophisticated, large-scale studies addressed the still contentious issue of whether childhood trauma can cause psychosis.

—John Read et al., "Childhood Trauma, Psychosis and Schizophrenia"

As regularly as I could, I went to visit my son—went to see how he was doing. Tito was still obsessed with the Mexico story on my next visit; he could not seem to shake it. Clearly remembering where he had left off, he started talking about life with the tíos, something he had not done when he returned from Rancho de Cosalima. He had never told me the story before.

"It was late spring of 1987, when I found myself in the fertile chile-zucchini-tomato-and-radish-carpeted valley of Tabasco, Zacatecas—in Mexico—trying to make sense of the craziness," he recalled. "Still couldn't understand what was happening. Didn't comprehend the mood changes, the strange noises popping into my mind. Was it the exotic birds around us? The wild pigs that roamed the mountainside or the strange Spanish words? It didn't make sense to me that Mexico would make me become who I was. It wasn't my own country. It wasn't me. Yet it was. I couldn't even begin to imagine how this foreign trip would help me reclaim my soul. Yet being there felt like a homecoming of sorts, and it helped me deal with something I'd never had to deal with before—me, inside, everything. There I was at the ranch with agricultural work to do and the expectation to tend sheep, goats, and cows. It was something right out of Freddy Krueger. Why did you do that to me, Momma?"

Without waiting for my response, he said, "It was out of my city-boy experience. I was an urban mall rat. Had never done more than mow the lawn. And even when I did it—made *trompas*—my lips hung to the ground as I wasted time away in the sun. As much as I hated it, I would rather be watching Tattoo greeting the plane on *Fantasy Island*—hearing 'zee plane, zee plane,' the taunt used by my younger brother and cousins, who compared me to Hervé Villechaize, the actor who played Tattoo."

Tito continued the story of his time in Mexico. His stay there was an intervention that his dad, Jorge, and I thought would quell his rebellion. "What did I know about animals?" he said. "Horses were too big. They scared me even more than dogs. *Chale*, Holmes. That wasn't for me. After a while, I got wise. Decided to not even try. This got me off the hook. I got to bum around. My tíos thought I was, at best, a distraction from *el Norte*. They got a few laughs at my expense, making fun of my gringo ways. My accent gave them a laugh. They mocked me when I mixed my English and Spanish, because I didn't sound like them. So I quickly learned that getting into the tíos' hair released me from my duties. That's how I got to hang out, just eating, drinking, and horsing around. It was in Tabasco that I learned to become just another *flojo* and *sinvergüenza*, a shameless and idle young man at their expense. At least that's what they called me."

Tito helped me realize that the trip to Mexico had been hard on him. His narration, while a way to make conversation with me, was filled with resentment. I did not respond. The only cues I gave him were nonverbal signs that let him know I was listening.

"Why did you send me?" he asked. Without waiting for an answer, Tito left me in the living room to ponder his query. Because he had no desire to spend time with me, my only option was to leave.

Early the next morning, when I returned, I ran into him in the garage. As was his habit, Tito was puffing away on a cigarette. Unaware that I had come to see him, he continued his nicotine ritual, the process that calmed him and helped him deal with the anxiety produced by the countless drugs he took, as he often explained to me. When he noticed me, he rushed to greet me and walked with me toward the reception area, desperately needing to talk to someone: loneliness is something he frequently complains about.

"Momma, I'm a real screw-up," he said. "What a disappointment I must've been for my tío and tía. They wanted to help me grow up. *Pero cague el pinche palo*—I screwed up, man."

He continued with the narrative of the time in Mexico as if no time had passed. "Don't get me wrong, Momma. It's clear that you all thought the tíos could help. And in the long run they did. That trip was better than living inside the madness of Santa Cruz. At least there, I didn't have to pretend things were fine. They didn't know me from a hole in the ground, as the saying goes. I was just another *pendejo* linked to their bloodline. With them, I could have a new start. I'm sure you didn't even guess what was beginning to come down for me. Away, at their ranch, it became easier to hide from the demons that were gnawing at me. Living with them allowed me to ignore the illness that was festering."

Incessant talking filled the space, like a faucet dripping without a pause. Tito didn't give me space to ask what was going on with him. He didn't look good. His eyes had that faraway, blank look of an impending break. I had to speak to the social worker so they could schedule him to see the house psychiatrist.

Voices and Recollections

Just wanted to get me outta your hair. Didn't know what to do with me. So you sent me off to Mexico with your relatives, as if that would have taken care of the problems that were coming. Already going outta my mind. You couldn't see it if it were biting you on the nose.

—Tito

I tried to engage my son in a conversation about Mexico. The last two times I'd seen him, he had told me about that trip. Before I broached the subject again, I asked him if he wanted coffee. He said no. It was strange because he usually looked forward to drinking coffee with me. I offered to take him to Starbucks, and again he said no. Given the practice in my family of asking three times, I asked him yet again, but he asserted he did not want any coffee.

We went to his room to put away the things I had brought him. He was happy that I was able to find an icon of Guadalupe with a chain that he could now wear around his neck for protection. However, his happiness dissipated within seconds. Soon I noticed Tito frozen in thought, motionless like a still frame from a movie. He seemed to be listening to someone or something; his head tilted to the left side. He was stretching his neck as if reaching out to some faraway sound.

Because I was so sleep deprived from the early flight to San José, I let Tito be with his thoughts. Then, without warning, he spoke to no one in particular in voices that were not his own.

HOMEBOY: "Yeah, right. But that's not what your *familia* thought, *ese.*"

GRUFF CHICANO ACTIVIST: "Damn, you thought you sent me on a journey to find myself in my cultural past, that you were giving me the medicine I needed for a difficult adolescence—you know, la *cultura cura*, as you used to say about your community mental health shit. You were hoping that it would be a lesson that could improve my terrible performance in school, help me to grow up, pay attention, get a job, and be somebody."

HOMEBOY: "Backfired on you, ¿qué no?"

He spoke to me without looking in my direction. And not really interested in my commentary or in a response, Tito went on.

"It's your fault," he said, pointing in my direction as he continued talking about his recollection of Mexico. "Instead I became a *borracho*, a hanger-on with newly found irresponsible *camaradas*—those long-lost relatives on either side of your lines. Kicked it with them. Instead of eating at home with the tíos, I wasted money on food. Then, when I learned that they don't card anyone in Mexico, I drank. I drank and drank and drank. By the third week the tíos must've regretted my presence in their lives. I wasn't improving, and I was giving them more work than they had bargained for."

Tito was trapped inside his Mexico experience; it was a delusional script he was unable to leave behind. He was trying to tell me something, but I was not getting his meaning. I wondered if perhaps I wasn't the right person. Maybe Tito needed to talk to his dad, Jorge. After all, he seemed to relate better to men. On the other hand, Tito had always been able to talk to me because I make an effort to give him space so he can tell his stories without pressure or expectations. I try to be patient and listen intently. Despite these efforts, sometimes it takes more than I can give, even though I am his mother.

Specter of Himself
Life Slides Off

Family members look expectantly to the newest medication or the next treatment, hoping that this will be "the one" to bring about a cure; and they find their hopes bolstered when they see incremental improvements in their loves one's condition.

—Larry Davidson and David Stayner,
"Loss, Loneliness, and the Desire for Love"

Apparently Tito's medication was no longer working. They gave him a complete examination and the psychiatrist decided to try new drugs. When I arrived at the residential facility Casa Olga, three weeks after the last time I saw him, he greeted me with the tíos' story again. Who knows why? According to the staff at the facility, all Tito talked about were the tíos.

This time the break appeared more intense; it was beyond story-telling or recalling the past. He voiced the sounds of a story, but I didn't think these were voluntary expressions. All I could do was listen to him and try to connect with the experiences he was sharing with me. So I did, although I was limited to reading his nonverbal language and it was hard for me to make sense of it all.

"My tíos were wonderful, nurturing, and caring persons," he said. "You and Dad were hoping that because of their success with their eleven children and through their generous offering of taking me in, that they would make me well." In an almost inaudible voice, he added, "But I'm not like their sons." Then he spewed the words in my direction as if to connect me with the experiences and said, "Yeah, I know. One became a doctor. Another found success as a well-to-do businessman in California, while yet another amassed a fortune in agriculture. And I was the fucked-up relative that brought the tíos special problems."

It was as if he was living inside that time. But why? He went silent, almost catatonic, disappearing to a place where he and I could not connect. He was somewhere else. I wondered what he thinks when he goes into silence. I could not help but gaze at my son, and he caught me staring. As if knowing what I was thinking, Tito blurted out a story about Belinda, my father's half sister, whom he had wanted Tito to marry so he could bring her to the United States. Heaving a sigh of disgust because she was his grandfather's own half sister, Tito transitioned to feelings of regret for what he could have done for her, for them, for their family to have a better life. Then he offered me an assessment of what he sees in himself, though he failed to explain the different voices that emerge from him at different times.

"Damn, I was the problem relative who didn't know his *culo* from a hole in the ground," he exclaimed. "Relatives and friends thought I was eccentric if not odd, to say the least. All of them, whenever they had a chance to throw it in my face, told me I didn't realize how lucky I was. Every time they could, they all reminded me of all that had been given and spent on me, throwing in the sacrifices my relatives made to give me what they lacked growing up. The tíos were just trying to help out, I guess."

Before continuing, he said, "Yeah, I agree" to no one in particular. Then he said, "You and Dad were trying to give me an alternative to the spoils of middle-class life. But I didn't meet your expectations of enrolling in school. What a fuckup I was! Frustrating your hopes to teach me about rural life, I didn't even help the tíos on the ranch. Didn't lift a finger to give them a hand with *la pisca* or tend to the *chivos* and *vacas*—the cowballos." He uttered the last word with a hearty laugh, reminding me that it was a word we had coined long ago to refer to the cows we counted along the highways as we drove to some place or another in our beloved California.

"Momma," he continued, "one thing I did learn was how to ride a horse. Only reason was 'cause Tío was a real vaquero. He was way patient with me. Made me learn by choosing the scrawniest and smallest of his horses. What a smart dude! Don't know how, but he knew that it would take multiple times and many falls before I could ride. What cinched it was that he made me cross the arroyo that passed by his house on horseback. Usually arid with shallow pools of water here and there, it would've been no problem to cross. It was during the rainy season—the rivulet gushed with strong currents of water. Knew how to swim, so the water didn't scare me. Still, my stomach made it difficult 'cause it became easily agitated, and having seen the pigs leave their waste, along with the stories I was told about the leeches in its waters, I held on real tight. Stayed glued to the horse like *mugre y uña*—quick to nails, as you translated my attachment to my cousins. 'Member, Momma? That's the way I finally was able to ride a horse—the only lesson I learned in the rancho."

Tears flowed down my face. His recollections, the memories we shared about the environment in which I once roamed, my mother's village, moved me to the core.

"It's OK, Momma," he told me. "This was but one small success, because every one of your efforts rolled off of me. Mexico didn't take. I didn't listen. Instead, in Rancho de Cosalima, I made myself believe I was on a permanent vacation at your expense. You'd think I was made of Teflon."

Foreign Context

Schizophrenic Trip

It is important to know how restricted and limited the social lives of people with schizophrenia [are] . . . recognize the painful feelings of loss and mourning . . . listen to the voice from behind the expressionless face, appreciate the obstacles . . . and continue to believe in and bear witness to that person's integrity and potential, even when things seem the bleakest.

—Larry Davidson and David Stayner,
"Loss, Loneliness, and the Desire for Love"

On my next visit, about a month later, Tito did not seem to be improving. He had lost his sense of time. He did not remember the last time I visited and acted as though I had just been to see him. He came in talking, as if I had never left. Giving him attention, I focused on him, hugging him and rubbing his back to let him know I was listening. Again he was consumed with the Mexican narrative.

"Momma, the one good thing about that trip was the Spanish I picked up," he said with a sense of pride. "You know what? I even learned the Spanish of your mother's land. That's how I got into singing *rancheras*, Mexican folk songs. I memorized 'La Puerta Negra' by Los Tigres del Norte, who originally came from Sinaloa before they became famous in San José."

He spoke as if I didn't know what he was talking about, almost as if dismissing the history we had in common, with my upbringing in San José. Then he began singing, a melodious song that was not distorted by the influence of his medications: "Ya está cerrada con cien candados / Esta cerrada y remachada la puerta negra" (Jesus, little did I know the black door of mental illness was closing in and shutting me out of my reality). "You know, all wasn't that bad," Tito told me as he returned to the experiences he had during his visit to my mother's village. "It was in Cosalima that I got the opportunity to become a gringo troubadour. With a pretty good voice, something I got from you, the Méndez side of the family, I gained access to the party life of borrachos in the rancho where I stayed. It worked well enough to get me free drinks. And I learned other songs to entertain people, giving them a hip-hop treat in English now and then."

Tito reenacted the stories he told me. He mimicked the movements and belted out the songs. "One time, at the center of Tabasco, *los amigos y parientes* convinced me to rap and do my dance moves—another love I got from the Méndezes. So I did several raps, stooping down to a couple by Eminem, but their favorite one was the one about the police. Playacted Ice-T. With a *cha-ka-boom cha-ka-cha-ka-boom* intro, I kept the first line and added my own:

Fuck the police comin' straight from the underground
Chinga la placa todos gritamos
Porque soy café y mexicano
Porque no soy blanco me quieren matar

"When I sang those English-language songs, they thought I was good," Tito said. "They thought all things associated with the United States were the best. Without realizing it, that village was a good way of numbing and silencing the voices. But it was also there that I perfected my drinking to stop the noise. It was where I became better at covering up what I was hearing, the illness that would never end."

Through the visits I made, I began to see patterns. When Tito went inside the chaos of mental illness, he paused for a while and then displayed a faraway look, where he stayed until he came back. I think it's a form a disassociation. The only option I have is to wait him out.

"Momma, why would you think that living in the town where my grandmother was born, which was not too far from your own hometown of Tabasco, would make me well?" Tito asked. "At best, I got to know both sides of the family, Grandma and Grandpa's relatives. I know you had hoped that I would learn about hard work. That I would understand my privilege as a middle-class gringofied *pocho*. One who never really knew poverty or deprivation, someone you wished would become a bilingual-bicultural Mexican American. Can't believe you thought that Mexico would be the cure."

Tito paused before adding a forceful "No." Then he said, "Mexico wasn't the blessing you guys expected. You know what I got? I got an earful of horror stories about my norteamericano family from relatives who were quick to fill my ears with *chisme*—they loved to gossip. To them, I was just another gringo *nalga prieta*, a dark-skinned white-assed guy trying to pass for a Mexican who had to be put in his place. They made fun of me about anything and everything. Every chance they had, they reminded me I wasn't one of them."

Without a hint he would do so, and with the recollection of their taunts, Tito went inside his silence. He hesitated, with a deep look of concentration, and seemed to be trying to sort things out. He must have been hearing voices again. I waited. Then, as I had been warned by the social workers, Tito suddenly began to speak the voices he was hearing. First came the throaty words of an older homeboy.

HOMEBOY: "Pinche *tragón*, how could you not? You ate twenty small tacos a sitting every time you had a chance. No wonder you got Montezuma's revenge."

Then Tito switched to a honey-toned, feminized voice.

SYRUPY GIRL: "If it hadn't been for the tíos, you would have been dead. You almost died in dear old Mexico."

"Yeah! Yeah! Yeah!" Tito retorted, trying to soothe the thoughts in his mind. Then, as if trying to gain his composure, he said, "Momma."

"M'ijo," I responded. "Are you OK?"

He didn't say much in response and soon continued his narrative: "Thankfully, my time in Cosalima was short, although two scary things happened while I was there: I turned seventeen and I got deathly sick—an illness that emotionally devastated me. Pushed my return to

California, where I came back carrying gory stories about my family roots. Something so horrible, I suppressed it, believing it to be true. It was shocking, Momma. Getting sick must have made the tíos realize that the experiment had backfired—it was a good thing I got sick. Otherwise, I don't know what would've happened."

Tito paused a moment then continued. "As it is, I left thinking I had knifed someone in one of the many *borlotes* in which I took part, when they called me pocho and gringo. Imagined it so well, I still have nightmares. Thought I killed many. Believed I put them to rest for having made fun of me, for trying to discredit me in public. My pinche relatives tried to make me feel inferior and less than even the worst of them. Their taunting didn't help. After a while, all the imaginary killings I committed became real to me. Couldn't wait to get back home; I wanted to feel protected by familiar surroundings. 'Member, Momma, I returned to the United States, thinking I was wanted for murder in Cosalima? Who would have thought? No one thought I'd go nuts. An obedient kid who loved to read and who dreamed of becoming someone from whom much was expected. No one in the family foresaw what was coming my way. I was an ideal child who never gave anyone problems."

Tito spoke reassuringly, as if to make what I was experiencing as I listened to him more palatable. "Both of you still pursuing an education, working to get your PhDs. You and Dad had tried to give me every opportunity you lacked, tried to help me deal with a very difficult adolescence. Don't feel bad, you did what you could."

He continued to talk about the experience, telling me how it shaped him. "By this time I had learned to see myself as a big screw-up who couldn't even get to school on time and didn't study. Recognizing this, when I returned home from Mexico, I promised to do well in school. Still, no matter how much I tried, I was unsuccessful at doing normal things. For me, concentration became a problem. It was only during the highs of the disease that I was able to do school. But it was difficult to stay focused. But I achieved the impossible. My street smarts got me by. My mind. I took and passed all my high school exams. In those chaotic six weeks, I did what I wasn't able to do all four years of high school—I got my high school diploma. You were so proud of me. The rest of the time, I continued to flounder. I remember when . . ."

Another pause. Tito's voice trailed off and I waited patiently, as I had learned to do. I gave him space. Joining him in the silence, I waited. Although the pause gave me time to think about schizophrenia, deep inside I was devastated because my son had now become socialized as an institution man who was more comfortable being overlooked, over-medicated, and left alone. So I let him be, telling him that I had to go because his grandma was expecting me.

Surprisingly, and not even aware that he was doing it, Tito said, "It's been a horrible, terrible, no good, very bad day." He walked away from me without even a good-bye and returned to his routine of hanging out on the third-floor balcony to chain-smoke his anxiety away. I walked away, too, without giving him a good-bye hug, puzzled that Casa Olga did not have a smoke-free environment. The home needed stricter rules to curb cigarette use. Smoking, after all, is an addiction that surely was not helping his treatment and was damaging his physical health.

Delusions and Misperceptions

Over the last half-century, thousands of studies have looked at the Moon's effect upon the behaviours. . . . Occasionally, one of these studies will show a correlation with the fullness of the Moon. . . . More thorough follow-up studies show absolutely no correlation at all.

—Karl S. Kruszelnicki, "Can a Full Moon Affect Behaviours?"

Tito continues to struggle with the illness that overwhelms him—his so-called lunacy. Wanting to know all, I have read everything I can get my hands on. Among the papers I've studied was one by a master's student of mine who was completing a research project in which she hypothesized that the new moon stirs the psyche in all those who are mentally ill.

One day, my patience tested in all directions, I grasped for whatever was available to rationalize Tito's behavior. He seemed to be bouncing off the walls, giving evidence to support my student's notions that the moon influences those who are mentally ill, and he had called me at least twenty times. Sadly, I did not fully recognize the signs that he was heading into a mental breakdown. I had read that it is not unusual for schizophrenic patients to go inward and refuse to talk, so I did not make anything out the silences that had preceded this episode, even when they became more frequent and intense. Maybe I should have done something.

But it was not my fault. I was not there to see him fall apart. According to the nurses, Tito became a holy terror, preaching religious talk like it was the end of the world. Tito believed all of this to be real. He took seriously the responsibility for warning everyone about the impending doom they faced—Armageddon was near. He scared the residents to death. He believed he was the savior incarnate, so he was trying to do something; he was not embarrassed to take charge of warning everyone, either. Staff said that he got in people's faces and told them to repent, warning them that there was still time to change their ways.

Others heard Tito goad the residents with whom he lived, encouraging them to sin or do whatever they wished. "'Cause after all the end is near," he told them. "We're all going to hell in a hand basket." There are times he makes it so real I can almost believe that we are the pathologically impaired ones.

According to the head nurse, who seems to hold a deep resentment toward Tito, my son frightened the older women out of their skins, especially some who stayed away for days. He liked that he did not have to put up with their complaining or begging for cigarettes. He couldn't have cared less about their emotional distance; he was in his own world. Thus residents in the facility saw Tito as the devil incarnate. They believed his stories, fearing his psychoses.

Maybe it's good that I don't live with him, I thought. Good that I'm not there to witness all the difficulties he confronts. Even when I come to visit, to advocate for him, I often feel helpless. There is so much to know about his illness. All I've learned in my social work education and all I've read is so dated and not always useful. I worry about being away from my son, feel guilty about not being there to help him, but the distance gives me the respite I need to deal with him.

Inner Voices

Holding On to Myself

How does the act of storytelling work dialogically, *not so much to claim others' recognition for the self's authenticity, but rather to fashion that authenticity out of recognitions that the story provides for? How are dialogical relationships both the topic of the story, its* content, *and also the goal of telling the story, its* process?

—Arthur W. Frank, "Why Study People's Stories?"

Three weeks after my last visit, I saw Tito again. With work and all the responsibilities I carry, it's difficult to come as often as I do. This time I took an early flight, and rather than land in San José, I booked my plane to San Francisco. After renting a car and driving to Palo Alto, where my son lives, it ended up being about the same distance. He had no idea I was coming.

Luckily, I found a parking spot in the garage of his residence. As I headed in the direction of the reception area, I spied Tito coming my way. He seemed calmer, though two months had passed since he started having problems. As I hugged him, I wondered if his medications had been adequately adjusted. He was happy but still looked anxious and distracted. As if uncorking a bottle of cider, one of his favorite drinks, he began to talk, picking up the story of his life where he had left off the last time I visited. It was Mexico, again.

"As I was saying, Momma, I came back from Mexico extremely

angry. You know, you 'member, I really came back with my mind made up to change. Wanted to reenroll in school, find a job, and become a part of our family, that's what I wanted to do."

Tito was very rational, into specifics, and even self-critical, displaying a deep need to reconstruct moments of his decline. "Why didn't you tell me that I didn't make things easy for anyone, least of all myself?" he asked. "That I walked around the house as if I was confined to it? It felt like a prison, and I acted like a convict, carrying and pushing my weight around. My brother paid the price, 'cause I picked on him every chance I got. In my confusion, I fought you guys all along the way, refusing to be held accountable for my behavior. I saw myself as a young man, but I acted like a three-year-old and became angry with you when you put a stop to my games. You raised hell when I smuggled that girl into the bedroom I shared with my brother, Corky. That, along with countless broken curfews, fights with you and Dad, and other conflicts, drove me out onto the streets. Thought I was all *chingón*—badass. So I went to live in Beach Flats, a seedy area of Santa Cruz, with two friends—a pregnant sixteen-year-old girl close to giving birth and her boyfriend, Bruce—where all the wannabe druggies hung out. Together, we moved into a small attic."

A gruff *pachuco* voice emerged from my son's lips: "¿Qué pendejo, no? What an innocent child." It was an unrehearsed pause that allowed him to gather his thoughts.

"But I didn't keep my independence that long," he continued. "Couldn't make it on my own. Don't have to tell you, you were the one who had to back me up when I needed food or money. Good thing my friend Bruce went to look for you, Momma. Told you how immature I was and that I couldn't make it on my own. They all knew I survived on the food you guys bought for me. That I kept clean by washing my clothes at your house. That wasn't the worst of all. Bruce confirmed your suspicions about my use of drugs. Told you he really was concerned about me. 'Rob is a little kid. He needs your help but doesn't know how to ask you for it. Go pick him up. I think he's really getting into dope.' I later learned that those were the exact words he used to get you to bring me home."

I nodded, listening.

"You took his advice. Picked me up the very same day. Got there before Bruce returned, appearing at the door of that shack that stood behind a large dilapidated house filled with a bunch of immature morons like me who also thought they could make it on their own in the Flats. You knocked. No one responded. You persisted. You stayed there until Bruce arrived. He let you in, pretending not to know why you were there, Momma. 'He's in his room. Go up the stairs and take a left,' I heard him tell you."

While I carry our shared experience, hearing Tito retell his recollections took me right back to that time and place. I could almost conjure the reek of cat urine in that blighted house. He seemed to connect to my thoughts.

"Worried about the sty we lived in, I prayed you wouldn't notice the house. It was filthy. Cat droppings all over the place, clothes strewn on the floor, and a kitchen sink filled with dishes that left little room for anything else. It stunk like rancid food and the curdled smell of vomit. You held it together; didn't say a thing. You didn't climb the stairs to my room. Instead you called for me to come down. When I heard you, I thought I was dreaming. So I turned around and tried to go back to sleep. Again, you persisted, calling me by my family name, 'Tito,' instead of Rob."

He repeated what I had told him: "'Tito. Get up! I've come to take you home. You have no choice about it. You're coming home with me. Right now, Tito. If you don't come down, I'll go up. I'm getting you out of here. Get up, Tito!' To save face with my friends, I pretended to be offended by your efforts. Groaning and babbling and still half-asleep, I finally came down. 'What are you doing here? Shit, just a minute. Let me get up.'"

Tito took a breath before continuing. "You were very patient," he said. "Don't know how you could stand the stench of the room, and even though I was still groggy from a restless night's sleep, I picked up my dirty *chonis*, T-shirts, and pants and stuffed them in my duffle bag, adding the clean clothes that were hanging in the closet without bothering to separate them. In a strange way, I was happy that you were taking me away from the *mierda*. The shit had lost its appeal. I came down like a timid and compliant little child. You couldn't tell that I was losing it. Luckily, apart from my disheveled and uncombed hair, I looked clean cut. My weight had not fluctuated greatly; I was the same size. By my appearance, there were no warning signs. I looked squeaky clean, just like you wanted to pretend I was. Right, Momma?"

I remained silent, listening.

"But you were like an angel," Tito went on. "I couldn't help but let out a sigh of relief—a way of expressing my gratitude. Didn't thank you. Instead I played the hard-to-get part, intent on feigning resentment, almost as if to guilt-trip you for forcing me back into a safe environment. What a shithead I was to you, Momma. I'm sorry. You didn't realize I was pretending, though. And if you did, you didn't let on. Always an action woman, a *lo que te truje Chencha*, you rushed me out. We didn't wait around for anyone to ask any questions or make any comments. Didn't say good-bye to Bruce or his girl, and not one single soul looked out the window. As quickly as you arrived, we left."

This was only the beginning. Our emotional teeter-totter was taking off.

"Once inside the car, we barely spoke to each other. You kept to yourself. I pretended to be upset at you for disrupting my fictitious happy life. Then you spoke. As the crisis solver that you are, you already had a plan of action. Had already hashed it over with Dad and wanted me to know about it. The two of you had agreed that I could return home, with the expectation that I would have to follow the rules. But you had a backup plan, and without taking into account how I felt about it, you and Dad had already talked to Uncle Ernest and Grandma about my staying with them in San José. I was lucky to have been born in a Mexican family. Because we help each other out. My relatives were giving me a chance to turn things around if I returned to school and graduated. All my aunts and uncles, who had a harder life than me, had graduated and most even attended college. How could I refuse? Right, Momma? You had it all planned out. You don't have to answer. Right?"

I nodded.

"Grandma's house was the outlet I needed. It was better than having to live under your rules or crashing on other people's couches. I'll give Grandma's a chance. I'll try my best. I told you what you wanted to hear. You appeared relieved, but also somewhat disappointed that I didn't choose to stay home. What better place was there for me? I could get the nurturing of Grandma and the support of Uncle Ernest. Still, deep inside I believed I would get away with less hassle at Grandma's. Once the decision was made, you didn't give me a chance to change my mind. We drove directly to Grandma's house. There, in a family meeting, Uncle Ernest and Grandma spelled out their rules. I agreed to what they asked. What choice did I have? 'So long as you're going to school, our family will help you,' Uncle Ernest told me for all to hear. In no uncertain terms, he made sure to let me know. 'You will have to go to work if you don't go to school, and I expect you to contribute your fair share toward maintenance of the household.'"

A change of environment for Tito had often appeared to be the solution.

"Away from all that distracted me in Santa Cruz, my friends at the Flats and the Boardwalk, where all the lost boys and girls end up, I made a greater effort," Tito went on. "Having been given another chance, I tried to follow their conditions. Do you 'member, Momma? It was 1989 when I went to live with Grandma, Uncle Ernest, and his girlfriend, Sue [now his wife]. I enrolled at Mount Pleasant High School in East San José. Still, even with their help, I wasn't able to keep it together. Despite having a warehousing job at a local grocery store and pretending all was well, I couldn't fool Aunt Celia, my uncle Tomás's live-in girlfriend. She was the first person I told about the voices and the smells that weren't there. Knowing what I knew about her, I thought she would understand. But she thought I was into drugs and dismissed it as hallucinations."

How sad, I thought. Tito must have been too scared to tell anyone else.

"I remember exactly how I told her. Aunt Celia would later tell Tomás that I could talk with birds and that they talked back. Apparently, I claimed to understand their language, when I let it slip that the birds and I communicated. I thought she could hear them, too. She didn't say a thing. Didn't tell anyone at first, either. She kept my secret. Didn't want me to get in trouble with my relatives. In her own way she was just trying to help."

With barely a pause, not even creating space for me to comment,

Tito spoke as if he needed to commit his stories to memory. When he stopped talking, he got up to leave and hugged me. He told me he had to go to sleep and I could leave now. He had visited with me and he was done. Not yet ready to leave, I gave him a hug and went to stay at Amá's. She was expecting me.

There were times that the only life I saw in Tito was in his stories. His imagination was boundless. Were it not for his concerted effort to keep it together, Tito almost could have faded into the depths of his fantastic worlds.

I came back to visit my son on Saturday and found him enveloped in the unpleasant smell of a 1930s couch that reeked of moths, chloroform, and almonds and that, according to the social worker, had been gifted by a rich donor in Palo Alto. Tito had finally found a home at Casa Olga. Unaffected by the sharp stench, Tito often used that sofa as his womb, a place where he went inside his mind to forget or to get lost in the chaos. Inside his recollections, he laughed out loud or shed buckets of tears. The mixture of his emotions might have frightened those who did not know him.

According to the social worker, Tito said he went there to escape. She told me, "It was a place that could be both eerily wonderful and terrifying, for him." As sad as it sounds, it was inside those moments that he relished reliving his life stories. He reeled them over and over inside his mind, traveling through time, reliving his life in an instant replay.

Those snippets of time made Tito feel alive. His stories were abundant. He thrived on his favorites; they gave him peace. Remembering allowed him the comfort of being close to me, his mother.

Unintended Disclosures

Voices Speak

Viewing delusions as stories that people with schizophrenia tell about their lives further suggests that delusions may play a role in the course of the disorder as "regulatory mechanisms" that help people modulate the amount of change to which they will have to adapt in the context of significant life events.

—Larry Davidson, "Story Telling and Schizophrenia"

I enjoyed hearing my son's stories; they gave me insight into the young man who lives among the discarded human beings of mental illness. He taught me what I have to do as his mother. Even though Tito was able to speak about his troubles, he still held too many things inside. Somehow, schizophrenia did not distort the memories he relied on to return to the past. It was a way to keep his integrity, which was probably why he uttered them to anyone who would listen, even when it was difficult to rouse their interest. After all, what would a disheveled, mentally ill Mexican have to offer anyone?

But I wanted to know what was going on with my son. I needed to understand all that I could about the illness that consumed him. As his mother, I was his captive audience. It was my job to listen. His stories took me out of my own reality and expanded my understanding about what happens with him when he is not faring well. Patiently, I sat with him and waited for him to talk, wondering what was going on as I mindfully listened to him. Then an argumentative and hostile voice lurched out. Tito wasn't making an effort to hide or restrain the voices that were coming out of him. I sat and listened to his inner dialogue.

SYRUPY GIRL: "Stories? Yeah. We have plenty of those inside."

HOMEBOY: "But we're not talking about that right now, ese. It's bad enough that I have to keep up with his *cabeza loca*—crazy head."

My poor Tito, he didn't look good. His eyes were getting glassy, and he was looking at me as if he were seeing through me. He intently listened to something, as though trying to sort out who was talking to him. The voices emerged. I sat and waited for it to pass, holding him by the shoulder to reassure him that I was here and would not leave. I heard a wispy, high-pitched, and childlike voice.

SYRUPY GIRL: "I still remember those days when Tito went around kicking and blocking everything and anyone in his path, sounding like a clicking lobster about to snap. With its open claws, trying to pinch or smack everything and anything that stood in his way. Kids in the neighborhood called him the Karate . . . *chavo*."

Then a know-it-all and judgmental adult voice interrupted.

ANGRY MAN: "Was that just plain anger that fed you? A walking volcano is how I saw you."

Advocating for Tito's right to express himself, a young adolescent voice pleaded on his behalf.

ADORING FEMALE: "Come on. You know Tito loved Karate."

Then the voices stopped. Tito went inward, displaying a sense of hyper-concentration, and while he simulated martial-art moves, the words continued to slide from his lips as if his memories had to be unraveled. To no one in particular, he continued talking about being five years old. As if I was not there, he uttered what the voices told him about himself.

SYRUPY GIRL: "He looked like a living Japanese cartoon character with deep-set, wide eyes and a modified Beatles haircut."

ADORING FEMALE: "Bubbly and talkative, he seldom lacked attention."

ANGRY MAN: "He was a motormouth. Never stopped to listen."

ADORING FEMALE: "He was the cutest kid you would ever

want to see, and what was worse is that he knew it and used it to the limit."

ANGRY MAN: "Tried every ploy he could to get attention. He didn't impress me."

ADORING FEMALE: "Yeah. He was a brilliant little boy who until the age of five lived with a single mother."

Clearly, each voice spoke what he heard inside his mind. However, I did not stop to ask Tito to explain. Even though my patience was wearing thin, I was sitting on my hands to stay with it as I continued to listen. The soothing voice of the adoring female emerged again, describing Tito's creative brilliance.

ADORING FEMALE: "Barely three and a half, yet he was a fun, creative, and smart kid who could already read. By the age of four, he could read a book upside down—a device he used to impress us."

Despite the chaos and confusion, Tito realized I was there. Then, as if pointing to an imaginary book, he said in an excited childlike tone, "Look! Look! I can read this book upside down. Come see! Look at me. Momma, that's when everything began to change, and I still can't believe that you didn't have a clue. You were a social worker, for God's sake. Where were you when all this was happening? Too busy with school, I guess."

As if reading my mind, a voice within Tito came out to comfort me.

ADORING FEMALE: "He had no clue. He didn't understand it. He was barely in kindergarten."

The syllables in his words stretched like saltwater taffy, and yet another voice appeared to remind me about his fantastic fears.

DRUGGIE: "Yeah. It was like being inside an acid trip in an overactive mind. Flying saucers and aliens were out there ready to suck him into spaceships. He was forever figuring out ways to survive UFO attacks, just in case aliens from outer space kidnapped him."

The voices stopped. So much was coming out. Sounds and words blurred together, making it difficult to keep up, but I made every effort. He drew my attention in the voice of an announcer broadcasting a mid-century baseball game.

SPORTS ANNOUNCER: "Drawn and repulsed by fear all at the same time, he watched frightening things. Even when they agitated him to the point of sleepless nights, Tito would continue to watch as if these programs were the answer. He was afraid of everyday things and most things around him, he would complain. It was too dark in his room. There were monsters inside the closet or underneath his bed. He hated all sounds out of the ordinary; they became something to be wary about. He slept with the lights on. Comforted him to know the lights were on. Still, it didn't keep the fears at bay. Dogs were after him. He saw them everywhere and they were all out to get him. He could not walk to school, even though it was short distance from his family day care. It took him forever to feel comfortable."

Then the scratchy, timid voice of an elderly woman popped out to assert his recollections as if to validate the memories.

ELDERLY FEMALE: "Yeah. I remember about the dogs. Countless times, his momma left work to pick him up."

All of a sudden, Tito called out to me as if I wasn't even there. The tone of his voice concerned me, but I reassured him that everything was fine, telling him, "M'ijo, I am here. It's Momma. I'll stay for a while."

Hinting that he was aware of my presence, he continued. He talked to me as the five-year-old son I carried in my heart, the beautiful child for whom I had wanted so much. He had such potential.

"Momma, come and pick me up," Tito said. "The black dog scared me. I don't wanna walk by myself. I'm scared. Please, please, please. Come. Pick me up. Please."

It was hard for me to witness what seemed to be a psychotic break. I stayed there, waiting patiently, if for nothing else than to give him the space to gather his thoughts. Telling him that I would not leave didn't seem to help. Soon he withdrew inside himself, but his mind was going a mile a minute. His eyes looked upward and to the left, as if retrieving some distant memory, scanning his brain with his eyes.

After a while, he lurched over a little bit, as if to hear more plainly what was being said to him. He continued to vocalize. He winced, as though someone has insulted him.

ANGRY MAN: "Jeez, what a sissy. Can you believe that crybaby?"

SYRUPY GIRL: "It was by the end of the first grade when he finally walked home from school. Took three years for him to feel safe.

Still, he was such a scaredy-cat. His parents tried to put him at ease, but nothing worked."

ADORING FEMALE: "That's right. Tito was not an easy child to figure out. He tried to please everyone around him. He desperately wanted to be liked and accepted. Who doesn't? Don't you? What a hard life he had. He was always trying to keep up appearances, while pretending all was right inside his mind."

SYRUPY GIRL: "Don't know how he did it. Still can't figure it out."

HOMEBOY: "¡Híjole! It was hard to make him listen, rejected speaking Spanish even when he knew how. Didn't like for others to think of him as Mexican—he was no wetback! Even though he enjoyed *folklórico* classes and Mexican jazz, he couldn't have cared less about Mexican culture. Those who made fun of him—friends, white people, and just old mean ones—had scared it out of him."

ADORING FEMALE: "But his momma didn't want him to be ashamed of his background. She did all she could to be there for him, to the point of incorporating him into her activism."

SYRUPY GIRL: "Yeah, I remember when he went with her to boycott Gallo wine. He really got into it."

HOMEBOY: "That's why he loves that blessed silver ring with the United Farm Workers eagle on it. He claims it reminds him of happier days when he helped his momma boycott Ray's Liquor Store near his grandmother's house in San José. He was only a first-grade *mocoso*. Got a kick out of the way the liquor store owner tried to trick him to get away from the entrance. Tito pleaded with customers not to buy the despised rooster wine of those geezers who refused to sign a contract with the union."

ADORING FEMALE: "At such a young age he was a Chavista. He really wanted to help."

HOMEBOY: "Homeboy *no se vendió* for a handful of candy. He didn't sell out for the few pieces they tossed his way to keep him from the door. The *carnalito* walked head high, with his chest out, marching back and forth, with his boycott sign proudly jetting above his round head, pleading customers not to buy Gallo wine."

ADORING FEMALE: "He turned many away. Just looking at him and his bighearted commitment was enough to send the customers to another store. 'Boycott Gallo! Down with Gallo! Chavez, sí, Gallo, no!'"

HOMEBOY: "*Chavalito*, that snotty little boy, showed them he really believed in what he was doing, so many left rather than break his heart. They couldn't ignore the passion he showed in support of the farmworkers."

Without warning, Tito stopped staring out the window. His eyes turned dark. Realizing that he had been narrating the voices inside his mind, he slowly turned my way and told me he had been remembering the things he did with us—his family—when he was a young boy. Prodding, and using the dialogue I'd just heard, I tried to have him elaborate and explain what all of that meant. But he said, "It's no use. I feel better already." He walked away from me, then turned around to tell me, "It's good to have you here. You give me a safe place where I can return to myself." All I could think was that I did not fear him, as would be the expectation.

Through Tito, stereotypes about people like him are eroding, such as the notion of their inability to feel or that they are detached from their emotions. He is connected to his emotions; he is unusually nonstereotypical. A very thoughtful and caring young man, he has allowed me to view mentally ill people in a positive light. Tito has taught me much about mental illness. There are those whose families remain connected to them. Then there are others whose families support them in material ways. Still others support and include them in their lives, although tightly bound to limits set by relatives.

Mentally ill people love and want others around them—they're not disconnected from themselves, they're just preoccupied or busy with the voices, fears, and hallucinations that have become part of their lives. From Tito, I'm learning about what he experiences, and I imagine what may be going on with others who are mentally ill.

Homeboy Remembers

No One's to Blame

Understanding that no one in the family is to blame for causing schizophrenia was the most helpful coping strategy of all. . . . The right attitude evolves [with the] resolution of the twin monsters of schizophrenia—blame and shame.

—Rose Marie Friedrich, Sonya Lively, and Linda M. Rubenstein, "Siblings' Coping Strategies and Mental Health Services"

Extremely upset, Tito wanted to talk about the lack of support from family members, claiming to be angry with each one of them. Feeling desperately alone and making an effort to unload it all, he said, "No one gives a damn." Dealing with fear and the delusions of his fragile state, it was emotionally difficult for him to sort out what was going on, but Tito was definitely connected to his emotions. On this occasion he was particularly upset that he doesn't hear from his brother as often as he would like to.

Ever the helping person because of my training, and refusing to get hooked on the blame game regarding his brother, I helped Tito focus. "Geez, m'ijo, there's a lot going on with you," I told him while asking him to concentrate only on one issue. If I don't use this approach, his anxiety escalates. "Find the six shades of yellow in the room," I said—a strategy I'd learned from one of the therapists with whom Tito worked to help him deal with tension and anxiety.

Tito mocked me for making it hard because the visiting room in which we found ourselves had been painted butter yellow. Nonetheless, he proceeded to accurately identify six yellow shades of color in the decorations of the room and in our clothes, pointing out that he hadn't counted the four walls of the room—that would have been the obvious choice. Though Tito was agitated and anxious, he was becoming more focused. So we tried again.

This time, I asked him to find six expressions of red in the room, a task he achieved quickly. He became more attentive and decided to talk about what was uppermost in his mind. It was as if he had been rehearsing it all along. Then he took a detour and I let him go on about how much we are alike. Soon, and with an "Anyway, as I was saying," he went on about my courtship with his biological father.

"Did they really think you were a loose woman?" he asked. "Did Tía Vicki really tell everyone that you carried a mattress on your back? Why would she say you trapped my father, Beto, into marriage like that?"

As if waiting for me to answer his questions, Tito paused. He went inside himself. He tittered to himself, listening to a private joke, then slapped his left knee as if to key in his thoughts. For some reason Tito wanted to tell me my story in my own words.

"There we were," he said, "two people with nothing else to do, with no future to speak of, who met each other and found the companionship we lacked in our own large families. The fear of being alone, of me staying an old maid, brought us together."

Tito continued to talk, and I just listened, thinking that reciting the events might help him reclaim that part of himself. Still, he talked to me as if I were a stranger instead of his own mother. Without changing his tone or mimicking me, he switched to his own voice to continue the story.

"Truth is, Momma didn't have me until they had been married almost three years. Had I been born a pachyderm—that's an elephant and that's how long they carry their young—the López family would have been right. Then the gossip mongering of Beto's sister, Tía Vicki, would've been true and it would've been Dumbo, instead of me, who was born to my parents."

I couldn't help but chortle at that comment, and he too laughed at his joke. Tito continued his story by dispelling whatever myths the family had spewed about me—his mother.

"Went to Reno, Nevada, and eloped. Ran away to get married—even though it wasn't the shotgun marriage they all imagined. Momma was barely nineteen. My father was about eight months younger than her. Probably felt safer being with a younger man. Must've thought he wouldn't hurt her the way her own father did. But there are different ways to hurt others, don't you think?"

Without leaving space for me to respond, he continued the story. "Theirs wasn't a very formal wedding. She said she wore a royal-blue wool suit. It was perfect for the frigid weather of that December day in Carson County, Nevada. That's where the courthouse was, not in Reno. Known as a peacock, Beto donned a gray suit paired with a white shirt with ruffles on it that were lined with blue embroidery—the color of Momma's suit. Just like those he wore to the prom or the *quinceañearas* they used to hit on weekends. Their marriage didn't last that long, though. They broke up. Talk goes that her own mother thought they were shacking up. When the divorce became final and Grandma read it in the paper, she realized that they had been married all along. Tell you more about that later, OK?"

Looking straight at me, Tito said, "You married for the wrong reasons. He wanted a virgin. And you wanted to marry before the train passed you by—before you got too old. You liked that Beto was handsome and that he had defended your honor."

As if guarding a secret, he added a quick "You'll see what I mean" before continuing the story. "He was the first one to stand up for you, Momma. No one had ever done that before. Made you beholden to him. Best of all, he seemed to like you. The way others saw it, he respected you above all else."

He shifted again to speak to an audience that wasn't visible to me, then continued telling his story.

"Marrying for those reasons didn't help, though. Innocence, virginity, and ignorance didn't create the necessary bond in that marriage, much like the sandy flakes of fool's gold Momma had collected at the river's edge of Tabasco, Zacatecas, where she was raised, were not real gold. They tried to make their marriage work by moving to Gilroy,

48

California, where I was born. Wanted a home away from the distraction of their friends and the meddling of families. You told me that you really wanted your own little family so that the two of you could thrive, right? Too bad it didn't turn out to be the way you had hoped. Beto turned out to be a major womanizer, just like your father. Guess in some ways the cycle continues. Right?"

I nodded in reply.

"Sad to say, it took a life-threatening accident, when Beto almost died, for you to find out," he went on. "Slipped into that coma for a year. Momma, you had to hear it from Beto's own mouth. Her name slipped from his lips as he was coming out of it. What's worse was that the other woman's name was Hermelinda. It's ironic, isn't it? That woman carried the name of your beloved great-aunt from Mexico who raised you. Don't know much else about your marriage. But for our small family, that was the beginning of the end. Talk. Gossip. Just heard about things here and there. Don't remember . . . I was just about three and a half months old. Nobody gave me any details, but I've heard the stories from my tías, who thought Beto was really cute and good, along with those you told me." And then Tito slipped back into voices that did not sound like his.

ANGRY MAN: "Ay si, no one gave you details. As if . . ."

HOMEBOY: "Come on, don't play the pendejo game. Your mother's told you the story before. Tell it. There's nothing to hide."

Turning his head to the right, my son said, "I seriously mean it, shut up!" Then he continued talking, as if he had not stopped, as if he were speaking to an invisible presence in the room: "To me, it's not like you to tolerate a night out with the boys. But Friday nights were Beto's. So hanging out with his buddies was not an unusual thing for him to do, but he never stayed out all night. The way you've talked about it, that evening of the accident was the first time Beto didn't come home at all. You Méndez women are known for your intuition, and you told me that you had a premonition that something was wrong. Also, Beto never failed to call you if he were going to be late. This wasn't like him. You must've been worried about him."

As I listened, I wondered how Tito was feeling. It was difficult for me to discern. He continued: "It was early Saturday morning, seven o'clock, when a policeman showed up at your Rosanna Street doorstep, at the two-bedroom duplex that was but a few blocks from the police station and Wheeler Hospital. It was then that your whole world collapsed into pieces, when the policeman informed you that Beto was in the emergency room. How sad, you didn't even have anyone to leave me with. So you wrapped me in a flannel blanket, like a tamale, and you took me to the hospital with you. I was just a little baby. 'He's not expected to make it,' the cop told you. 'He most likely will die. Prepare yourself.'"

Turning to his right, Tito said, "Lucky thing, she didn't drop me when she saw Beto on that gurney. And better that I was young enough to not remember what she saw." Then he faced me to say, "Poor you. It must have been terrible. The way I've been told, Beto's head had ballooned to three times its size. It had bulged—when he was thrown from the car onto that garlic field—that chilly early winter morning. Who knows how long he had been there? Doctors even told you. It was the cold that kept him alive. He had been exposed to the elements for at least six hours. No one could see him in the dark. How could anyone report it? It was when the workers were going to their jobs that someone saw two bodies on the ground and reported the accident to the police."

That was not the way for a proud man to be found, I thought.

"When the cops finally arrived," he went on, "they found his friend Al—dead. When they checked on Beto, he still had a faint pulse, barely alive, hanging by a thread. Soaked in blood the color of chocolate, he was covered with small mounds of caked body fluids in some parts of his body. His scalp spread out like an open cabbage that has had its core taken out. His ripped scalp exposed part of his brain on the left side. His pants and shirt, partially torn like he had gotten too big for them overnight, made him look like the Incredible Hulk."

Even though I recognized this time as part of the life I had lived, Tito's narrative didn't stir any pain or hurt for me. I had dealt with this part of my life. However, Tito showed feelings of regret, or sympathy, as he continued to tell me what I now perceived to be his origin story.

"Poor Momma," he said. "It must've been so hard for you. People recalled that you held it together pretty well, though. Guess you had no choice, huh? Luckily, Uncle Rick, my other runaway uncle who wanted to distance himself from the bad influence of my biological father's family, and his wife, Lala, who lived across the street, had returned from their trip. You dropped me off at their house so they could take care of me."

Tito looked in my direction, as if to gauge what I was feeling. Seeing that I was listening without interruption so that he could tell me the story that gave him life, he proceeded with the tale, looking off to the right as if to retrieve the narrative.

"Among many of the stories of that time, you told me about riding in the ambulance with Beto. The forty-five-minute drive to Valley Medical Center in San José seemed never ending. You would later tell me that you were consumed by the flickering electric signals and beeps that filled the crevices of the ambulance. Every one of the machines hooked to his body made a noise that you didn't understand. The incessant jerking of his limbs scared you. You signaled the attendants to check the machines that kept him alive. I know you felt helpless and that you were frightened for all of us. Besides praying, what else could you do? So spent from too much thinking and too much guessing, you tried to take everything in, tried to make sense of it all. But you felt useless, anyway. With the ambulance siren wailing full blast, you finally reached your destination. Arrived at the trauma center—the Neurology and Brain Injury Unit at Valley Medical Center, which would become Beto's home for the next year."

Tito stopped talking. He became quiet, and again, silence took over the space we occupied. As I had learned to do, I waited for him. Used to my son's processes, it seemed to me that he was hearing voices. I reminded myself to tell the nurse and his doctor. I couldn't overlook it or take it for granted. The last time this had happened, my son was hospitalized. But Tito was not done. He continued speaking as if others were talking for him.

HOMEBOY: "See what I mean? *Sonso, sonso, pero no tanto*—he's not dumb at all."

SYRUPY GIRL: "He's the best storyteller ever. See why he has movies inside his head?"

HOMEBOY: "This is where Tito cut me off. He took over the story."

ADORING FEMALE: "So that's how Tito's mother found out about Beto romancing that neighbor behind her back, huh?"

HOMEBOY: "Híjole, she worked at the same garlic plant?"

ADORING FEMALE: "The one who bore the name of her beloved great-aunt?"

HOMEBOY: "Yeah. Hermelinda, the one he worked with at the Gilroy Garlic Factory."

Tito's own voice had returned, and he resumed telling me how Beto had betrayed me: "Beto and Hermelinda hooked up during the latter part of your pregnancy with me. His excuse was that he didn't want to hurt me in the womb or make you feel uncomfortable. So he went looking for it elsewhere. Can you believe that? What a sorry excuse for a man."

I didn't respond audibly, but I nodded in agreement with his statement. I couldn't help it. My son paused as if to catch the thread of the story he was telling me, nodding his head when he caught up with the strand.

"After your divorce, it was really scary to be around Beto. I still have those memories swimming inside. I know I was between two and three years old, but I remember, Momma. To me, Beto looked like he was part metal and part man, like the centaurs I later read about in school—half man and half machine instead of stallion—rolling from one place to the next in his wheelchair. He terrified me. Later, when he started walking, he had a strange gait that didn't make sense and scared me. He was a bit like a Frankenstein in slow motion, with hands reaching out as the mummy of those old black-and-white movies. He also made funny noises and was forever salivating, choking, and hacking as he rolled those big wheels with his arms."

Through the story, Tito voiced concerns he had about himself as well. He so desperately longed to be part of the norm. "He hated to be abnormal because they made fun of him, because whatever abilities he had were stripped away with the accident," he said. "Can you imagine? He aspired to become a bodybuilder like Franco Colombo, Mr. Universe, or Arnold Schwarzenegger. Instead he became a pretzel man. Beto blamed all his problems on the accident. Doctors said some muscles and nerves had failed him with the brain damage, so his fingers were permanently fixed in an arthritic pose that looked like he was about to grab a doorknob. How sad."

Tito paused, remembering. "The first memory I have of Beto was when you took me to see him in the hospital. His head was tilted to the left and he could hardly lift it to look at me. I could barely walk, but I remember. When he tried to hold me, I ran away from him and into your arms. His hacking and spitting and trying to grasp for words made him more ominous the nearer he was to me. After witnessing my terror, you didn't let me stay for those weekend visits. Ignored visitation conditions and didn't complain 'cause he could barely tend to his own needs. It was hard to be around Beto, he was so intimidating. To boot, he didn't even have any patience with me. It felt like he could barely tolerate me. Left me to his other relatives to tend to."

As if to convince himself that his father made no difference to him, Tito made it a point to remind me that his uncles, cousins, and my professional friends were around until he was almost five, when his stepfather, Jorge, whom he calls Dad, came into our life. He told me that even if there had been no men around, I was strong enough to take care of him.

Fully immersed in the awareness that I was there in front of him, Tito asked, "Was I three the last time I saw Beto?" Wrapped inside what appeared to be fear and confusion, he added, "I never had a chance to know him. So how could I miss him?" With tears in his eyes, he said, "Raised by you as a single parent, I had no need for a male figure. I just loved being your little boy. It wasn't until Jorge came into our lives that I had a male influence. Although everything was perfect when it was just the two of us—you and me. You and I, all by ourselves, we were just fine—didn't need anyone else. Jorge should've stayed with those other women who pursued him. Then I could've had you all to myself."

Then Tito told me a story I had not heard before: "My resentment and dislike for Dad was short lived, though. Time taught me to get over my self-pity, and I later learned to love him. He became a big part of me. Won me over with his love and discipline—respected me and expected me to treat him the same way. With him, I learned to have a trusting and loving relationship. He became the dad I should have always had."

After finishing the story, Tito began to get edgy. Then, without warning, he got up and left. He must have had enough.

It is always amazing to hear the stories Tito carries. He does not censor his narrative and his feelings are not blunted or repressed: he cries and laughs just like any "normal" person. His emotions are connected to the stories he tells and congruent with what he is saying or remembering. When he is angry, the emotions show on his face and in his eyes, and when he is most irate, he expands his upper torso just as those blow toads do when they are threatened with attack. Still, Tito does not frighten me.

Self-Medication

Hiding from Help

While schizophrenia is often made worse by stress, it is not caused by bad parenting, "cold" or over-involved mothers, or any other known psychological factor. . . . emotional stress—including pressure from well-meaning family members—can make the illness worse.

—Ronald Pies, "How Families Can Cope with Schizophrenia"

My son's stories are timeless and compelling. They fill his need to reclaim and remember the life he has led.

I had not seen Tito in two months because he had been stable and was dealing well with the illness and his environment. I wondered what our visit would be like and hoped that sharing his memories would make him feel good. Still, I wondered if Tito would be upset. Soon enough, I would find out.

"Nice haircut," I said when I met him. "It's short. Did the barber use a lawn mower?"

"It's not funny, Momma. It's in style," he retorted. "It's in right now. Had the house barber snip the long hair, just got tired of the rattail. It didn't go well with my look."

I was surprised by Tito's appearance. He was dressed in a semi-formal style with a coat and slacks he had purchased on clearance at Just for Men; he looked like a businessman who had slept in his suit overnight. It was great to see him "all decked out," as he called it.

I was glad he had gotten rid of his oversized Dickies, white T-shirt, and Pendleton shirts buttoned up at the neck. His appearance would help him to not be persecuted or picked on. He was making an effort to shed the gangbanging image I despised. I celebrated his attire, clapping as he entered the conference room for our visit. It was good to see him. I imagined that he had less difficulty with others because of his self-presentation.

As soon as I sat, Tito talked to me about the onset of his illness, as if I'd not been around when it happened. I didn't protest. I listened to his story.

"It's hard to really remember what went on the first few days," he said. "I thought the hallucinations were a result of the LSD—I had dropped a few hits. And the smells only I could detect, I dismissed as unimportant. Always been frightened, so I didn't pay any attention to my growing paranoia. I was stuck like gum to your hair, Momma. You had to take me everywhere, and when you went to the university, I had to know how to reach you 'cause I didn't want to stay home by myself. Didn't cut you any slack, gave you no break. I made you take me everywhere. Then and now, I still try to guilt-trip you into making me your sole reason for living. Always telling you that I only feel safe when you're around. Back in those days, you did as much work at home as possible. It was so you could be there for me—those first two years, 'member? 'Member?"

Listening intently, I nodded.

"You were preparing for the oral exams. That's when the shit hit the fan. It was then that it became too hard for you and you tried to get me help. Yet agencies that treated drug addicts, like Pathways and County Mental Health, had their rules. Each one treated a particular problem and kept people separate—locos with locos and dopers with dopers. Housing them together was potentially combustible. No one could provide us the assistance we needed. You became desperate, exhausting all the resources you knew about. There was nothing else to try, and my only option at the time was to resort to folk-healing practices."

Tito went on: "It was when you decided to take me to a curandero. He was a former Chicano troublemaker or activist, depending on who's telling the story, who was jailed in 1968 for fighting the cops at the Fiesta de las Rosas Parade, which supposedly celebrated the town's Mexican heritage. Chemo was now a healer. You drove forty miles plus to Hollister. Wanted to see if he could do something for me. I felt safe around him. Chemo didn't scare me. Somehow, he made me understand that I was living in a reality that wasn't the same for all of us. Told me to let go of the fear. Suggested I needed to do whatever you asked so you could help me. He told me, 'There's a time in a man's life when one's mother has the wisdom to help us; we have to accept that help.' Chemo did a spiritual cleansing using palm leaves. He prayed over me. You knew about this stuff. Your relatives treated you for *mal de ojo* also with an egg rub and cleansed you of evil energies with sage smoke. It was not a big deal to you."

How does his mind work? I wondered as I briefly detached from the narrative. Returning to Tito's story, I was in awe of all he remembered.

"So when Chemo began crossing me in the four directions with his healing lemongrass, he asked the Great Spirit to purge the evil from me," Tito said, continuing with the story. "Then he called my spirit back by whispering my name in my ear four times on each side. Don't know why, but after he finished, I felt calm. But his *curación* didn't take. Things got worse by the end of the day. Withdrew into myself. I began to see and hear demons, telling me to hurt myself. Remember, Momma? The demons were taking control. They were so evil and gross I could only be around my immediate family—you guys were the only ones I trusted. Even then, there were times I didn't even trust most of you."

As he took me back to those times of delusions, I could almost touch the fear Tito had felt.

"Messages inside were of doom. Told me to kill myself—wasn't worth living anyway. Having tried every option, Momma, you finally took me to Barbara Arons Pavilion, the psych ward at Valley Medical Center. You forced the mental health professionals to do a seventy-two-hour hold. They kept me for three days to evaluate me. That was my first hospitalization. If you had not known to take me there, I'd still be going from place to place—drug agencies and mental health wards—without any help."

Those days were difficult. Even though I was a professional insider,

I learned firsthand the frustrations of not getting help. Recalling this brought back the disappointment.

"But I didn't appreciate your efforts," Tito continued. "I felt like you dumped me for others to take charge. Wanted you to take care of me, as if I was your baby. Couldn't get you to understand that. With that first hospitalization, the psychiatric facility finally confirmed that I would forever have this fuckin' illness. I was diagnosed as paranoid schizophrenic. That slippage into mental illness changed the way I saw the world forever. But their diagnosis didn't prepare me to live with it. At least now we knew. But how to deal with it was another story. So I migrated to and from every board-and-care home and homeless shelter in Santa Clara County, sometimes sleeping in the streets of Santa Cruz and the New Brighton Beach woods, before I finally understood that this damned condition could not get cured with pills, that the pills could only put it in check. In the early days, I faked taking those damned drugs. That's why they couldn't control the illness. I refused them. With time, I finally understood that schizophrenia never goes away. At best, it can be silenced with pills."

You made your mind up to rely on the medication, I thought. But you would still resort to taking flights into health when you got tired of it all.

Tito went on, "Medicine would be my only source of relief—for the rest of my life. But the pills make me sick. They turn my stomach and make me dizzy. While they quiet the sounds and noises inside my mind, they're a blessing and a curse all at the same time. Make me fear the drooling, zombie-like behavior and dreaded drug shuffle that will follow with time. Don't want to end up the same way as those old men I roomed with or turn into a stupefied retard like those who live here at Casa Olga. End like a stupid *baboso* unable to make sense of my every step."

Tito looked at me intently. "You can't even begin to understand that. Despite all your education and ability to read all you could about the disease, you don't walk my path. You can live your life, while I live inside the illness, however silent. You know what? It was the horror of living inside the *loquera* and those damned delusions that finally convinced me that I could only find relief living medicated. It was better

58

than having to survive the name-calling and the dares to kill myself because I was a worthless human being—the muscle pains, slurred speech, and the accelerated tapping of my right foot became a better option to festering in the lunacy of the disease. With your help, I finally understood that schizophrenia was forever. That the only thing that could silence the madness was pills. I accepted the diagnosis and regularly took the medication I was prescribed."

Was he telling me what he thought I wanted to hear? It wouldn't have been the first time.

"Yet this wouldn't be without taking multiple flights into health, when I made those of you who took care of me and who remained in my life, along with myself, believe that the pills had cured me, that I could live a normal life again. The first time that happened was when I made myself believe I would be safer among the Norteños, or those who claim Northern California as their gang turf. I returned to the life of the streets and gangs—to live with my former in-laws and their hoodlum— to show them I was just fine. Didn't last long. No more than three days passed before I began harassing you to come and pick me up."

His fear was such that retuning to those people was no longer his option. He didn't feel safe anywhere. I particularly remember that call.

"I thought my-in laws and their lackeys were feeding me human flesh—believed they were going to kill me," Tito said. "Everything I ate tasted like human blood to me, or so I thought. Made myself believe it, even though I would not have known what it was like. Only thing close to it was the taste of blood in small cuts I licked to stop the bleeding. It's always those delusional trips that bring about many near disasters for my family and me. I'm sorry I put you through all these troubles."

Then, in an angry voice that didn't sound like him, I heard, "Don't feel good. Why you recording me?" With that, he walked away. What was going on? It was obvious to me that he was not doing well. Could the staff not see he needed their assistance? The threads of his story aligned exactly with the experiences we had lived. I needed to tell the social worker and head nurse that my son needed an evaluation.

Why is it that those who serve Tito (and people like him) minimize his condition? Why is it that providers fail to see that he is decompensating?

✝

En route to San Antonio, Texas, I wrote in my journal, recording what had transpired with Tito. I could not help but conclude that he was exhibiting relapse symptoms. For instance, as he had done in the past, without notice and looking very upset, he just up and left me when I was visiting. This time he talked to me about what happens to him when he has an active case of psychosis; some of the voices spoke. However, when he was done, as if in a performance that was timed, Tito left me there, making me wonder about his state of mind.

I could hear and see how difficult it was for him to go through the emotional turmoil. There were hints that he was nearing a break. It wasn't the first time he had jetted out when I was visiting.

When Tito is doing well, he can't tell me enough how appreciative he is that I have come to see him. But he can fall into a relapse without being aware of the extreme emotional pain he carries. Still, judging by the stories he shared with me on my last visit, his intuition and level of awareness is amazing.

I was concerned that another flight into health was coming—one of those times when Tito pretends there is nothing wrong with him and he can go about living his life as others do. He was trying too hard to create as "normal" an environment as possible for me. Even though Tito understands his condition better than most patients I have met throughout his years of treatment, he is not always aware of his jumbled reality: his hallucinations—images, sounds, and smells; his delusions— eight fictive communities that include gangbangers and demons; and his uncontrollable, extreme fears. I hoped he would not be committed to the psychiatric ward. I prayed it would not come to that.

Urban Upbringing

Running from Self

The importance of management practices in determining how involved residents are in the community supports the notion that facility staff and administrators' explicit and implicit expectations play a major role in determining the client's integration in the larger community.

—Jean M. Kruzich, "Community Integration of the
Mentally Ill in Residential Facilities"

My son was moved to an intermediate facility—another name in the string of happy names that are incongruent with the conditions of the people housed within these facilities: Golden Living Center, Heaven's Gate. For some reason, Tito wanted to talk about the agricultural fields, *los files*, and about the dreaded short hoe, *el cortito*, that gave our parents and *abuelitos* and *abuelitas* the damaged backs that forced them out of work for the rest of their lives. Maybe it was because I carted him around with me when I did support work with the United Farm Workers. "It was the only work those who came before us could do," I had once told Tito when he asked me why our ancestral work legacy was connected to agriculture. Both sides of his family had worked the fields of California and South Texas, until the Méndez family settled into urban life in San José, just as his López ancestors had done.

Tito began to tell me the story he had often requested when we were doing our time at the secondary grape and wine boycott, at those places where organizers tried to deter many from shopping. "Even though my family history is connected to fields of the Garden of the Hearts Delight, what the Santa Clara Valley was called before it became an urban space of silicone, farmwork was something we all had in common. Talking about family backgrounds and the poverty we experienced is good to talk about, don't you think, Momma?"

I nodded in agreement with my son. Keeping some thoughts to myself, I said, "It's good to talk about our history—for both of us." While Tito sat in silence across from me, sorting his thoughts, I continued to explore ways to help him.

Even though talk therapy is not the focus of treatment for people with schizophrenia, I have learned to recognize that our talks are useful to Tito. Our *pláticas* help him refocus and deal with the depression that comes with his illness. I have noticed a pattern in his narratives. Most of his stories are positive. Tito tells me that he wants to keep us, his family, as close to him as possible. But I also have noticed that a key story line, and a source of loss for him, is his lack of a relationship with his biological father, Beto López, even though any comment to that effect is often followed with a statement that his father did not matter. "How could I miss him if he was never there for me?" he said on our next visit. "If he had really cared for me he would have stayed in my life."

That was all he needed to venture into talking about Beto at length, not because he had missed having his father around but because knowing his biological father would have allowed Tito to know himself better, or so he argued. Tito regrets not knowing much about his father, and he verbalizes what he has heard along the way, as if to get me to confirm or support the knowledge he carries about Beto.

As he has been known to do, he launched into a story about him. "Beto had a very hard life to overcome early on," he began, quickly moving on to the height they have in common (they're both short men). "My biological father's stature had earned him the street name of Little Man, right? He was the seventh youngest in a line of fifteen children."

Without looking in my direction, he said, "I know, I know," as though I had commented on the two facts he had recalled about Beto. Then, repeating something I had told him when he was about fourteen, he said, "My early life was trouble free. The main thing we had in common was the absence of fathers who failed to assume responsibility for us as children."

Silently, I agreed with the thread of his narration. I continued to listen.

"While I had tried to be an ideal child, Beto had earned the reputation of not putting up with anybody's demands. Hotheaded and fiery as the jalapeños that sprout in Mexico, where our ancestors originated, both of us shared the same bloodline and temper. That's another thing he and I had in common. That's how we were."

He continued telling me the story, speaking as though I were unfamiliar with it, as though it were not part of the life I have led.

"My father, Beto, was born to doña Vera Otero, my Apache grandmother, who boldly claimed her line to the tribe. As if she were royalty, doña Vera, what she liked to be called 'cause she was too young to be a grandmother, often referred to herself as an Apache princess—ha, we know they didn't have royalty. Could have been more like the chief's daughter, but you know the tall tales they spoke. Anyway, Beto had been a product of Vera's first marriage to Abuelo Pedro López, a Mexican immigrant who worked in the fields of California. Gonzalez and its artichoke fields, Salinas and iceberg lettuce, Watsonville and strawberries—these were but a few of the places where they picked fruit or cleared land to get it ready for harvesting."

Tito commented on the narrative he was sharing with me: "Like their mother, my tíos and tías also claimed their Indian ancestry over their Mexican roots, because they long had learned that it was better to be an Indian than a Mexican in California. I learned that line from you, Momma. Some of my relatives even tried to prove it by getting recognized as American Indians by the Bureau of Indian Affairs. The way they saw it, if they were certified as the real thing, at least they got money as members of a tribe, even though they had long left the reservation to live in the city. They didn't want to be Mexican—those interlopers who thought this land was still theirs. Shit we were all a mix and none of us were pure bloods. But that's the way the story goes."

Tito took a pause, playing out in his mind the story I had lived in my own skin, then added, "Beto thought they were full of it, my uncle Lario told me." Like his biological father, Tito saw himself as the most

Chicano of them all and often mocked those who rejected their Mexican heritage. Just like Beto, my son went about sprinkling Spanish or barrio slang words into his conversations. Unlike Beto, Tito did not start a social club that would give him friends and a sense of belonging.

Not bothering to provide a transition to his story, Tito continued: "We both went to the Diez y Seis and Cinco de Mayo parades that were held at Downtown San José. He to strut his stuff and pick some fights if someone threw him those mad-dog looks. It was safer to take it out on one of your own than on the gringos or cops who came after you to teach you a few lessons. I went to enjoy the culture and music of our people."

Pointing to his Apache nose, which he claimed to have inherited from doña Vera and which was also his father's nose, Tito bragged about having his Mexican father's spirit to wander about with and noted the dislike they both had for farmwork. "See, I have their nose—of course I'm a López," he said, as if rebutting a challenge to that fact. "Momma, did you know that the López called Beto a 'roamer'?"

"No," I said. "I haven't heard that term. I recognize 'runaways' or 'pushed-out youth,' but not 'roamers.'" I was captivated by Tito's way of describing Beto's displacement as he went from one relative's home to the next, never having a permanent place to live. He slept in whatever bed or sofa was available and sometimes even on the floor.

Laughter erupted, and it brought me face to face with Tito. It wasn't clear at first what he found so funny, and he offered no explanation, but he made an uncomfortable observation. "That allergy has you all stuffed up ¿qué no?" he said. "Man, you were digging up there as if mining for gold instead of snot." Embarrassed that I had let my social graces down, I was at a loss for words, and Tito continued to laugh. Rather than add to the situation's discomfort, I waited for my son to pick up where he left off.

"You see, Momma, in the López family, there was only room for so many. My father, Beto, was known to say that what pushed him out was his refusal to be one more sibling fighting for space. El Duke," he said, recalling another nickname Beto had earned for his regal presence and his ability to seduce girls, "refused to be just another mouth to feed. So from a very early age, Beto tried to make it on his own. Didn't care to be in debt to anyone. Don't know why I'm telling you this story. You lived it with him."

By way of a pause, Tito said, "Shit, can't stop now, I have to continue." He returned to his narrative: "With the streets for a home, at the age of fifteen and no parents to care for him, because there was only so much they could give, Beto tended to his own needs in whatever way he could. Some claim he even took what wasn't his—stole! While others said that it was not beneath him to go to his sisters' or mother's to find what he could to make do—food and loose change. Talk goes that he even resorted to adult-movie trysts with the manager of the local dollar show. Later, when his mind froze at the age of fourteen after that dreaded accident, that time when he realized he was a permanent Chicano Peter Pan, he told you that he'd let Bill Brown do hand jobs at the back of the movie theater for money to get by, adding that it didn't make him a *joto*—queer. He believed that so long as he was receiving, there was no way he could be a *maricón*. The ones that did it to him were the pinche *maricas*.

"How sad, Momma. My biological father and I have another thing in common—our memories of what was. For him, it was the accident that left him locked up inside his past, except Beto only remembered the bad times and his messed-up adolescence. He was forced to live without a past or a future, and I have to remember my past so I can stay in the present and not get lost inside the madness. But in his youth and despite all he had experienced, Beto thought himself a warrior. He did what he had to do to survive. So he formed a social family—were you one of them, Momma? Did you hang with his gang, the Dukes? You never told me that part of the story, I heard about it from my tías, your sisters. Apparently, he was a great dancer. He would hold you so close to him you appeared as one. Liked to drop his right arm at your side and sway you to the slow sound of the oldies you both enjoyed. And wouldn't you know, one of his favorites was 'Duke of Earl.' If I close my eyes real tight, I can just about imagine the two of you dancing."

Tito began singing that song in a familiar way, almost as if he had lived it with us. He was on tempo and on key, and he stirred memories I carried about my life with his father. He brought Gene Chandler to life: "As I walk through this world / Nothing can stop the Duke of Earl."

65

Without waiting for a response or noticing he had stirred my emotions, Tito listed the names adopted by those lost boys who ran with Beto. He continued telling me his story, because by now he was invested in the narration as if it was all about him.

"Buzzard—so called because of his beak of a nose and because of his will to survive," he said. "He was on par with those birds that scavenge to live. He really stood out. Another one was Kat, who earned the tag when he enlisted a martial arts teacher to learn karate. That's when Danny became Kat. And Alex, whose head was slanted slightly to the left, was named Five to Twelve, because he looked like he was permanently stuck at that time on the clock. He was always there before anyone, arriving five minutes to whatever, challenging distorted notions of Chicano time. Despite their special names, they were only small-time players. Beto's chosen family were his best friend, Joe Martinez, and his girlfriend, Jasper Jimenez, even though the two brought others along with them. What they had in common was a difficult life that sometimes pushed Joe to pick fights just to feel alive. They learned that with a good fight they felt alive. Sometimes I feel like them, Momma. It's as if I have to give someone grief so I can be noticed. Why didn't you tell me about the glue sniffing?"

Tito asked the question without making a pause for me to answer, then continued telling me about the Dukes: "And then there was the glue sniffing or inhaling one or another substance to numb it all, to help them forget or just because they liked the high. Does it ever make you wonder if that's what got me the way I am? They say that substance use by one's parents may be a contributing factor. Do you know?"

Again he didn't wait for me to give him an answer, and he continued with the story, providing his own transition back to the narrative. "But this is not about me, it's about Beto," he said. "Let me go on. You knew about Manito, their friend who burned out before he was twenty-one. He sniffed airplane glue. Don't know much about how it's done—'cause I'm not even that loco to try that shit—only that they place the glue in a baggie to inhale the fumes. I was told it got so bad that Manito couldn't even remember his name. His speech had become so slurred, like me when I'm overmedicated."

He looked in my direction to give me a point of reference. "Even people who knew him couldn't understand what he said," he continued. "Got to the point that Manito could no longer keep in the waste. That's when his mother's full-time job became keeping her son out of his own filth. It's sad, huh? You know what? Her name, Angustia, translates to 'anguish'—that's probably what she felt caring for Manito. At least you don't have to take care of me that way. You know what you have to deal with, unlike that poor ol' Angustia, who didn't even understand how her son ended up that way. She never had a clue as to his drug use. Never noticed any difference in him. He had always been quiet and kept to himself. At least you don't have to be like Angustia, who had no choice but to live with her charge, practicing what she believed—children are yours for life. And so Angustia carried her cross. What else could she do? Put him away? Never!"

He didn't directly tell me that I should be like Angustia and leave it all to take care of him, but I knew that was exactly what he was intimating. He wanted to live at home with my husband and me, for me to be his caregiver.*

Yet again, without warning or adding another word, Tito just up and left. He didn't even say good-bye. He seemed angry about the notion that a mother would abandon her child. I know he often feels abandoned. Maybe that was his way of showing me how he feels. With several days left in the Bay Area, I'd have more time to visit and let him know that I dearly love him.

---

* Tito now lives with Jorge and me in San Antonio, Texas. He has been with us since December 24, 2014.

Stories Are Life

Schizophrenia is a devastating illness, not only for the person who is ill but also for the entire family.

—Rose Marie Friedrich, Sonya Lively, and Linda M. Rubenstein,
"Siblings' Coping Strategies and Mental Health Services"

All Tito has are his stories and the memories he carries inside him. Listening to the tales he feels compelled to narrate, I have learned to see them as a sort of map that guides him outside the comfort of his middle-class upbringing. Also, they help Tito get unstuck when he finds himself in between so-called normalcy and mental illness. When he tries to sort it out, the staff has informed me, he shares his stories with anyone who is willing to listen, not just those who run the facility in which he lives. Their tendency is to ignore him or just pretend they're listening.

It is my belief that my son is trying to make sense of it all, one story at a time, as if he is committing to memory the life he has lived inside his illness. My hunch is that for him, forgetting would mean the loss of his self. That, I am beginning to believe, is how Tito keeps it together.

Still, even with the stories, there are times he appears confused, and at those times, one is tempted to doubt his tales. The narratives he carries about his father, even when they came from other relatives, make him feel alive. For Tito, these stories have become a way to be with us, his family. It is possible that in the haze of his illness, when he feels disconnected from himself, they are a way to reclaim his family relationships. He wants a family of his own so desperately that he has to experience it vicariously through others or in his memories. The last time I came to visit, Tito told me that the stories feel like sacks of luggage he has never unpacked: "These stories are the connection to my family when I'm lonely. They keep me alive."

He has always left me with the desire to hear more. His tales help me separate the guilty feelings from the detachment that allows me to spend time away from my son as I pursue a professional life. Tito's stories give me a view of his thoughts, making me wonder about the narratives he will spin the next time I visit, if he is in the mood to do so. Even though I become anxious when the tales unfurl, I cannot blame my son for my feelings. I am responsible for the emotions I carry; my feelings are my own. I'm doing the best I can, as is he, with what we have been given.

Sometimes his stories make me feel like a voyeur, like I am on the outside looking in and not involved. It's almost as though I am looking to him to provide answers to our problems. That's not fair. No one has the answers. Still, the stories of his life unfold like a telenovela I anxiously wait to view. As a receptive audience of one, I will be there to listen.

With Family Tales, Loneliness Goes Away

It is important to address all issues with which patients, families and carers need assistance, and to take a well-informed, creative approach to pharmacological treatment, using medication according to individual patient need rather than mechanistic adherence to guidelines.

—Ann M. Mortimer,
"Another Triumph of Hope over Experience?"

Two months after my last visit with Tito, I returned to see him again. As if time had not passed, when I arrived, Tito picked up the story where he had left off. His long-term memory is exceptional, though I did not expect this, given his appearance. Despite his disheveled look, his rancid body odor from lack of bathing, and his grimy teeth, my son appeared lucid. Nevertheless, his hygiene and appearance gave me cause for concern.

After a quick hug that lasted long enough for his body odor to cling to me—smoke mixed with sweat—he gave me a kiss, as if slurping me in order to fuse my presence to memory. Again, departing from family yarns, speaking as if he had been a spectator in my and Beto's story, Tito returned to a tale he had told me several times before, that *Westside Story* about our time in San José.

Laughing, he let on that he could have become one of Beto's boys—punctuated with a scream. Then, without warning, he gave me a blow-by-blow account of my courtship dance. He pulled me back into the past, painting the scene in precise strokes, even though the voice with which he told the story did not sound like my son. It was more like a *lucha libre* announcer broadcasting the lineup for a wrestling match.

"Lost among the guys," Tito said. "Going at it. Challenging life. Daring life to give them their due." He paused. Maybe his heart wasn't in it or he paused to capture the essence of the story. Patience would take us there. "Two young Chicanos," he began, "not yet eighteen years of age, came to blows over a rumor that you had been deflowered—not a virgin anymore—by one of them."

As though narrating a David and Goliath story, he told me about the gangly giant who had been challenged to that fight for spreading lies about me, Beto's girl. The evil guy, Mike King, had spread rumors that I was a loose girl with whom boys could do whatever they wanted. Tito described Mike, who had been reduced to Jell-O by Beto's fists and feet. He detailed the brawl as centering around a Rita Moreno–like protagonist, refusing to soil me, his momma, in any way. It was something he never would have done, except for the one time he called me a bitch because I had put a stop to his hanging around with negative influences—druggies at his high school.

He had had a conversion experience. Tito now thought "a Chicano's mother is next to God." It appeared that this particular story connected Tito with his male side. Conjuring up Beto's effort to set the record straight was important to him, especially knowing that Mike King had not even gotten to first base with me. I had remained pure and special for Beto—intact.

Thus he continued with the story, emulating a narrator in a boxing documentary, describing the gang choreographies of the day, reenacting the shenanigans of the social group his biological father had amassed for support. The story moved on: "With the Dukes and the Kings as an audience, two groups who dared each other's manhood to pass the time, mostly socializing and sometimes fighting to push away the boredom, Beto set out to cleanse your name, Momma. He mostly wanted to protect your chastity because he was known for only going out with pure and unused girls, regardless of the discards he left along the way. He would have never done the same for those he pawed and dumped; they weren't good girls anymore. But you were. So he set out to prove it."

Tito paused. It wasn't clear to me if this was for effect or if his mind was embroiled in the auditory delusions that he had to sort out to follow the story. Or maybe the voices interfered with the narrative. He expanded the silence, squinting, as if to make out a figure in the distance, as if sorting through the images he carried. I could imagine him picturing Beto. He grimaced from invisible punches, aping and mimicking a contorted face and body receiving invisible blows, playacting every punch.

Storytelling with his body, Tito shifted his face as if to evade blows directed toward that Apache nose he had inherited. The internal vignette he carried came to life with bits of acting, and a lot of bravado, displayed for anyone who was there to witness it. Tito brought the story alive. As quickly as he paused, he continued again, narrating what he saw in that boxing announcer tone.

"Left punch, right jab," he said. "Undercut to the chin. Fist to the gut. Did I tell you that every punch given or received, one blow after the other, failed to stop Beto until he got the best of Mike? It wasn't until the slanderer got his nose busted and his pride exposed raw that the fight ended. Everything stopped. Beto didn't have to say a word. Had no need to. Didn't even curse. He just stopped. Having given Mike a lesson for daring to soil your reputation, Momma, and for bringing shame to his name, the fight finally set the record straight. Pendejo, Mike knew it. All messed up like a rooster that lost its bout, with blood spurting from his beak, and finally on the floor, Mike King tried to talk, to apologize. Words were barely audible, though."

Tito's words took me back to the scene, and I imagined Beto leaning over as he tried to make out Mike's words. I could almost hear Beto speaking to Mike in the words uttered by my son: "I didn't hear you. Apologize for all to hear."

Tito went on with the story: "With a bullhorn of a loud roar, Beto commanded Mike King to say he was sorry. It was so quiet everyone could hear the shallow breathing of those frightened wannabe gangsters. One by one, each person could hear their breath growing louder.

After an eternity to them, Mike, the defeated street warrior, finally obeyed the victor's command. He knelt to do just what the smaller one of the two told him to do, in that bout for purity. With lips curled like an inflated, upside-down *w*, Mike King finally expressed his regrets. In a voice that was barely a whisper."

Recalling Mike's words, Tito said, "Beto's right. Nothing ever happened. I made it up because she didn't want to go out with me. I lied. *Lo siento*."

The narrator again, Tito said, "Those who knew him best could tell he really didn't mean it. They knew it was a fake sincerity, but they said nothing because they felt sorry for Mike—he had had enough blows for the day. He thought that by throwing in a couple of words in *castellano*, he would convince those who retained the language of his parents, saying he was sorry in Spanish. Sorry, like the gringos who took away his great-great-great-grandfather's land in south Texas and only left him with the name. But like them, he didn't mean it."

Tito's sense of awe was acute; he appeared to be foreshadowing things to come. As he continued, his story brought me back to earlier times. "Beto, having been around the block more than once, called Mike out on his lack of sincerity and didn't cut him any slack. After all, his pride and his girlfriend's reputation were at stake. Mad-dogging Mike, with eyes sizing him up, Beto's razor-sharp stares delivered invisible stabs that made Mike sweat like a running water faucet. 'You said what?' Tito said in Beto's voice. 'Didn't hear ya.' Unhappy with Mike's weak-assed apology, my dad, Beto, demanded that he do it again. 'Can't hear you! Say it again.' For a second time, and more to himself than those who patiently awaited the apology, Mike King's cauliflower lips screamed for all to hear: 'Lo siento. Disculpame.'"

Tito hesitated before continuing. "My father, Beto, accepted his apology. Then, digging his fingers into Mike's arm as if to call attention to his remarks, Beto told him not to do it again ever—not to his girl or any other one, ever. He meant it. 'Don't let me catch you talking bad about our *huisas* or you'll be sorry. It's enough that they have to put up with pussies like you, Miguel Rey.' Purposely translating his cattle-baron name, Beto insulted the wannabe white boy who had always refused to speak Spanish. Beto was not satisfied, wanted insurance, asked Mike King to apologize again in English, threatening him with a pummeling if he refused to comply. 'I'm sorry. She's a *virgin*. I *never* touched her.' They shook hands, as if to signify that all was OK."

Without turning to me, he added, "Can't believe you let him get away with it. He treated you like a prized ear or tail from the bull that had just lost to the matador in a bullfight. Just like that, it was over. The contenders made peace. The crowd drifted away before the cops came. They left no evidence behind."

Tito didn't stop until he could take me to the end of the story I had told him: "The midday slow-moving shadows of slightly gray and blue-white clouds—heavenly cotton candy where members of the Dukes imagined artistic images during those hot summer months—faded along with the lost souls who disappeared at the end of the brawl. The rays of the sun unveiled them, exposing their bodies for all to see. Others went to the José Theater—the dollar movies of my childhood—to see a Bruce Lee movie about a dragon. Still others went behind the bushes to make out, a dangerous way to pass the time. Their stories are my story."

Tito looked to me. "Momma," he said, "sometimes stories are the only thing that can soothe the pain. It helps me to tell them. Medicine is not enough. The feelings and hurts wrapped inside the confusion and the anxiety create a need for me to talk to someone. I'm so glad you listen to me. It's better than just popping pills into my body, as if that frees you from having to deal with me and the madness that's my reality."

Tito had finished the story he wanted to share with me. Clearly, his stories, like the fight he spoke about, humanize him and take him beyond the perception of him as another drugged-up resident who kind workers listen to instead of casting aside. They keep him anchored to something.

Even though this was one of the best places in which my son had resided, I was beginning to notice the pecking order in it—a pecking order described by many experts. Here, as in other such places, psychiatrists were always busy dispensing meds, while psychologists were not accessible for talk therapy—taking their wisdom to money-making counseling sites instead—and social workers were left to pick up the pieces where neither psychologists nor psychiatrists dared to go. Even though the resident psychiatrist believed in the efficacy of talk therapy, he was too busy to talk to the patients. I guess that is one of the reasons they hire psychiatric nurses. They're cheaper and, I must say, the only professionals who seem to listen to the residents and help them keep it together when they are coming undone.

Even though there are times I would rather not listen to Tito, listening is the one way I can be there for him. His recollections of it all—the lives he has shared with those he loves, his movie sequels or reruns of the past—seem to calm him.

Bed-Wetting and Past Lives

[Twenty-one] percent of the schizophrenia patients experienced child-hood bedwetting, compared with 11 percent of their unaffected brothers and sisters, and 7 percent of those in the other comparison group. This suggests that childhood bedwetting indicates abnormal brain development that contributes to the development of schizophrenia, the study authors say.

—Thomas M. Hyde et al., "Enuresis as a Premorbid
Developmental Marker of Schizophrenia"

I wondered if it was the story about Beto and his friends that inspired Tito to talk to me about the few friendships he has had in his life. The subject had always been difficult for him. Or maybe his willingness to talk was related to an argument he had recently engaged in. It was a serious altercation with Bryan Benson, one of the residents. The manager of the facility reported it to me, telling me that while words had been slung, no physical violence had been involved. The argument was over Bryan's intrusion into Tito's locked nightstand. Apparently, Bryan had helped himself to the cigarettes Tito guards so dearly.

When I first heard the story from Tito, through one of his never-ending telephone calls, he told me he was getting fed up with the abuses. He was tired of covering for Bryan. However, he hadn't told anyone yet because he didn't want to be "a fink or a rat." He followed a code of honor and ethics that made him loyal to a fault. Concerned about my son, I called the manager to tell her about the incident. That was the beginning of Tito's "finks" and "rats" talks—along with his talks about having lived two thousand years and having had multiple lives. He was not doing well. The director told me to call the facility's psychiatrist to tell him what had happened, assuring me that they would keep an eye on Tito.

Why do I have to do their work? I wondered as I talked to the director. Why can't they speak to each other?

"We need to watch him," the director added. "I'll tell the psychiatric nurse to monitor the intake of his medicine and to keep an eye on his actions."

The calls about Bryan continued. Tito was obsessing, and he called me to clear his mind. "Remember, how hard it was?" he asked me. "It was never easy making friends. My mere presence seemed to annoy even people who were my own age, and when I lost what you used to call my 'cute button appearance,' even those adults who paid attention to me became less patient. So I was often alone. You well know that the only friends I had in the whole world growing up were relatives my own age within the extended family. But even they didn't really want to be with me. They just tolerated me. Put up with my eccentricities because I was part of the family. You know that."

I listened and acknowledged his recollections with a nod.

"Don't have to tell you," Tito continued. "From very early on, I lived a lonely existence, where name-calling became my only defense. I doled out those names as easily as they were given to me. With nicknames like 'CB' for crybaby and 'TC' for Top Cat because I thought I was the boss despite being barely able to handle my own business. I don't recall one single friend from elementary school. Only had one in middle school—the Filipino who liked to come over and eat with us. Remember? It was Sammy Duclaydon, a nerd reject just like me who nobody else befriended. When we finally found each other, our friendship ended when I spent the night at his house. I had an accident—peed on his bed. So embarrassed. My shame and his mother's anger over the incident tore us apart. Although we remained friends at school, we never visited each other again."

Feeling sorry for himself, he began to whimper. He said that the only people in the whole world who had ever supported him were those in the family who came to visit, because not all of my relatives visited or provided him with the support he needed. He reminded me, as he continued with his story, that Tía Felisa, Grandma, and me are his only sources of support.

"Do you remember Sammy?" he asked. "That's really when the family became my only source of social support. Among them I felt safe, but not always, because of the name-calling I was telling you about and because of the teasing ways that went among us. It hurt to be called names, even when I flung them at those who did it to me. We thought of it as normal and as a way to communicate affections. Remember that my crying spells and the fact I preferred to associate with girls earned me the nickname 'sissy' from the boys and men of the family? My tattling didn't help. The male cousins shunned me, but I learned from them. They were as *chismosos* as the rest. An easy target, I gave them plenty of reasons to pick on me. So when I complained about feeling picked on, my words fell on deaf ears. The bantering took place among peers, and it was a back-and-forth thing we did; the older relatives saw it all as kids' games. But it hurt. They didn't notice the violence in the behavior of my peers. I hated that no one liked me."

Tito paused. It sounded like he was crying along with the story he was telling me. I tried to encourage him to talk, saying, "I'm listening" as the cue for him to continue. My son was silent for a little while longer, then he returned to the issues of friendship.

"I'm mentally ill but not dumb, Momma," he said. "In the sixth grade, after beating all the intelligence tests they gave smart kids, I was placed in a gifted and talented program. Finally, my odd and peculiar behavior was suitable for a crowd among whom *I* could fit—head always buried in the books, always looking for those by Stephen King, dressed in high-waist *brincacharcos*, or high-water pants, and talking like an adult with all the twenty-five-cent words I could use to impress those around me, opened up the possibilities for making friends. But I still felt like a tortilla in a breadbasket because I was a Mexican at a white middle- and upper-class school—I didn't fit their expectations. My cultural background became a reason for taunting. I wasn't embarrassed about that, you know. I did Mexican dancing and learned to speak Spanish. I was still ostracized, but for different reasons."

No matter how hard he tried, I thought, Tito always seemed to be out of place. "Although I fit in among a group of 'weird kids,' as an ethnic person I didn't belong," he told me. "School became another place where others made fun of me for different reasons. That's when stupid banter like 'How many smart Mexicans do you know?' became another way to tease me. Then we moved to Santa Cruz for Dad to work on his PhD, and I entered the ninth grade. There I attempted to become part of any peer group that would accept me. In an effort to become a part of something, I tried the surfers. Rejected. Didn't look the part, despite the built-in tan. After that, I sought the nerds—after all, I was very bright—and they ignored me. They weren't used to smart Mexicans, so I was told. The socialites, or 'socs,' as they liked to be called, didn't want to bother with me. They said I wore the wrong clothes and didn't come from the proper families in town. Everyplace I turned to, I didn't fit. It was then the druggies, the users, became my only refuge. Joining the army of lost souls who drugged themselves to deal with their own isolation, I finally thought I belonged."

The loss and pain in Tito's words made me a more mindful listener. He continued with his narration.

"However, because I was afraid of you and Dad, I only became a pretend druggie to fit in somewhere. Didn't want you and Dad to find me out and be disappointed. I mostly stuck around the house making excuses that I had strict curfews as the reason for not partying with the druggies. But in school I was one of them. The druggies understood what it was like to be a high school outcast. With them, I almost felt at home. Life only became worse after that. That's when I began to smell strange things. It wasn't enough that I had no friends and that those who took me into their group only did it because I pretended to be like them, and that I was still having accidents in bed. Didn't tell you until I got sick, but just about when I turned sixteen, I began to smell things that weren't there—olfactory hallucinations, as I now know them. These strange smells were a constant part of my torment, especially since there was no evidence for them. It was also then that my behavior became bizarre. I started to become compulsive about grooming, taking two to five showers a day or more if you two weren't around. Found myself controlled by my grooming needs."

The extreme cleanliness was so frustrating, especially during severe drought days. They forced us to monitor the newly developed cleansing rituals he devised to deal with the phantom scents. How could I have suspected? I thought.

"Momma, I know you didn't know what to do, but I tried your patience and limited what you perceived as my indulgences, while my dad, Jorge, chalked it up to the eccentricities of a difficult adolescence. When I finally asked you if I stunk, you reassured me that I didn't smell, emphasizing that my grooming and hygiene were probably the best of any adolescent in the world. Still, you soon could not tolerate my waste of water and limited me to one shower a day. Yet you didn't abandon me and made every effort to help me make sense of it all. I could barely make sense of my own situation. But you and Dad tried, tried to figure it out, get to bottom of it—both of you made adjustments to help me deal with things coming my way."

I recalled the troubled adolescent he had become. The continuation of his story brought me back, and I listened attentively.

"Of course, I didn't tell you what was going on inside my mind or how I felt. I didn't even let myself believe that this was happening to me. Didn't want you to think I was going crazy. Still, you both talked to me and asked questions. Questions that pushed me away from you, distancing me even further and alienating me from you, and I dismissed and disregarded your efforts to help me at every turn. Despite the problems I gave you, you and Dad continued to provide a healthy environment for me: he as the disciplinarian and you validating and affirming who I was every chance you had. Momma, I know you did the best you could, given that your life has been no 'bed of roses,' as Cuauhtémoc said to the Spaniards when they were putting his feet to the fire during the conquest of Tenochtitlán. 'Member, I learned that from you? Had no clue that this would be just the beginning of our personal torment."

Tito's stories are a way to keep me connected to the life he knew before schizophrenia. It's clearer to me now. As if reading my mind, he added, "Momma, I still have my stories to keep me alive. These tales are a type of coping strategy for me, for when I feel the loneliest I just have to recall the efforts you and Dad made to help me and I don't feel so alone. Feel supported and loved by you, because you have never left me."

It's not clear to me if Tito fully buys all that he tells me, but it is evident that he carries a great deal of memory and history inside him. My son is amazingly intelligent; the way he copes with the disease puts me in awe of him. His exceptional ability to retain information inspires me. I remind myself that I am his mother, not his therapist, recognizing that my intuition guides me to work with the voices because it is during those dreaded appearances and his paranoid episodes that Tito becomes a bit more confused, although he has learned to sort out the voices and focus on his own.

I am beginning to wonder if our pláticas are helping him. They seem to soothe him. I have tried to test this possibility. At times I have asked him to explore if the voices are telling him something about the ways he relates to or interacts with us or if the stories are a vehicle to bring family members back into his life when he misses them. Recently, he imagined or dreamed that my sister Felisa and I were both named Amy and that we were out to kill him. He narrated the entire episode. I listened patiently and reassured him that I love him and that my sister and I would never harm him. As he talked, I asked him to think it through and process it with me. After a while, he became convinced that I would never harm him and that I love him. So he stopped talking.

While not always able to control these auditory delusions and hallucinations, Tito makes an effort to understand the voices and the messages they may bring. Apparently, as the literature in England and Australia shows, there are researchers who are developing a way to treat people who hear voices. Yes, I know I'm not my son's therapist, but if it helps for me to better understand and help him deal with the disease, I may have to try these strategies out. It doesn't hurt to try to place what I do with Tito in context of what is being done by others.* After all, no one is giving him the opportunity to vocalize what he experiences in his everyday life.

---

* Hayward et al. (2009) make a case for a therapeutic approach in which those who hear voices learn to work with their dominant voice. Through case studies, these researchers arrived at three conclusions that allow for an examination of voices as evidence of the social relationships of those who hear voices, the reciprocity of the voice-hearer relationship, and the possibility of change through an empty-chair conversation or a Gestalt approach.

Therapeutic approaches aside, I am concerned about my son. His speech has become labored; his words slide like molasses from a jar. In his desire to be understood, he works to stretch out every word. It is then that my listening skills are tested and I have to rely on the patience he has taught me. I thought I knew so much, but I am barely scratching the surface. The textbooks offer only a glimpse into what someone with his condition experiences on a daily basis. With him, I have come to realize that my knowledge is limited and I have much more to learn. I have to continue my research. Maybe then I can find more than is available to me now. My journaling is a big help, as it allows me to compare and contrast the patterns in my son's behavior and lets me know when he is entering the abyss of psychosis. And then, in those times of desperation, I can harness the patience I need to hear him and to comfort him.

I have to remind myself to stay with it, to not give up. Still, there are times I feel so alone that I imagine myself being the only one dealing with this problem. While it's not always clear that my efforts help Tito, I will continue to do my best, especially since he places his trust in me when he hears the voices.

God, give me the patience to hear and listen to my son and the strength to help Tito as he narrates his stories and tells me about his life. There are times I feel like I'm in his shoes, that I too am becoming mentally ill, but he reminds me I need to stay together so I can be there for him.

Seeking for Silence

At Rope's End

Our findings suggest that during inner speech, the alterations of white matter fiber tracts in patients with frequent hallucinations lead to abnormal coactivation in regions related to the acoustical processing of external stimuli. This abnormal activation may account for the patients' inability to distinguish self-generated thoughts from external stimulation.

—Daniela Hubl et al., "Pathways that Make Voices"

One evening, another one of the dreaded telephone calls came. I lifted the receiver to answer and Tito told me he wasn't doing well. His voice had an urgency that frightened me.

"Momma, will you help me sort out the voices? They're loud and I can't even hear my own. Will you listen?" He told me he has no one to talk to because he does not trust anyone, not even the staff. Tito was calling me from the social worker's office; she had allowed him to use the telephone to make the long-distance call without consulting the director. Because I was cooking dinner, I asked Tito if he minded being on speaker. He said it was fine with him, but I detected hesitation and fear in his voice. He whispered, afraid someone would hear him, and described what he was experiencing. He didn't sound well—his words were labored and he wasn't focused. I imagined that the social worker who remained in the room was also struggling to understand what was going on.

"Momma. Momma. Momma. I can't. Can't. Can't. Can't. Can't take it anymore. It's killing me. I can't take it anymore. The devil is winning."

Tito continued to talk in spurts, as if to physically grasp the words so they wouldn't slip away from him. Just as he was trying to capture the words, I was making an intense effort to listen to my son, trying to not let anything he said escape my grasp.

"Feels weird," he said. "Inside. Feels strange. Things move in and out—head's about to pop. I'm going crazy. Lots, lots, lots, going on. Going crazy. Don't know what's happening. Can't take it. Mind splitting."

His words seemed to be directed elsewhere. Tito didn't feel safe. Not wanting to push him, I waited for him to continue.

"What? Whatchu say?" he soon said. "It's not that bad. Who are you to say? How do you know? There are times . . . there are times I get the biggest kick . . . makes me laugh, and I, I can't figure out why. Then I'm sad. Oh, so sad—can't get out of bed. Is it funny ha-ha? Or just ha? Shit! Shut up. Don't even. Let me think. Momma, just want to make sense of things. You know, tilt-a-whirl, mind spinning, not making sense, and can't get anything clear. But try, yeah, I try. Have to try. Got to try, trying."

The words came from his lips to the tune of a hip-hop song I've heard before, then he jarringly screams for it to stop. "*Stop.* Just *stop.* *Stop*, OK? *Stop*! Talking forever. Never stops. My brain—home of too many voices—how many does it house? Why you care? That's enough! Stop. Doesn't stop. Sad. Lonely. Confused. Depressed. Often cry and I don't know why I'm crying, crying, crying."

In the form of an old doo-wop song, he cried out words of caution to an imaginary voice inside his mind.

ANGRY MAN: "Shh! They'll hear ya. They're watching ya."

Then Tito returned to his own voice. "Kablooey. It's home. I'm back home. I'm . . . in my parents'—your house. Again. Coming or going? Going and coming. Don't know which way I'm going. I couldn't live with you. You didn't understand."

I realized Tito was now talking to me, so I tried to let him know that it was not about wanting, it was about not being able to tend to him because of the responsibilities I have with my job. It was then that he began to talk about his illness in a film metaphor: "Movies flash inside. Mind lit by color films. One. Two. Three. Four. Five. Six. Seven. Eight. That's enough! There are eight channels inside. Let's see one, two, tres, cuatro, five, six, siete, and ocho. Yeah. It's eight. It's too loud in there. Can't hear myself think. Confused. Can't make sense. Have to listen. See what I see. Hear what I think I hear."

The tone and timbre of his voice changed to the point that I believed someone else had taken hold of the telephone. I said, "Hello, hello," thinking that my son had handed the phone to someone else, but he didn't respond to me—just continued to speak.

HOMEBOY: "Yeah. That's the one . . . 'bout the good ol' days."

"Concentrate," Tito's self said, hinting at the voices he was trying to sort out. "Focus. Adjust . . . there . . . there . . . you've got it." Then there was another comment that sounded like someone other than my son.

ADORING FEMALE: "It's funny. But it's not. It's tragic."

"My life," Tito said in his own voice. "How sad!"

HOMEBOY: "No shit, ese. You're loony, Holmes."

DRUGGIE: "So what's worse than being Mexican and crazy?"

Tito's voice broke in, saying, "*Vato* inside asks. He's number . . . ahem, ah, forgot."

HOMEBOY: "It's like a hole in your pants. They see it but pretend not to. First they see you. Then they don't."

SYRUPY GIRL: "I'm see-through? Peekaboo! I'm see-through like the fabric in a tutu."

HOMEBOY: "Deep doodoo, ese. Stop already. Heard it all."

Tito again interrupted the voices. "Momma—" I think he's finally talking to me, so I can respond. But he is talking at me, instead of with me, so I try to sort out what's going on. Can't figure it out. Scared of 'em. Live among white old bags, *viejitas*. Dudes that pee—peepee, chichi, and caca—have no control. But they really like me. It don't matter to 'em that I'm nuts—a crazy Mexican. Not like the others. Knows how to act. They say, 'Good manners.' Really like me. Most people really, really like me."

Tito was enacting the voices he heard inside his mind. He had performed them for me so I could hear what he contends with when he is not doing well. It was not clear that he was doing it "so I can walk in his shoes," as he has been known to tell me. He continued speaking the various voices as he tried to sort out his thoughts.

ANGRY MAN: "Hey, don't. Stop. Stick to the story."

DRUGGIE: "Hurrryyy. Here comes another one. Listen. Look. Can you see it?"

SYRUPY GIRL: "Don't forget. *Don't let it get away.* Don't get lost. Watch out! Don't let it go. Stick with it. The story."

HOMEBOY: "Right. Right. Gotta focus. Can't . . . can't . . . can't lose it!"

ADORING FEMALE: "Stay with it. Keep it together."

The pain, confusion, and anxiety were palpable. I was reduced to silent tears of the sort I usually keep hidden because I don't want him to think I am coming undone.

"Nooo," Tito continued. "Don't wanna remember. Being homeless is no fun. Time and again, lost. Hungry. Lonely. Alone. Away. No parents. Run, run, running from confusion. Protect 'em. Hide."

HOMEBOY: "Came back. Home again, home again, jiggery jig."

"Scared them," Tito said. "Was skinny. So skinny pants were held up with a Jerry Garcia tie from a trash bin. 'Twas my belt. Swimming pants. Puddled at my feet. Big. Not cool. Must fold. Fold. Fold. Fold. Cuff. Cuff. Cuff 'em. Roll 'em up. Roll 'em up and put 'em in the—"

HOMEBOY: "There he goes, *se sale*. Pat-a-cake. What a baby."

Tito said, "Came back to save face. Told, told 'em, to, to, to figure it out, hoping for an easy life."

DRUGGIE: "'Member? Ate everything. Couldn't get enough. Slurped bananas, with one swallow. Drank milk. Made noodle cups. Left 'em. One cup. Two cups. Three cups. Saved 'em, for later. Stomach couldn't take it. No more. No more. Later."

"Eyes look at me, gawking," Tito said. "Slurping sounds made 'em stare. Bet you don't know Momma . . . wild berries kept me alive. Lied. Wanted pity. Ate homeless leftovers. Protected me. Harassed me. Newbie. Had to learn. Didn't panhandle; too proud to beg. Resold bus transfers at the Metro station. Above begging. Half price. Ate. Didn't beg. Didn't beg. Didn't beg! Worked for food. Worked for food. Worked. Worked. Almost begged—embarrassed—under pressure. Homeless. Rip-offs. Took advantage for being too short. So young and they thought I was real stupid. Took what I had. Ripped me off, took my bike. Ate discards. Penniless. No money. Proud. Had dignity, you know."

In a voice that didn't sound like Tito, he chastised himself for ranting.

HOMEBOY: "Jesus! Stop this loco. Not making sense."

"Momma," Tito said in his voice, "I know the family gets tired. Every time I, we, return. You tried to keep me there. Make me part again. Had my room. My things. Coming. Going. Leaving. Returning. Love me. Got tired of me. Disappointed. Loved me. Came and went. Love me."

My precious Tito, what a horrible life he leads, and I have no control over what happens with him. As a mentally ill adult, he gets to decide whether or not I find out about his condition. Only he can give those who treat him permission to talk to me.

Immersed in my own thoughts, I heard my son tell me good-bye. "'Bye, Momma. Gotta go, I'm making a big bill on their phone. Aren't you glad they let me use it to call you?"

Vermin and Other Things

[Expressed emotion] was the single most potent predictor of clinical relapse, although patients who lived with high EE relatives were substantially protected from relapse if they regularly took antipsychotic medication or were not in frequent contact with their high EE relative.

—Janis Jenkins et al., "Expressed Emotion in Cross-Cultural Context"

After all this time dealing with Tito's illness, I should be ready for whatever comes my way. I find myself thinking that I need to learn to not be surprised by what he does. But he still throws me for a loop. There are times when I am at a loss for how to respond.

Yesterday he called me. He was crying, screaming, and sometimes roaring with laughter as if listening to his own private jokes. It was another marathon phone session. Tito talked to me as if he were in a performance, backed up by an audience. He asked me if I remembered the time I took him to a beauty shop in Santa Cruz's West Side, when he was infested with lice. Without inhibition, he spilled out what was on his mind, describing a scene in which both of us took part—our experience at a swanky beauty shop where I got my hair and nails done.

"I see it," Tito said. "It's the Golden Tresses Beauty Shop. That time . . . long ago . . . when I embarrassed you, Momma. There it is—a director's chair. Fancy shop. Haircut place. Not in the gutter. By Julian Street Inn. Homeless shelter. San José. Laughing. Hopelessness. Bearded tramp. Scraggly hair. Smelly. Dirty teeth. Unkempt. At the Golden Tresses, there, there I am. Sitting in the director's chair."

He was hearing the voices again. He was confused and didn't seem to hear me when I tried to interject to let him know I understood, I was there. "They asked me to stay away from the shop," I told Tito to no avail. So I made an effort to listen as best I could.

ANGRY MAN: "Wasso funny? Can't control it. Laughing at no one in particular. Everyone who isn't anyone."

HOMEBOY: "Pinches *piojos*. Lousy bugs make me laugh."

ADORING FEMALE: "Instant replay. Back up. No, no, yeah. There. There."

HOMEBOY: "Piojos pinches. I had piojos. Piojos."

"Itch, scratch," Tito said in his own voice. "Stinks. Lice medicine. Itchy head. Crawling all over me. Talked to me. Sucked my blood. Talked to me and told me."

ANGRY MAN: "You're no good. Shut your trap!"

"Oh, no," Tito said, his words melding with those of the voices he was hearing. "Draining my brain. Killing the gray matter, demyelination." Even though he was only talking about lice and nits, he perceived them as being much stronger. "No. No. Oh, no. Sucking it out—their fault—lousy piojos sap my brain. Talk to me. They tell me, 'Do yourself a favor—do yourself in.' Can't. Won't. Maybe. Think about it. Momma, I don't want drugs. It's my head. The way it works. Scratch. Itch. Scratch, s'more. Dry scalp. Dandruff? Piojos? Got Momma thrown out. Unwelcome. No chances. Can't come back. Delousing cost. No room for Mexicans or homeless, anymore."

SYRUPY GIRL: "What did you expect? No one wants lice."

"Lost a lot of bucks," Tito continued. "High-class people left. Afraid of Mexican piojos and a homeless bearded man, but they didn't tell you. Couldn't explain. Still, it was so funny. So funny, cracked up! Momma, you know what? 'Louse and Mexican' has a funny ha-ha ring to it. Laughing at myself? Things. Life. People pass. Stare. Could care less. Scratching. Unaware. Lice live in my head. Camping inside, they drill my brain, talk, tell me jokes about me. Piojos tell me things about myself I don't even know. Distorted titters distract. Delayed tears ready to come out. Out. Out! Damned piojos, leave me alone. Get out! Scratching. Went inside. My head. Head. Tears. Alone. Missed. Family. Hug? No hugs. No one to hug! Yet alive! The maze . . . my brain . . . awful inside.

Screen to screen, channel to channel. Reality. Insanity. Can't make sense."

Tito yelled at someone and dropped the telephone. It bounced against the wall. He shouted, "It's a telenovela with a twist." And as abruptly as he had dropped the telephone, Tito returned. His marathon monologue continued uninterrupted. He was unable to hear any of my questions or the statements of sympathy I uttered. "I live inside it," he told me. "Try to make sense. Reality. Insanity. Heaven? Hell? Madness! What is it?"

Then, as if explaining to me, he added, "Momma, you wanted to know. It's never-ending noise. Chatters. Inside. Loud. Louder. Loud. Louder. Loudest. Firecrackers burst. Guns blast. Bang. Bang. I have amplified special effects inside my mind. Never stop. Numb noises with meds—though they're still there whispering—my blunted mind tries to sort it out. You wanted to know, so now you do. Now you know why the street drugs made things normal. Walking in a haze made it normal. Had a reason to get high. Didn't have to explain or make sense of the demons. Noise. Prattle. Confusion. Every waking minute. You can't even begin to imagine what it's like. There are many living inside."

He disagreed with me before I could even get a word out. "No, not like Sybil," he said. "No, I don't have a multiple personality disorder. My mind hears voices and has imagined communities living inside and I have no control over them. My mind is clear. Then it isn't. Confusing. Breaks down. Voices live inside. Don't make them up. They just show up and take residence, without paying rent! TV set always on. Inside. It's a challenge. Have to watch out. Stay with it. Sort it out."

HOMEBOY: "Gotta look out. Have to hear what sonsos say. What to do!"

ADORING FEMALE: "Control serious battles. Inside. Outside. Making noise. Wanting to be heard."

DRUGGIE: "But I just ride with it. Put up with seven other dummies. Yelling. Screaming for attention. Trying to come out."

ELDERLY MALE: "Sorry. Didn't mean you. It's the other ones I'm talking about."

HOMEBOY: "Híjole, what bugs me is the way they treat him.

'*Ta loquito* and all, but he's a real sharp dude. Real sensitive. Caring. More people should be like him."

ADORING FEMALE: "Compassionate. *Buena gente*—good guy. He'll do what he can for you."

HOMEBOY: "When viejitos at that House with the Name of a Woman—Casa Olga—need help, he helps. Finds 'em cigarettes. Gives 'em a shoulder to cry on. Lends 'em a helping hand. Don't matter, if it's men or women. Black or white? Fat? Skinny! Young! Old? He really cares about their illness. Helps 'em."

ADORING FEMALE: "Compassionate. Loving."

ANGRY MAN: "Shut up. Stop it! Don't say that."

HOMEBOY: "Pobrecito homey. He waants looove."

"Momma," Tito interjects, "sometimes, loneliness wins. I've tried to end it all."

DRUGGIE: "Yeah. Almost jumped from the eighth floor. Serious. Wanted to do it. All believed he would. But my voice told him to walk up the stairs. Listened. Climbed each one, almost out of breath. One floor. Two floors. Three floors. Five. Six. Seven. Eight floors. He made it. Didn't take the elevator."

DRUGGIE: "Good thing he walked. Otherwise, kaput, you're a goner. Legs and arms flailing . . . cracked eggs and all, you know what I mean. You know. Would've ended up in pieces."

ELDERLY MALE: "Up on the eighth. Out of breath from the climb, and that horrible chain-smoking-I-hate-and-wish-he-would-quit-at-this-very-moment habit didn't help. Sat. Cried like a baby. Hard lesson. There's no one there to give him a hand. Just has to listen."

ANGRY MAN: "Jiminy Cricket! Stop it! Want peace and quiet. Give me some."

HOMEBOY: "Enough! Stop it! Don't wanna hear it."

ANGRY MAN: "Don't confuse me. Buncha crazies. I'm his only sanity. Keep him away from the voices. Chase his paranoia. Get him the hell out of his funk."

ACTIVISTS: "Shh! Leave him alone. No. No. Told you—it's not a Sybil story already. It's the way his mind works—paranoia and all—with depression to boot."

HOMEBOY: "I take care of him. Language unites us. Voice came through that trip to Mexico. That time with the tíos, running from the demons beginning to come up. Had no clues about 'em. Thought it was drugs."

ANGRY MAN: "Good grief! Thought Mexico would straighten him up. Shit, didn't really know him, did they? Why would they think that garbage? Good ol' American boy like him."

Tito returned: "Momma, you remember, the only thing I cared about was hanging out. Taking it easy. Kicking back—good practice for later. You, the old ones were so busy you didn't see it. Paid no attention. Good for me. Just wanted to kick it. Your precious education. Didn't have time for me."

DRUGGIE: "Got lost in the fray. Lost it, man."

ANGRY MAN: "Stop talking that shit. Speak English, damn it. Don't wanna hear it."

HOMEBOY: "Be quiet. Don't put down my language, ese. If you wanna know, Spanish got him to listen. Helped him make sense. Talked a mixture of Nahuatl and Castilian. Mexican."

ADORING FEMALE: "Yeah. For a young pochito he's real good at it. And what's best, he likes to speak it, not like his friends who hate Mexican Spanish. Makes 'em less worthy. But we know better."

HOMEBOY: "Language made us one. *Entiendes*, Méndez? We understand each other, ¿qué no?"

DRUGGIE: "Crazy homey. He loses it!"

HOMEBOY: "Good thing I arrived. Taught him 'bout the streets, you know. Knows I'm here. When he needs me, he thinks in Spanish too, ese. When he does that, I'm there for him."

ELDERLY MALE: "Smart *cuate*, right? Knows just how to reach me. Finds me."

HOMEBOY: "He's a lady's man. Loves the women."

ACTIVIST: "Loco or not, he's had a lot of 'em. Now he's with Sharon. Don't care that she's older. Age is no thing for him. Just wants to love. Be loved back."

Deep in thought, I imagined ways to get a conversation going with my son. I wanted to talk to him about the voices inside. What were they trying to tell him? As I was trying to figure out what to do next,

Tito stopped as suddenly as he had started. He hung up the telephone without even saying good-bye. It was so unlike him. He's not rude, especially not to me, though sometimes he can get demanding and ask for too many things. But that day, while my son was losing it, I would have given him my mind if it had meant he would find his.

Creating Family from Scratch
Found the One

The lack of research in this area and the emphasis on negative outcomes rather than building on strengths are in conflict with the recovery literature and fail to provide adequate direction to mental health professionals who are working with individuals confronting these issues.

—Shirley M. Glynn et al., "The Potential Impact of the Recovery Movement on Family Interventions for Schizophrenia"

Sounding like himself again, Tito called me. He told me he was getting married to Sharon, his new girlfriend. "She is the one," he said, serious as a heart attack—or a mental break. I wasn't surprised. With at least three of his former girlfriends, he has tried to create a family. He desperately wants a family of his own. But Sharon cannot have any children—she is already a grandma. I guess that is one way to have a family. I didn't say a thing to Tito, I just listened. He sounded more urgent than ever before to make marriage happen. While Sharon seemed to care for him and was concerned for his welfare—as Tito was for hers—it was likely that the marriage would take place only because they needed each other.

But what do I know? There I was, speaking to a so-called deranged man, and I had yet to talk to anyone at work about my difficulties. I talked myself out of these thoughts by getting back to thinking about

Tito and his new relationship. Hopefully this thing with Sharon would last beyond the next shipment of cigarettes.

Anyway, the way life is for Tito, you never know when things will change. His new girlfriend was the most recent in a string of prospects since he became mentally ill. On my next visit I'd make a point to talk to Sharon and Tito. I was concerned about the choice he was making, especially because of the delusions, hallucinations, and paranoia he had been displaying. Then again, I thought, maybe marriage is not so much a problem as a solution to some of the difficulties Tito already confronts. Married, he wouldn't be alone. He would have someone there with him when the voices come.

Acting the Part

Psychotic Performance

Our clinical impression is that the family members who effectively deal with their relatives with schizophrenia are those who hold reasonable social expectations (perceive some controllability) and encourage their relatives to achieve certain goals.

—Amy Weisman et al., "An Attributional Analysis of Expressed Emotion in Mexican-American Families with Schizophrenia"

What I thought would happen did. During my next visit, Tito's active psychosis was evident. It was surreal. I wondered if he was "suckering me," as he has been known to say. Tito didn't seem to mind that I was witnessing what he was going through, reminding me that that was the way it was for him when he first became ill. He was confused and could not sort out the voices. He had to concentrate on his own thinking to get around the noise pollution. "Under medication, the voices are more like soft whispers," he said. "So I don't have to pay attention to differentiate my own voice."

Still, even in soft whispers, he said, the "noise is always there. But do not be fooled that I cannot think or talk because I'm mentally ill. I'm really sharp and sensitive. Most people dismiss me, but I am aware of my feelings, my surroundings, and the ways in which others perceive me. I'm very smart. You know that. But then there are those times when I'm obsessed and I go on about things, repeating whatever is uppermost in my mind."

Suddenly, almost as if reading my mind, he talked for me, uttering the very words I was thinking: "Yeah, I do think. And I do feel. My mind doesn't work like that of others. But when it does, you wouldn't figure I'm mentally ill." Then Tito's face mellowed out. He smiled, causing me to wonder what he was thinking about, but I just waited. I didn't ask him what he was thinking or interrupt his thoughts. He would tell me when he was ready. As I waited for him, I revisited a conversation we had.

"All I ever wanted was to start a family of my own," Tito said. "Have children to love. I want children. Children. I wish I could have children."

Instead of being the family man he had always wanted to be, at thirty-two my son was warehoused in a lonely institution, where he ambled the halls, a lost spirit trying to find his rightful place, scaring others and frightening himself, wanting to stop voices over which he had no control. He had finally accepted that this was his condition, and he was both rejecting and not rejecting his lot in life. In other words, he was not embracing schizophrenia but had come to understand that the illness would never go away. He had it and he would deal with it as best he could. (Although there were times he would escape into the self-medication delusions of normalizing mental illness and all its symptoms by scoring street drugs.)

It had taken him almost ten years to get to this point. Finally, Tito had learned to live among those overripe men and women who forgot to shower and forgot their names. After six years at Casa Olga, the residents had almost become his family, but Tito still experienced periodic psychotic breaks. To this day I don't know how he handles it. In that fairy-tale way of his, Tito has told me that he has an empty space for a heart, as he desperately tries to find love. He aches for those children he has finally convinced himself not to have. "I'm too far gone to be a father to any children," he has told me several times.

Tito still misses the child he believes he made with a runaway girl from San Diego, a supposed consequence of that first flight into health, when he lived in the Flats. That was when he allowed himself to believe that he could make it on his own and desperately tried to prove it. Working for minimum wage to take care of her—there was no one else who wanted her—he really believed that he had someone to hold on to.

Tito comes alive with the thought of having had a baby of his very own. Now that child who might have been has become part of Tito's imagined real estate in his mind, where all he has to do to be with that child is beckon it to memory. The way he sees it, the mere thought of that child makes Tito more human, less despicable. Tito lives with the hope of someday finding himself face to face with that baby.

There are days when Tito just sits and waits for that child to appear. Then out of the blue, and to anyone who will listen, and even to those who don't, he goes on about finding his lost baby because it would be the only thing that could fill the emptiness inside. It is so sad, there are times I sit and cry for him and those with this dreaded disease. What it does to human beings depresses me. Lately, I've begun to shed tears over any little thing.

Tito has learned to accept Casa Olga as home. He loves and hates it all at the same time. He lives mourning the loss of the child he imagined he had. Thankful for having a roof over his head, there are times Tito can almost bask in the safety of that haven—but for the memory of that child. While Casa Olga shelters Tito, it also keeps him trapped because he cannot leave and have his own life so long as those fictive communities of devils, gods, Norteños and Sureños, and petty thieves are embedded in his mind. He is free to go, but he does not have the independence he craves: a job, marriage, children.

Interestingly, it is during psychotic breaks that talk of the child surfaces. That memory keeps away the Armageddon of good and evil that holds him off balance. Thoughts of having had a child anchor Tito's mind as he struggles to not relapse. Letting his imagination take him where it wants to go, yet fearing the ride, Tito has made the child reality itself—it is almost Tito in better times.

For Tito, schizophrenia is not a physical or mental illness. He has learned to understand its complexity all too well and compares it to diabetes: "It's like diabetes. A sentence I will carry for the rest of my life. There is no cure, just respite."

"At least you are not taking insulin," I've often said to him. I usually add that "diabetes is the silent killer that destroys the body organ by organ, and the worst thing that could happen with this illness is the tics that emerge from extended use of medication." But I soon stop, reminding myself that he has no control over the breaks that will continue to come. "Can't even predict when the psychosis comes on," Tito often says. "Then I comfort myself with the knowledge that the psychiatrists just need to adjust or change my meds."

The workers at the facility tell me that Tito is a compliant patient. Not refusing the assortment of pills they give him, he clings to the hope that a cure will soon appear to erase the delusions, snuff the paranoia, and silence the distorted thinking brought on by the disease. But my son is tired of the voices and images that surface and of the extreme fears that can come with these symptoms.

In our talks about his condition, he has taught me to expand my views of schizophrenia. He sometimes explains it in interesting and complex ways: "Schizophrenia is a religious illness. Good and evil come through in images of saints and demons. I even get to talk to Jesus." He proselytizes his beliefs about the illness. To him, schizophrenia is creativity itself, explaining why he is, looks, or acts in the manner he does. Often, and without warning, Tito will offer more information, talking to the residents in the home—the gerontology patients who are just too old to remember and who have no one to care for them.

"Mental illness is about the struggles of good and evil," Tito says. "It's demons against God. It's a philosophical battle for life, where I have to fight to stay in control of that reality that everyone holds so dear, that so easily eludes me. It's like the fog, I've tried to embrace it with my arms, but it too dissipates like the passing thoughts of the madness from which I cannot free myself."

He has such depth, such interesting ways to introduce mental illness to people who are ignorant about it. There are sane people who cannot even find that awareness—even among my family. Then there are those who are blinded by prejudice, who blame the mentally ill for their own circumstances or even dare to accuse them of faking their condition. But as Tito notes, the "struggle is as real as my conversation with you, Momma. I can hear it. See it. Feel it. Just as well as I listen to your words, but it's not always evident."

In the darkest of times, Tito reminds me what it's like to be schizophrenic. He keeps me on my toes. "That damned illness lives inside me," he says. "Just like everyday life. The only way to gain control of it is to end it all. Kill myself. Put an end to it. Die. But I'm such a coward. I'd rather live with the dreaded illness than take the easy way out. Put up with it rather than make my loved ones go through grief. Promised Grandma I would hang in there. And I will."

He is like a walking book—so clear about what the psychosis does to him. He knows how it all works. Sometimes, seeing the humor in it all, he tells me not to take life too seriously: "There are times I can see the irony of my life and I have a real laugh at my own expense. Other times I'm too sad to see the humor. Still, I hold on to the possibilities. Living on hold, I await the dispensation of my meds to numb the reality that is my life."

When things become the saddest for Tito, with feelings he equates to the Chicken Little story of the heavens falling, he still clings to the dream of a life he wanted. In Casa Olga, he searches for the good life. Even so, he has to contend with his illusions of health.

Tito can have such clarity about his life: "Here I sit at Casa Olga, a lonely man who dreamed too much for himself. I'm stuck inside those dreams that will never materialize. I am a young man who lives hoping for a life that may never come. I live a life on hold." When Tito speaks like that, he brings my emotions to my throat. I cry for him and ache for the loss of my son as he used to be.

Tito 24

Starving the Demons

Those families who cope well with their disturbed relatives may be those who maintain a delicate balance between perceiving some control while recognizing that some of the odd or disruptive behavior is an inevitable side effect of a genuine illness.

—Amy Weisman et al., "An Attributional Analysis of Expressed Emotion in Mexican-American Families with Schizophrenia"

Tito greeted me, laughing out loud. I had just arrived from San Antonio to visit him. Unable to shake memories of that time in Mexico when he lived with my tíos, he began by reminding me of the time he ate twenty mini-tacos in less than ten minutes. "Lately food seems to be the only way that I can stay connected to my body," he said. "So remembering your cooking and the feasting in Mexico makes me feel better. Food seems to be the only real thing to me. I've been losing it here and there. Had never felt this way before. No. Take it back. That's the way I felt when I was in Mexico. Maybe that's why I'm remembering the food."

I wondered if another break was looming. Shaking my head, I reminded myself that I could not think that way. I had to remember that in addition to all the positive symptoms that were not really positive—such as delusions, hallucinations, and paranoia—his condition was undifferentiated because of the depression.

The staff told me that they have told Tito to brush his teeth more than twice a day and have made him shower daily. "He is losing sight of his physical connection to his body," they said.

"Why did you send me to Cosalima?" Tito asked me without expecting an answer. "There I began to experience what I had never felt before. My mind moved in and out of the reality that was around me. Others' voices sounded foreign, nonsensical—not like a language I knew, even though I spoke Spanish. Words from people's mouths came out like strings of saltwater taffy—too long to understand, yet in short bursts like light on a firebug, breaking here and there. The sounds from their mouths terrified me. Could not string the words together inside my mind. Plugging my ears made it worse. It was not what they were speaking, it was as if my mind was weaving, pulling, creating what came out of their mouths for me to hear. In flashes of reality, I could read the fear in their eyes. They were looking at me weird."

Uttering things he didn't mean to share, he began a tirade of negative and derisive comments.

HOMEBOY: "Gringo loco. We do not understand you."

SYRUPY GIRL: "You're talking like a baby dog in a language we don't know—you must be possessed."

ANGRY MAN: "*Está endemoniado*—'ta loco. He's possessed. Be careful."

"It was at the taquería," Tito said in his own voice. "Scared them away with my actions. Did not want to deal with the craziness that was coming out of me. Having eaten what I bought for them, they had no use for me. Often ditched me and left me where we went. My body was not my own. I had no control over it. My mind had turned upside down. Entangling me in a world of death and deception, I believed I was in a fight for my life. One of the guys who had given me a hard time the week before was tormenting me. Dared me to fight. Pulled out a knife that I made vanish with my thoughts, easily transferring the weapon to my own hands. I killed him. *Piquetitos*. Stabbings. Splat, spurt, splat—blood sprayed all over everyone but me."

Tito took a pause before continuing. "What made it more terrifying was that the dude wouldn't die. Tried to put him and me out of our miseries. But he kept coming back for more. Stubborn—wouldn't give up. He kept coming back for more until I finally pierced his heart. It was then that someone tapped me on the shoulder. Brought me back. Filled with a sense of victory, I basked in the power that one gets from slaying a tormentor who taunts one for being all wrong, all stupid—for not fitting in. It was horrible. Both there and not there all at the same time. 'Member, I finally told you that I had killed someone in Cosalima. Couldn't live with the burden in my conscience. It would not be until much later I realized that the one I had killed had been me. Tito had died. Never to come back, the person that I used to be before that day was forever gone."

I could not help but cry as my son told a story I had already heard. Somehow, the story helped me capture the complexity of his life. It was hard to imagine that Tito had kept all these memories inside him, many years after his return from Mexico.

"It took me several years to get that the murder scene had been a hallucination," he continued. "To this day, the smell of blood, sweat of the fight, and color of blood turning brick red from its contact with the air when it escaped from his wounds, feels real. The guilt of believing I had killed someone became another excuse to numb my mind with drugs. Until I told you about it, I kept that agony to myself. It wasn't until you checked out my story with our Mexico relatives that I finally realized it had been my imagination. Unfortunately, that incident had opened the door of mental illness. Don't get scared. I'm not violent. I don't want to hurt you or anybody. Sure, I get upset and throw a tantrum once in a while, but I only harm myself in the process, like that time I hit my fist against the wall and hurt my knuckles. Or the time I hit my head on the wall to stop the voices until the workers at the hospital restrained me. And those times I self-mutilated to numb the pain."

Near the conclusion of our talk, Tito said, "Good thing I've seen the error of my ways, for now. I'm so frightened about death that I've even given up on committing suicide or hurting myself in any way. Depression brings me to the brink, but fear saves me. It's not so much that I'm afraid to die. It's that I dread living with the disease. What keeps me here is my love for you guys—I don't want to hurt you. I want you to be proud of me because I've tried to live the life I was given as best I could."

Memories and Loneliness

The only way for a person with schizophrenia to feel less isolated and alone is to be with other people, real or imagined, who care for and accept the person despite his or her illness.

—Larry Davidson, *Living Outside Mental Illness*

Mexico is still in Tito's mind. Every chance he has, he wants to talk to me all about the time he spent there. It makes me wonder about the baggage he carries and the torment he unlocked on that trip. Laughing and crying at the same time, Tito once told me about the muck he uncovered in Mexico—the secrets and buried skeletons. Some relative, whose name he didn't even remember, had told him that he was the product of rape—that his own grandfather was his father. No wonder my son went mad. That would have been traumatic for anyone.

"Momma, I came back devastated from that Mexico trip," he told me. "With the hallucinations and all that I was feeling, I didn't know who to talk to. Kept everything inside as long as I could, until I could no longer hold it. Despite the pain and confusion, I finally went to your sister Mary, who had been spared the reasons for the family breakup. You had told me about the abuse, but I had no idea how savage it had been. It was something so shameful to you—the three oldest sisters— that you even kept it from Tía Mary to protect her, to spare her the horror. 'I know cousin John and I are products of rape,' I recall telling Aunt Mary. My auntie didn't know what to say. Told me I was crazy, making things up as usual."

How sad that he had kept that from me, I thought. "She had known my father, Beto, and could attest to my origins," Tito continued. "Wrestling with her discovery, Mary did not immediately tell or ask anyone about it. 'It's worse than stupid—I can't believe you are dumb enough to bring them back and spread them around,' was all she could tell me as I began to peel the secrets off of our family closet. Soon enough, watching TV one day, Auntie Mary broached the subject with my cousin John, whom we called Negro because of his chocolate brown color. I can still remember every word. 'Negro, I know how you were born.' Mary's comment didn't seem out of the ordinary. John's mother had let him know he was a product of violence but had never identified or named the perpetrator. Without malice, or intending any harm, Mary said: 'Did you know we have the same father?'"

That's the way the family secret had unraveled, but it was all for the good, I thought as I listened to Tito. "This unplanned revelation sickened and shocked my cousin Negro," he said. "Didn't mean to hurt him. I just needed to unload that awful truth. I waited what felt like a lifetime, but John said nothing. Could hear the silence in the room like cold air that whizzes past you when you're in the presence of a spirit. Then Negro came apart. But he tried to keep it together, and even then I heard him say, 'Now, it all makes sense.' Accusingly, Negro glared in my direction, telling Mary, as if I wasn't there but wanting me to hear, 'This has to be a cruel joke. Are you trying to make life more unbearable for me?'"

Tito paused in his recollection of Negro's words, bringing tears to my eyes. "Momma, he thought I was playing tricks on him. As if. Why would I do that? Felt horrible. Went inside my own self-pity, especially because I still believed that I was in the same straits. Didn't want to be part of such an evil man. Rather than face it, I regretted being the carrier of those questions. I felt horrible for having unlocked the secret. Why did I have to do that? Negro had never been ashamed of being the product of rape. He had learned to accept that. But being the son of his own grandfather! After this, the thought of suicide played like a broken record inside my cousin's mind. He wanted to end it all. Negro didn't even look in my direction, much less talk to me about all of this drama that came out. But he couldn't fool me. I knew the fact of his conception continued to slap him in the face. He stayed away from the family because he was afraid to let on that he knew about his origins. I could sense, those times he wanted to scream, that he knew. The anger was so palpable I thought he could explode into the infinite."

My poor son and his cousin. Life was not a bed of roses for them. Tito's voice led me back to the story. "Momma, you told me that things would be all right. That we would sort it out. That when the time was right for John, he would see his mother to tell her that he knew. And a few months later, you told me John had gone to talk to her, and they fell into each other's arms—*dos brazos*, or what he calls the hugs they gave each other. They cried. Talked. Best of all they put the past in its place. Negro pledged to continue living as best he could, to honor his mother, who sacrificed her childhood for him."

Even though his stories are real, sometimes, as on this occasion, it feels as though Tito is fabricating them. They are so fantastic, it makes me wonder if he's entering a delusional phase. On this visit I decided to talk to him about it later. He was upset, and I did not want to add to his burden. As a sign of not wanting to discuss it, he gave me a hug and left.

Sometimes Death
Is the Only Option

Awareness and concern by mental health professionals about sexuality in schizophrenia emerge only in the context of its inappropriate occurrence in hospitals or when sexually transmitted diseases or unwanted pregnancies arise as consequences of uninformed sexual activity. . . . For most providers of mental health services, the sex lives of those with schizophrenia are preferably out of sight and out of mind.

—Alex Kopelowicz, Robert Paul Liberman, and Donald Stolar,
"Schizophrenia and Sexuality"

I hadn't detected Tito's suicidal ideation the last time we talked, but he must have been more devastated than I was able to discern at the time. After our visit, he tried to kill himself, but he didn't really want to die. It was a call for attention, so no one notified me about the attempt. I found out about it when Tito called to inform me that he was in the psychiatric ward. As I listened, he took me back to other times he had tried to kill himself, as if to find a pattern. It wasn't clear to me that he wanted to explain what he had just gone through. Rather, it was as if he aimed to punish me by telling me about it.

"There I was again, deep in the depression and the loneliness, and having to deal with the impending feeling of ending it all," he said. "This time, it was not so much the voices or that I was feeling sorry for myself—it was not even depression. I was fed up with it all. Momma, can you believe it? A sexual predator who lived in the same board-and-care home came on to me, confusing my loneliness and need to have someone in my life as a desire for sex of whatever type. This guy tried to convince me that I was gay, that he could take care of my physical needs. He petrified the shit out of me. You see, what scared me more is that I had entertained the possibility that being gay with someone was better than being straight with no one to hug me, to care for me, and to make me feel alive. So panicky was I that I made up my mind to kill myself—to end the confusion, to stop the loneliness, and to close the opening that made me contemplate that possibility, if only to be held and loved, not just for sex."

As if I had not been a part of the process, he told me, "Even before I called you, Mrs. Salud telephoned you, leaving several recorded messages about my attempt. Momma, do you remember me asking you if you would love me if I were gay? 'Of course,' your response came. 'Yes,' you said, as if making sure I heard you. 'Yes. I'd love you anyway—gay or straight. You're my son, my firstborn, my baby.' What else did I expect? Still, Mrs. Salud left a message as I was there waiting to hear your response. Freaked you out, right? 'Robert tried to kill himself. You better call. Please, call by nine.' Anxious over my problem, Mrs. Salud telephoned you several times. She was worse than me on a bad day, calling, calling, and calling you. I laughed thinking of you, as if you were sharing a joke only you and I understood."

Late from an evening class, that string of calls was the last thing I'd expected to hear. With my heart in my hands, I called to speak to Tito. "Gloria Salud left these messages as she tried to deal with my madness," Tito said. "Guess it comes with running a home for people like me—most of those people work for minimum pay and aren't at all equipped to deal with the problems we bring. The easy money they expect for our room and board comes with consequences; they have no idea what they take on. Poor lady, she had no clue as to what was going on inside my mind. Only thing she knew was that I had asked her to move Paul out of my room. Told her he had made advances at me. Of course, I later used that as another excuse to have you take me away from my surroundings, as I tried to strip myself away from the madness I could not shed."

Tito hesitated before continuing with the story he and I shared: "'Robert has cut his wrists. Please call me.' Somewhat more desperate, she continued trying to reach you. Becoming more anxious with her lack of success, my taunting didn't help her. 'You know why. You know why. Tell her. She needs to know what kind of place you're running here. Tell her about the horrible food you feed us.' All riled up and obsessed with the problems, as well as being infuriated about those sexual advances, I tried to restrain myself so as to not disobey the no-screaming signs posted in her office. I made an effort to hint at what had gone on, but I couldn't tell her that I was afraid of being raped by the guy who lived in my room, who didn't want to honor the limits I set for myself. Then I started to feel guilty, but with the kind of satisfaction that came with making you concerned about my situation—it was the case every time I tried to end it all. Mrs. Salud seemed afraid to know more because it would force her to tell you and Dad the reason. So she said nothing about that resident who'd made sexual advances at me. She kept it to herself."

Tito talked rapidly, not letting me get a word in edgewise: "The telephone rang while I was in her office. Mrs. Salud answered the call, repeating every question you asked, as if to keep me informed about your response. 'Are the wounds superficial?' Clarifying, more for her own benefit than for you, she added, 'I think it's just a cry for attention from your son. He is very lonely.' After that comment, Mrs. Salud handed me the telephone. You and I felt spent, consumed. You had had it with the incessant calls, and I felt tired of being perceived as incompetent, incapable of handling my own life affairs. Only thing I could do was to start the conversation I knew you hated to hear. It wasn't about dying. It was about living in institutions and not being independent. It's always been about that—board-and-care facilities are only holding tanks for the mentally ill. I wanted to be home with you and Dad. I pleaded to your conscience and used guilt like a Stradivarius violin to convince you to bring me home. 'Momma, I wish I could live on my own. Being with you would make everything all right.'"

Tito still wouldn't let me get a word in. He wanted to make sure I understood how he feels when he is in the throes of the illness. "You don't understand what it's like," he said. "You think you do, but you don't.

Staying with you would give me the freedom to come and go as I wish, without having to fear being accosted or ridiculed. Feeling trapped by the paranoia and delusions, and the sexual violence that comes with room-and-board living, all I could think about was getting out, going home to you, Momma, and the comfort of what was for me. Suddenly, coming to the realization that this was as trying on you as it was on me, I tried to get a grip on myself. I'm not the only one affected by my illness, I think to myself, trying to downplay what's going on inside me. Minimizing the horrors I live with every day, I stopped talking to you."

He continued his effort to make me understand how alone he felt, telling me, "I get it, I've pushed away most of my family. You all fear me. Aware that the illness is a burden for all of us, I tell you that I will try to cope with it as best I can. The ways the disease impacts my life frightens all of you, but you can leave it behind—goes with me wherever I go. See, I know why you don't come around much. It's no wonder I feel lonely. It doesn't make me happy to know that until the end of my days I will be living in such institutions. Some are better than others, but they're still institutions. Momma, being almost two thousand miles away from me, the distance insulates you. The damned telephone—just a gadget—is no substitute for you, but at least I feel reassured knowing that you are as near as the phone. I know, I know."

Tito barely gave me time to sort out the story I already knew. He hated where he was and wanted me to make arrangements for another facility. "Those damned telephone boundaries you place on me. You must dread hearing it ring as much as I dislike that damned recorder that keeps you away from me. Won't admit it, but I know you screen the calls, and to spite you, to get your attention, to not feel so alone, I keep ringing until I wear you down. There have been times when I've left thirty messages or more. Disabled the recorder with messages. Still haven't learned that it doesn't work. It just cuts me off from you, filling the recorder with my sorry words only cuts me off, can't leave you one more desperate call. But your detachment doesn't last long. You don't fail me. Even if it's from afar, you're there for me. If you weren't around, don't know what I would do. I can count on you. You call me, know when I need you. Not clear how you know, but you do. You can sense my depression and isolation."

Tito paused as if to sort out all he had told me. The phone went silent, and not even static in the line broke that silence, emphasizing my son's isolation. Then he continued to talk about schizophrenia in a voice so clear it felt like he was right next to me, in the living room. He grabbed my attention by exclaiming, "Shit, I'm your schizophrenia."

With a pause for effect, he waited for my reaction. He wanted me to respond, but I was at a loss for words. I waited for him to continue.

"I am the voice that never goes away and always returns to you," he went on. "I am the noise on the telephone that will come through again and again. The one that's always gnawing at you, keeping you alert about my every move, making you uncomfortable enough to wonder what will come. Just as I deal with the voices, paranoia, and delusions, Momma, you must live with the impending crises of my illness. We both live inside a recurring nightmare. The illness shows up when we least expect it, though you seem to be better at predicting the breaks before they come. Still, it keeps you off-balance and always focused on me. Poor Momma, I don't ever give you a break. Damned if you do and damned if you don't. It's a no-win situation for the two of us."

Tito paused again, then placed the telephone on a hard surface and left me waiting there, without saying anything. I hung up the telephone and continued with the everyday chores of my life. All I could do was hope that he was all right. Nevertheless, I called the office to inform them that I was concerned for my son.

TV Programs Inside

Voices Alive

The lack of research in this area and the emphasis on negative outcomes rather than building on strengths are in conflict with the recovery literature and fail to provide adequate direction to mental health professionals who are working with individuals confronting these issues.

—Shirley M. Glynn et al., "The Potential Impact of the Recovery
Movement on Family Interventions for Schizophrenia"

I have learned to capture Tito's perception of his life, including his sense of humor, as a television sitcom without direction. That is the way it is for him. His stories change and shift along with the voices or delusions invading his mind. If he were clear of the illness, his mind would be a goldmine for *Ripley's Believe It or Not.* Tito could be a source of television material a la Fellini—all the excitement, all the fantastic possibilities.

His thoughts are fleeting, plentiful, and dramatic. Often he tells me that his mind is like floating sparks in a kaleidoscope, constantly in motion. Images flickering inside, motion pictures projecting to the point that they interfere with his own voice and his own thinking. He is constantly trying to sort out his own mind. When the stories are about us—family—they are the lifesavers he needs. Those recollections awaken his spirit.

Then there are the desperate times when Tito becomes laden with sadness; these are the "icy periods" he calls to talk to me about. With these stirrings, his death wish reemerges and the cycle starts all over again—the never-ending pressure of mental illness.

Contemplating reasons for his being alive, the stories in Tito's mind keep him connected to his past, his former life. They become the foundation to a reality that he struggles with daily. Inside the distractions, there are times that, if Tito focuses enough, he could almost bring his family to life. So he tries to listen intently, to tap into those times for which he dearly longs. He tries to remember. He forever seeks to find meaning and reason for his entrance into the world.

Sometimes, these emotional vistas paint smiles on his face. At other times, these fragmented and disconnected messages give him the humor he needs to carry on with his life. His memories bring him alive and out of the reach of schizophrenia. Even when he is experiencing a psychotic break, for good or bad, we become part of his delusions—his fictive communities. And when he feels the most defeated, the most useless, these stories bring him back to himself as he was before the illness.

His favorite story is the one about his birth in Gilroy, California. Remembering it, Tito gets engrossed in the tale. He doesn't care who is there with him or what his or her purpose is, because that story is central, and as he tells it, he thrives. And even though I am a central character in this plot, Tito told me the story on my next visit as if I had been a detached spectator: "Shit, what's going on? No. Here it goes again. Hot damn! There it is. Momma, I'm on TV, walking through the maternity ward at the hospital. Nurse Ajo Head, so-called because of her pointy garlic dome, utters her commands. She stands at attention, croaking each name. Ha-ha!"

Tito laughed at the recollection. Unaware that he was telling me the story yet again, he called out the action like a director reading the dialogue of an inner movie—and voicing all the parts, to me, his mother.

"It's your sixth child, Socorrah," he began, imitating the nurse. "Stop your screaming. You knew what to expect. Don't play coy."

"Mean old bag. Can't she see? It hurts. Ay! Stop it."

"If you didn't want to hurt," he said, again playing the part of the nurse, "you shoulda kept your legs crossed, Nancy. Better yet, you could've put an aspirin between your knees."

"God-awful. What's up with her? Get Nurse Ratchet! Anybody. Somebody else."

"I know about you people. You think you would learn. But no! Here y'all are. Kid after kid, and you're still screaming. Stop opening your legs!"

"Thinks we're roaches. Multiplying. Taking over. Hey, not a bad idea. Let's make some more!"

"Quiet, Susana! Take it like a man. Stop crying."

"Even this nut knows. Men don't have children. Pendeja."

"Quiet! All right already!"

As though reciting dialogue in a play, Tito acted out the story. Almost as if he had heard me wondering about the nurse, he described her for me, exactly as I had when I'd told him the story of his birth.

"The nurse was built like a trapezoid," he said, "with the wide part of her upper body connected to a small cylindrical neck, which was attached to a head shaped like a garlic bulb with sparse bristles that stood on end for hair. Nurse Ajo Head marched up and down the hallways putting the fear of God into those mothers-to-be at Wheeler Hospital, where I was born. Told everyone who was listening or trying to ignore her to take birth control or stop having sex. Made the women feel like they're in some type of military drill, hearing her march up and down the hallway. Chastising them for having too many children, blaming them for their condition. You know, it takes two. You taught me that—my fault as well if someone got pregnant with my baby, not just the girl's."

The nurse returned: "Hup, two, three, four. March. Hup, two, three, four. March. Hope this is your last one, María. What would anyone want with seven children? You can barely feed the ones you have."

"Aren't you happy? More workers to pick your food, *gorda*. What country do you come from? More hands mean more money."

"Didn't you learn your lesson, Martha? If only you had some control over your fever, the rhythm would've worked, and you wouldn't be screaming now."

"What rhythm? Dancing got her pregnant?"

"Quiet! All right already! Stop the judgment."

"Shh! You'll scare the others. Stop making such a ruckus."

Again Tito narrated the story: "Dispensing judgments, Nurse Ajo continues to make the rounds, giving unwanted sermons to deaf ears. Like *aleluyas* at a communist convention, her words went for naught. She warned everyone not to frighten the 'greenhorns,' what she called those who were having a baby for the first time, complaining about their failed fertility lessons. Among them at Wheeler Hospital, awaiting my birth, you were just another member of Ajo's captive audience. Unsuccessfully tried to shut out her words—Ajo's marching chants didn't make anything easier, especially for Momma, who also was a first-timer. Told me you didn't have an easy pregnancy and my birth was hard and lasted sixteen hours. And I had the umbilical cord tied around my neck. The trauma of my birth gave me a deep-purple, wrinkled appearance that made me look like a small, withered grape. My whole body was the color of the spot Grandmother Vera would later seek on my lower my back. You see, unless she found it in her sons' offspring, she only recognized her daughters' children as grandkids."

Voicing his grandmother, Tito said, "The only grandchildren certain to be mine are those born to my daughters. With them, it doesn't matter who made them because they're born from my flesh."

"How could she?" Tito said, going back to his narration. "Her lack of trust must've really hurt you. She couldn't wait to get her hands on my backside to check the spot where my gluteus maximums ended for the sign. No sooner were the nurses gone than she did just that. Wanted to confirm that I was her progeny—didn't want to recognize somebody else's bastard. She took my five-pound-six-ounce body from you and flipped it upside down as if I had not experienced the trauma of that long labor we had survived. Without making a fuss over me or even giving me a peck on the cheek, she placed me on her lap. Like she was unwrapping the Christmas tamales she was so fond of eating, Vera peeled off my diaper. Checked for the Apache sign—a blue-purple triangle on my lower back—the Mongolian mark of her ancestors. Claiming to have originated from Apache chiefs, she wanted to make sure I was of her bloodline. And she did. It was there for her to witness. Her grandchild, I was. Since that mark was the only way to prove our blood link, she wanted to make sure. So that September 16, my grandmother Vera Organista recognized me, Robert López Jr., forever known as Tito, as another child of her family line. Whether it was good or bad, I never found out. We both know that Vera was never a part of my life, but for that unusual rite."

Tito stirred memories inside me, making me recall statements made to me when Vera's daughters were about to deliver her grandchildren. "Apparently, this was the ritual she exercised with most of the children produced by her daughters-in-law," he said. "Only exception was *la japonesa* that she didn't approve of—those children were Lan's. She was the woman who married one of my uncles against the wishes of both sides of their families. They were spared Vera's recognition. Their parents were banished for marrying outside their groups. For this, they were denied Vera's love, of which she had little left to give, having always made her current paramour the priority. Unlike me, los japoneses never had to show their Mongolian mark. Never had to prove anything to her. The thing we had in common was that we never had a relationship with her. How sad!"

As Tito does every time he feels he's talked enough, he hung up the telephone and went off to mourn the loss of what could have been. I imagined that he went for a cigarette break because cigarettes give him the comfort he needs. I was glad he called me and wanted to speak about the story of his beginning. He had been feeling out of sorts, and talking about the past and the stories he carries always provides him a sense of relief.

Grateful for the stories that keep my son connected to his self, I feel thankful that they give him some respite from the illness that controls his life. They allow him to imagine the life he would have liked to have had but did not get.

At Another Time, I Would Have Been Don Quixote

He was a dreamer and a fighter, and most of all he expected rejection along the way. "The mentally ill invite rejection," he was fond of saying, and that extended to his work on their behalf. He fancied himself a Don Quixote, tilting at windmills.

—Rebecca Birnbaum, "My Father's Advocacy for a Right to Treatment"

Oh, how the stories feed Tito's soul. He lives through them and because of them. Tito has many favorites. But the one that often surfaces is one I made up for him when he was in the second grade, when he started to feel confused about the meaning of truth. The clinical literature I have read notes that children who will become mentally ill have problems deciphering the truth, as it is typically understood, though I didn't know that when Tito was that age.

Looking back, it was about the time Tito was in second grade that he began telling tales too fantastic to believe, especially when he got in trouble or feared the imagined consequences of his mischief. One such time, when he was eight years old, he took a group of his friends to Alum Rock Park without permission —Tiburcio Vasquez's hiding place when he was running from the law in those frontier days of early California.

Near the mountain peak called Eagle Rock and compelled by Tito's dare, the kids agreed to play catch with yellow jacket honeycombs that hung in the trees, thinking the wasps would not sting. Well, they all got stung. And when they were found by a cadre of people who volunteered to comb the park, Tito's tales became epic. The stings magnified a thousand times; he told anyone who would listen that he had taken thousands of stings to protect the younger ones.

Consumed by my memories, I did not hear the telephone ring. One of the psych techs at Tito's facility called to tell me that the night before had been particularly difficult for Tito. He thought I should know that it was another sexual predator that had stirred him up. It wasn't the first time Tito had experienced this; he would talk to me about being accosted again. Apparently, a resident jumped into my son's bed and tried to have sex with him.

Later that same day, Tito called to tell me about the incident. Things were becoming more unbearable for him. He was extremely upset and claimed the staff was doing nothing about the situation, all the while chalking it up to things a "loony" would do, as if to anchor the conversation in what he knew or understood. Not wishing to add pressure to the troubles that already consumed him, I decided to listen to his side of the story. But it didn't sound like my son. The voices that came through the telephone were in a tone I was not familiar with.

DRUGGIE: "There you go, storyteller, can't seem to get you outta your funk, huh?"

HOMEBOY: "What's with the stories anyway, ese? Is another break coming?"

SYRUPY GIRL: "You think he's gonna have another episode?"

HOMEBOY: "Híjole, it gets old in here, cuate!"

ELDERLY MALE: "I remember when his momma tried to help him distinguish between truth and lies. She wanted him to understand what he was doing. Teach him a lesson at the same time she told him a story."

ANGRY MAN: "Of course I knew the difference!"

HOMEBOY: "Estoy loco, ¡pero no menso!"

"Sorry, Momma," Tito said in his own voice, "think I was reeling in that story you wrote for me when I was not yet six years old. When I was still trying to figure out what I could get away with, especially when you got together with the man who would become my dad, Jorge."

Still trying to sort it out, Tito continued with the story. Just listening, I decided to respond only when he asked me a direct question.

"Boy, I remember the ways you tried to discipline me," he said. "Used *cuentos*—tales about your own upbringing or those you made up as needed—because you didn't believe in spanking or hitting. So you made up that Aesop fable a la mexicana called 'Titotzín's Truth,' after your endearment for me. You explained the character's name, telling me that adding 'tzín' to Tito, which was a redundancy to my nickname Tito, for Robertito, made it 'Little Tito's Truth.' If that was your intent. Not sure how much it helped me with lying, though. But I really liked the stories you wrote, to the point that I memorized every word. I know you meant well, just trying to help me sort out the difference between lies and truth. Don't know if you realized it, but I've learned to use that story with the residents. They get a big kick out of it. Keeps them occupied. Sometimes they even stop lying. Wanna hear it?"

Committed to responding only when he asked a question, I grunted in agreement and Tito immediately jumped into the story. I dismissed my busy schedule so I could hear him tell it.

"Titotzín, a gifted child, came from the planet of Verdatl," he began, "your invention to convey the meaning of truth. It comes from Spanish and Nahuatl. Why am I telling you that? You already know. Titotzín had the ability to see what others couldn't. In his planet, they emphasized truth. Uncertainties, half-truths, and lies, even so-called white lies, were not part of that world. Still, Titotzín was curious about lying. One day he asked himself, 'How can I know truth if I don't know its opposite?' With that question in mind, he set out on a journey to Earth to find that which was absent in his world—lies.

"Along the way, he met many people and confronted multiple truths. But his most vivid confrontation began when he ran into two noisy birds perched up on a live oak tree limb—Urraca Grackle and Eagle Aguila, who I'll refer to as Urraca and Aguila for short. Titozín found them entangled in a shrieking and cawing contest, arguing back and forth. Actually, come to think of it, it was the most heated argument Titotzín had ever witnessed. So he stopped to watch them. He thought, 'In my world we don't fight. We accept each other's differences and respect one another for our similarities.' Still, Titotzín, trying to make sense of the birds' noises, sat under the tree to listen. Listened with his heart."

As Tito retold the tale of those two disparate birds, I wondered which of them he identified with. "To Titotzín it looked like the bold and powerful eagle aimed to impose her truths on the scraggly black-bird," he added. "She tried every which way to push her views down Urraca's throat. Titotzín couldn't believe it. It was such an infringe-ment on Urraca's rights. From what he could tell, Aguila didn't care to consider that each one of us has individual perceptions. Poor Urraca. She had to contend with everyone's judgments. The hyena or pig of the airs, perceived as a good-for-nothing that only exists to pilfer and pol-lute the environment, Urraca's lot was a legacy of struggle and survival. So she attempted to tell her truth to Aguila. Yet uncertain about her place in the world, she asked Titotzín to witness the debate."

Tito paused before continuing his narration. "Titotzín accepted the charge. With this task, he hoped to better understand the meaning of truth. 'Well,' Urraca said to Aguila, 'my children are the most beautiful in the world. Their chants are the most melodious. And they fly more gracefully than sea gulls in the middle of the ocean.' From the corner of his eyes Titotzín saw Aguila shaking her head in disbelief at Urraca's words. Trying to intimidate Urraca, Aguila strutted about, barrel chest arched, exaggerating her physical difference in an effort to undermine the scraggly blackbird. Not bothering about the witness, who took in her every move, Aguila continued aping Urraca's fidgety movements to bully her into defeat. As if she were a show bird on exhibition for a prize, Aguila alternated between postures of arrogance and threatening and annoying screeches, sending shrieks of power that sounded more like Urraca's than her own. She didn't care about Urraca's feelings. All that mattered to Aguila was being right and imposing her might.

"For Titotzín, those charades showed that Aguila was not inter-ested in being fair or just. None of Urraca's concerns mattered to Aguila, who was posturing to win the bout. That was all Aguila cared about, winning. Urraca attempted to restate her point. In the middle of all these pantomimes, she tried to tell her truth. But Aguila would have none of it, as she laughingly interrupted and mocked poor Urraca at every pause. 'You're crazy! Are you blind? Your children are the most despicable. They make horrid, terrible sounds, and when they sing, if you call that singing, they drive you wild with their screeches. To top it off, they can't even fly.'"

My beautiful Tito. He had such a difficult time believing he was loved. As he continued, I wondered how much he saw himself in the story.

"How sad for Urraca to hear those words. They were piercing the deepest crevice of her heart. So painful were they, her soul wanted to take flight. There! The bold Aguila stated her truth. After all, she didn't see those babies with a mother's eyes. Titotzín's stomach was about to burst from the tension; it twisted and wrung itself into little knots. His guts ached so that he had difficulty talking. Seeing the deadly pain in Urraca, Titotzín forced himself to share his thoughts. Because of his resolve, Aguila withdrew, realizing she was about to be judged by a little boy from who-knows-where: 'Man, I don't have to justify myself to anyone. I know my truth is right. Nobody can tell me I'm wrong. I never make mistakes or tell lies. That's just the way it is. Around here, I'm queen.'

"Having made her statement, Aguila ascended to the highest branch. Took her perch. Looked down and around, daring someone to kick her off the pedestal, resting on her greatness. Then, as if to intimidate Titotzín and Urraca, Aguila swooped above their heads. All that mattered to Aguila was her own views. All she cared about was the way she saw it. She believed fairness and justice were just illusions for those who have no power or who lack the authority she had as the ruler of the airs. With all the tolerance he could muster, Titotzín told Aguila to return. But she ignored him. Her actions gave Titotzín the resolve to tell the truth. Then, when he was about to speak, Titotzín realized he might hurt Urraca. So he measured his words. Trying not to hurt her, he said, 'Aguila is right. I have never seen such spent birds or ones so deprived in looks or ones that sing so poorly. But they are in this world for a purpose. Truth is in being who we are. They are beaut—'

"In his compassion, Titotzín tried to tell Urraca what she wanted to hear. He didn't want to harm her. He tried again. 'Miss Urraca, your children are beaut—'

"He stopped, realizing he had almost lied to protect her. That's when he came face to face with truth. Regaining his composure, Titotzín weighed the facts again. Gave them more thought. Finally, Aguila came down. She wanted to hear what he thought, even if to get a good laugh at his expense. Still struggling, speaking like a good diplomat, Titotzín said to Aguila: 'You are the same, but not alike. You're both birds that can fly and you have your own language to speak. I admire you for your differences but I respect you for your similarities. Those sounds that you call screeches are songs of love for Urraca. How can you put down the words a mother has for her children?'"

Tito waited a moment before going on. "It wasn't that difficult after all. They had much more in common than they thought. And most of all, they were all living creatures trying to do what was necessary to survive. Titotzín continued, trying to be just and fair to both of them, without hurting either one in the process. To Urraca, he said, 'I respect your sadness. Aguila has hurt you by telling you her truths. But what matters here is your own truth. In reality, her truths are different from yours and mine. If you see that the distinctions among us are what make us unique, your pain will be lessened. The three of us were born to be only who we are—us. Not identical but distinct from each other. Your looks do not make you less in my eyes; I do not devalue you because of them. You are just as important as this royal Aguila and me. You are beautiful and significant in your own way. You are.'

"Titotzín noticed Urraca's receptivity. And Aguila eyed him thoughtfully. Neither said anything. Satisfied with having done his part, Titotzín left to continue his quest. He had tried to be as just as he could under the circumstances. He felt at ease and good with himself. 'Good-bye. I wish you friendship.' As he left, Titotzín sighed from the depths of regret. 'By God, I almost lied. So this is what it means to tell partial truths? I almost made a deceitful act.' It wasn't difficult for Titotzín to realize this. The animals and people he encountered on Earth were similar to those characters found in the fairy tales of his land. Now he was beginning to understand what truth was all about."

Finished with the story, Tito said, "Momma, I'm not sure that I really understood what you were trying to teach me. It was a great story and now I know I saw myself as the Grackle, but at that time I didn't realize that my family and I didn't understand truth in the same way. It would not be until later that I would get the full meaning of the story. There's a second part to it. I'll tell you it the next time you come to visit me."

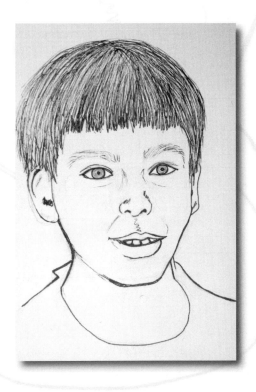

Reality Is Imagined

They freely exchanged stories. The lights proceeded to engage a symphony-like dance, corresponding with the exchange of words and tones. . . . The dark forces began to yell at Jim. Demanding he do the force's bidding, a thrust of energy came for Jim to handle the current situation.

—Vincent Macraven, *Tales from the Mind of a Schizophrenic*

In the six long weeks since I'd last seen my son, I had contemplated tape-recording Tito when we talked. I finally decided against it. Inside his psychosis, he was bound to believe I might use his words against him, even though he knows I'm not involved with or connected to the Norteños gangbangers he fears. Still, his narratives are informative, and because of the effect medicine has on my son, I decided to take notes as we spoke—just the main points and not in front of him.

I expected my son to continue the Titotzín story because it gives him a sense of who he is in relation to those he loves. As he came toward me, I began to take mental notes about his appearance and demeanor, jotting keywords every now and then on a palm-sized pad. "It's so I don't forget the key things you tell me," I informed him to let him know I was not spying. As I expected, my son returned to the story of Titozín. It wasn't clear to me why he had this need, but I was learning to recognize that the stories provide him a sense of reality that he does not always have. With them, he can return to the days of wellness, before the disease took over his life.

"To show you I remember the lessons you taught me, I'm retelling you the Titotzín story, Momma," he said, continuing his narration as if he had never stopped. "Deep in thought, and after walking for what seemed forever, the night descended upon him. Tired and sleepy, Titotzín decided to seek refuge. But there was nothing around him, just trees and animals. Then, in the distance, he spied a little house in the forest. He walked toward the house, wondering who lived there. 'Will I learn more about truth?' he said. 'What will be my lesson there?' Distracted by what he saw, Titozín didn't realize he spoke his thoughts aloud. 'By George, it's inhabited by a witch. She looks mean and is accusingly pointing her forefinger at a child.' In his quest for truth, he went to investigate and got closer without exposing himself. He knew it wasn't right for him to eavesdrop. But his curiosity got the best of him. Deep in thought, Titotzín did not recognize the screams until they invaded his ears like a bugle call to war. Without hesitating, he ran to help.

"*Knock. Knock. Knock.* No one heard him. Or his knock was ignored. *Knock. Knock. Knock.* The door remained closed. He tried finding another way to get their attention. He couldn't. So he ran to the side of the house, where he saw a shadow, a person lifting its arm to strike a smaller figure. Creeping around the window, he tried to see and hear more clearly what was going on. Soon he realized it was a little girl. She was sobbing, pleading her case. 'I didn't do it. Believe me. I was cleaning the dresser and it fell. It was an accident. Please, believe me. I am telling the truth.' It was a heartbreaking scene. The pleading tone of the young girl's voice tugged at Titotzín's heart. He could just about feel her pain. In his world he had learned to identify truth by the sounds of words and through facial expressions. But all Titozín could make out was sadness, fear, and confusion. He couldn't figure out what was going on. 'You lie. You never tell the truth. You're trying to cover up your fumbling mistakes as always. Look at all that I've done for you. This is the way you repay me?'

"Wanting to help, Titotzín tapped on the window as loudly as his manners allowed. Finally, the taller of the two answered the door. The woman greeted Titotzín almost as if she were expecting him. 'I'm glad you came. Now you can tell my child why she's such a bad daughter. She is so unappreciative. Always ignores her poor mother's wishes and directives. When I give her errands or chores to do, she does them begrudgingly. She never listens to me. She always lies. She never tells the truth.' Eyes squeezing giant teardrops, like melons, the woman stated her case as if she were a victim of her own child's lies. But Titotzín could see right through her. Barbara—that was her name—was as easy to read as a giant tome, although she wasn't aware of that. How unfair. The poor little girl stood accused in front of a stranger. Without the benefit of being heard, she was being judged. In a you'll-pay-for-it-later tone, the child's mother feigned encouragement for the child to tell her side of the story; in that warning-not-to-tell voice, Barbara egged on her child."

In the stories he tells, Tito captures the ways in which others perceive his world or interpret him in it. As he narrated this story, I understood what he was trying to tell me.

"'Go ahead, m'ija,' she said. 'Come on, my daughter. You know I'm too good to you. But go ahead, tell him you think I've done wrong. You know I've done nothing that calls for me to change. I stand here an innocent soul. All I've done is for your own good. I'm good to you. Aren't I?' Titotzín was confused. In Verdatl there would have been no reason to suspect an adult. Thoroughly perplexed, he didn't know what to believe. But to him, Barbara talked out of both sides of her mouth. And Barbara seemed to be succeeding at her game. All her child could do was quiver in fear. Having spent her tears, Raquel—that's what the woman called her daughter—stared at the floor. Hurting as she never had before, Raquel continued to stuff her feelings. 'My mother doesn't care about truth,' she thought, not daring to say that out loud. 'If I tell him what I feel, that she's not done right by me, will he hear me? She's always accusing, always scolding, always griping, always condemning. Treats me like her arms and her legs—get me this and get me that. Obey, be silent, and do what I tell you. She cares not what I think or what I feel. Only how she looks to others.'"

Tito stopped a moment and looked my way before continuing the story. "Raquel had not said a word, but Titotzín read her mind. The words were trapped inside, but her face told the story. The way he saw it, the little girl was drowning in her own feelings. Tangled in the pain, Titotzín failed to recognize that Barbi—what other adults called

Raquel's mother—had forgotten about the broken bottle of expensive perfume, the reason for her rage. Righteousness prevented her from admitting her inadequacies. It was even sadder when Titotzín came to the realization that Barbara would never seek help for her drinking, which would benefit both mother and daughter. It was no use. Right? Wrong? Truth or lie, power or powerless, good or bad, which one was it? Or was there an in-between place? With flooded eyes, Titotzín spoke to both: 'I do not see of what service I can be. If I stand between the two of you and hold you on the palm of my hand as if to balance your truths, I could never do either of you justice. You see, my truth is not yours. And fairness would be an issue, because I sympathize with Raquel. I identify with her pain.'

"Titotzín began to cry. He would have no part in imposing one truth over another: 'I'm sorry, ma'am, but I cannot become an accomplice to your deeds. I have seen your selective deafness. I don't want to help you pull the strings that control your child. As a person, she deserves to become who she was meant to be. I don't want to be part of her mistreatment. While I don't want to leave her in your hands, I have no choice. What is most sad is that I know I have no control over what you say or do. Now, I must really go. I hope and pray you open your mind. That you get help and create a new path for the both of you.'"

As if to give me time to catch up with him, Tito briefly stopped the narrative before going on. "Here was a child whose heart was withering and whose spirit was dying. This experience was difficult and painful. Titotzín finally lost all desire to figure out the world of lies. He realized that his quest to understand the difference between truth and lies was immaterial compared to the pain Raquel was living. Feeling more confused and sad than when his favorite grandmother had died, Titotzín decided he was done. For him, truth had always been in view. It came in many forms: the person telling it, the listener hearing it, and the interpreter translating the values of those whose ears selectively heard their own truth. Sorting it out was a painful process, and power and control were the scales that weighed it. This journey had finally made him see that he had always known what he sought—truth. Still, with a heavy heart and eyes flowing like rivers of salt, he returned to his home planet. As he ascended to Verdatl, Titotzín wailed from the complexity of it all. When he left, the earth became mute; the birds stopped singing, the wind stopped blowing, and all that made sounds became silent in reverence of the boy."

ANGRY MAN: "What a crappy and sappy story. Can't believe it. This is your favorite one!"

DRUGGIE: "What were the other ones like? Bet you ate it all up, ese."

ADORING FEMALE: "Aesop, maesop, and those dreaded morality tales."

HOMEBOY: "How boring! You bought that shit?"

I savored such times. I could sit and listen to Tito tell me stories forever. Even the pauses he took to listen to himself, as the tales unfolded, were fascinating. It felt good to visit my son.

When Tito had finished, as if to gauge my reaction to his story, he looked directly at me. Then he mockingly teased that I had tried to mimic *The Little Prince* in the story of Titozín. After stopping for a few seconds as if to listen to one of the many voices that live in his mind, he audibly chastised himself: "My truths have value, not just the system's truth. What I see, say, and think is important."

ANGRY MAN: "Geez, you were no Little Prince, Mr. Sissy-Boy-and-All. Can't believe you fell for that shit."

Realizing he had voiced his thoughts, Tito tried to minimize whatever was going on inside him. The smile on his face told me that he felt better now than he had before I'd arrived. But most of the time, listening to him talk, I could have cried for him.

Imagination Begets Life

It is one thing to write as a poet and another to write as a historian: the poet can recount or sing about things not as they were, but as they should have been, and the historian must write about them not as they should have been, but as they were, without adding or subtracting anything from the truth.

—Miguel de Cervantes Saavedra, *Don Quixote*

Even though Tito thought himself more akin to Sancho Panza, he loved the adventures of Don Quixote. But he had more affinity for the little boy from Verdatl. He didn't admit it, but Tito often imagined himself as Titotzín, "sorting things out both inside and outside the real world." He went about trying to make sense of his surroundings. Like the characters he described, Tito wanted a fairy-tale ending. It was a way to cope with the abuses and mockery he experienced about his looks and about the way he saw the world. Later, when he finally spoke about the abuses he had kept hidden, the fears that gripped him, and the terrors that had dominated his life, he surprised me. But on my next visit I had no clue as to what he would talk about, especially since I hadn't visited him in almost two months.

"Momma, you know things didn't get any better," he began. "Wish my life had been a happy story, but it wasn't. Adolescence was a nightmare; I could never do anything right—everybody let me know about my lack of competence. But the way I saw it, I was alone. And my imagination, which always had helped me deal with my fears, became my worst enemy. Every noise, every scent, became a source of suspicion. It was when I became a teenager that I started to smell rancid waste—feces. Remember? You guys put a stop to my bathing. Yeah! That was the reason I always showered. It was a source of strife for you and Dad, but you two were most concerned with wasting water in our ecologically conscious Santa Cruz community. You had no clue and I wasn't talking."

Tito paused, and his pause was almost calculated, as if to give me time to take in his comments or to choose his next topic. I wasn't sure if he was testing me or if he intuited that I, too, had been concerned about him "back in the day," as he often put it. When he talked about the early signs of his mental illness, I became uncomfortable. I felt guilt over having missed the cues. Even though he had had a somewhat healthy childhood, I always wondered what I could have done differently. How horrible it was for my son—for all of us. However, I was tired of carrying the burden, of trying to figure out what else I could have done.

With both of us deep in thought—me trying to figure out my part in his illness or how I might have contributed to it and Tito sorting out what to say next—he finally returned to the story of his adolescence, again as though I had not lived it with him. His mind was sharp and crisp that day. He almost sounded like the professor or attorney he had dreamed of becoming. He reflected on his adolescence.

"You know, Momma, even though our teen years are about growth, for me this time was not a rite of passage into adulthood. Instead, my brief life became replete with extremely chaotic and traumatic shifts. By this time I had become an expert at covering up or using deception to handle the chaos in my brain. Never told you before. And I denied it until I couldn't hold it in no more, but drugs covered up what was coming my way. Getting high helped me to normalize the madness I was experiencing. At least that way I could blame it on something."

Tito's efforts to stay focused told me that the voices were back. I saw him struggling to hear something far away. He paused once more, giving me time to take in what he had already said. I hoped I was able to listen as he wished. I was a bit distracted, but I responded, "Now, I get it. So that's why you got loaded. Why didn't you tell me? We could have done something. I could have had you speak to a counselor."

"What for?" he replied. "I needed the drugs to make it all seem normal. That's when I began to use them. Feeling like a failure, I decided to become the best mess-up I could be. Confusion and dejection were my guides. Even though I didn't understand anything that was going on inside me, I was too chicken to tell you guys what was really wrong with me. What a baby I was. That's when my school problems began, 'member? I couldn't concentrate or complete schoolwork, any work. That's when my body and mind began to turn against me. That wasn't even the half of it. My problems ran like a movie frame inside my mind—I could still see it all. First crisis was a very public one. Remember?"

I nodded.

"It happened on a trip we took to Mendocino County to visit our friends, Lorelei Hammond and Tim Brooks," he continued. "It was there, while on a hike on the coast of Point Arena, California, that I had a major seizure. It was Tim Brooks who noticed me slumped over the rocks, with my body jerking uncontrollably. Couldn't call for help. Didn't understand what was going on. Too frightened and out of control, there was nothing I could do. Couldn't talk. I had no control of my movement, even though I was aware of it all. Shit. Tim tried to be real smooth. Discretely, he called my dad to come help him."

ANGRY MAN: "No kidding! They really tried to keep calm about it."

"I've never seen anybody get anywhere so fast while feigning to take a leisurely stroll," Tito said. "Zaaazzz, before you knew it, they both were administering CPR. Tim and Dad stabilized me with their efforts. Deep into your hike, Lorelei and you had no clue as to what was going on at the beach below. Then you spotted a group of people surrounding me. Tim and Dad trying to keep calm. Not knowing what else to do, you froze on the spot. Just like that salt-pillar woman who tested temptation and turned into a statue, except you were staring in our direction. Couldn't decide whether to come where we were or remain where you stood. How scary it must've been for you. I was shitting in my pants and pretending that it didn't matter. I was here and not here all at the same time. Lorelei was trying to calm you. Keep you out of the way."

As if to draw me deeper into the conversation, Tito said, "How lucky we were to have friends like them. They've always been there for us." I was there with him, listening to his every word. "You were petrified," he went on, "and every once in a while, you looked our way. Your face, like the one you make when eating lemons with salt, was fixated in a state of horror. Confused, you stood there, unable or unwilling to get to where I was. However, I could see that you felt pulled by the desire to make sure I was OK. Instead of coming to where the crowd gathered, you helplessly paced, alternating between crying and praying—too afraid to come near me—thinking the worst. It must've been terrible for you. Corky, my younger brother, who always acted like he was the older one, became the go-between. That young boy in an old man's mind tried to reassure everyone that all was fine, making every effort to calm us. He really tried to keep things together. No one seemed distracted by the commotion. I became the priority."

ANGRY MAN: "Isn't that what you're still trying to do with her? With your calls for cigarettes, money, and all those collect calls for attention? Aren't you holding her hostage, so she can make you the priority, the number one in her life?"

SYRUPY GIRL: "Shh! Trying to talk. Stop! Stop interfering."

"Don't know how long that took," Tito continued in his voice. "But finally, after what seemed like an eternity, the ambulance and emergency medical people arrived. First thing they did was to disperse all the *fisgones*, the onlookers. Then they went about tending to me, to make sure everything was all right."

Tito had an urgent need to tell me about the onset. It was as if I hadn't even been there when the incident happened. So I just listened, trying to understand how he experienced it all.

"When they were done," he said, "they placed me in a helicopter that flew me to Santa Rosa Hospital for medical care. Aware of what was going on, I made every effort to impress anyone within ear range with a description of my surroundings. To show that I was conscious, I wanted anyone who cared to know that I recognized them, waving good-bye and calling them by name, while introducing myself to those whom I didn't know. Wanted to make sure they knew I was OK. Had learned that trick in the movies."

ADORING FEMALE: "Yeah. Like the time you cussed out the immigration agent who wouldn't let you back into the States. Taking a lesson from *El Norte* and with your best English, you put that Asian man in his place. Them curse words worked like magic—*fucking head*, *shut the fuck up* and other words did the trick, just like in the movie, huh? You thought you were all bad!"

HOMEBOY: "After that, the pinche *chinito* had no doubt you were American, ese."

"At the hospital," Tito continued, "all tests came back inconclusive. I was released to the care of our family physician, to Dr. Johansson. He knew I took drugs. I'd told him about it, particularly my use of LSD. But he didn't tell. Dr. Johansson kept his oath, even though chances are the seizures might've been due to drug use. Still, I couldn't cover the sun with my finger. Believe me, I tried. Every which way I pretended that all was fine and it was my imagination taking the best of me. However, soon enough, my parents, particularly you, Momma, became suspicious about that Point Arena incident, tried to relate it to drug use. But I never copped to it. Never admitted it to no one, not even you."

SYRUPY GIRL: "Stop it! You're interrupting. Let me talk."

"Some time after the Point Arena incident," Tito said, "and upon your insistence, a neurologist evaluated me. Again the tests were inconclusive, but they showed areas of my brain with dead gray matter that wasn't making quite the right connections in my brain. It freaked you out, Momma. Remember?"

HOMEBOY: "Neurons weren't transmitting anything, ese. A few *canicas* loose in the cabeza, no?"

SYRUPY GIRL: "Told you to stop interrupting. You're pissing me off!"

Tito gritted his teeth and pressed his hands against the seat, as if to lessen the distractions. Whispering something or other at no one in the room—I was the only one there—Tito continued. "The doctor couldn't explain it. After this, you requested a psychological evaluation. Because the family doctor deemed it unnecessary, our insurance carrier did not approve it. They let it slide, denying further tests while reassuring you that the clinic would keep an eye on me. But things continued as they were. Only saw the doctor when I complained. But nothing was ever done. It was the beginning of the end for all of us. Those were really confusing times. It didn't help that both of you were graduate students. You were too busy to pay attention to my shenanigans. Made it easy for me to stray and hang out after school with my druggie friends. They became my haven. They became my excuse."

I had thought he was just acting like a difficult adolescent. At the time, I never imagined that his life was continuing to devolve into mental illness.

"Still, suspecting drug use," he went on, "you tried to get information from the doctor. You wanted to rule out drugs as the cause of my condition. But the doctor wouldn't tell you. With privacy and confidentiality as the reason, he denied you access to my files. He thought he was helping, but we later found out different. He should have told. Maybe I could have been treated sooner. Every family member, from you guys to my grandparents, tried to understand what was going on with me. But it was too confusing. It was too scary to acknowledge that I was going off the deep end. But you didn't give up. Tried to find an answer. You read all you could about neurological disorders, and even I began to scan the medical journals. However, without the guidance of medical personnel who could assist us in understanding my condition, we all settled for the more acceptable illness—epilepsy became the official diagnosis. All of you accepted it without question. It helped us cope, and we all tried to go on about our lives. But soon I became unmanageable. Became more bizarre. And you eased up on your suspicions that I was medicating myself with illicit drugs. Testing your boundaries, I continued getting over them."

HOMEBOY: "No kidding, ese. You tested them every which way, exhausting every excuse you had at your disposal."

DRUGGIE: "They must've been really busy not to notice all the stuff you tried to get away with, dude."

"Failing to get the support we needed," Tito said in his own voice, "you soon gave up your search. Then you were too busy to put all the pieces of the puzzle together. So I fell through the cracks. Ever since then, I've wondered if early intervention might have helped. One never knows. Without realizing it, I was masking the symptoms of mental illness and getting deeper into drugs. Got good at covering up the problem for you guys. So good that I even began to believe that all my problems were drug related. Didn't have to try to figure things out. I just did the best I could."

I could not even conceive of how difficult it had been for my son. Looking him in the eyes, I conveyed my thoughts without speaking.

"Every so often, Momma, you would gather information about my symptoms, hoping to rule out serious mental illness. Don't know, but you might've suspected the beginning of schizophrenia. One by one, those eccentricities I had exhibited escalated. It got to the point that you could've discerned the symptoms of my illness. However, no one was looking at all of them or piecing them together. My irrational fears intensified. Even the slightest noise or the faintest sound petrified me. Weird delusions abounded. No one liked me. Everyone was out to get me. My overactive imagination had no limits. While some people might have thought there were space aliens, I actually saw them and hid. Olfactory hallucinations emanated from inside me; I smelled things that had no outside source. Made me confused."

I just listened to my son. I tried to hear what he had to say about everything unraveling for him. He wanted nothing more than to let me know what all of it was like for him. So I applied my listening skills, taking in his every word.

"If that weren't enough," he continued, "the gray matter in my brain was fading like those bed-wetting problems I had left behind only a couple of years before. But I later learned they were also symptoms of the inevitable. None of you recognized or acknowledged the symptoms. Didn't want to believe I had serious problems. Finally, you began to put the pieces together. Started when you read some articles about bed-wetting—it was an early symptom. After that, other pieces fell into place. For example, having an exceptional and gifted mind. Experiencing difficulty socializing, especially with age-appropriate peers. The seizures and the dissipating gray matter in some areas of my brain were also associated with the condition. Momma, you were close to uncovering my self-medication with illicit drugs. But I didn't let you in. Kept myself to myself.

"Don't think you really wanted to see it, though. Denial protected you. It kept you from acknowledging my illness. You, like the others and me, were not ready to see it. Even though the pile of evidence was mounting in front of us, we all closed our eyes to it. It was too painful a possibility. So we went on with our lives. If I felt like it, I took medication for epilepsy and you numbed yourselves to my problems, buried in your intellectual work. Secretly, most of my relatives hedged their bets on drug addiction instead of mental illness. They knew about that problem, having lived in and around it, and it was easier to deal with."

My son had become a timing expert. He could talk without pausing for about forty-five minutes. And he told me his story as though I were one of the social workers he speaks with about schizophrenia. "You know what, Momma?" Tito said. "Wish you had paid more attention to your concern about drugs, but you feared going there. It must've been your alcoholic father. You were clueless about drugs. Can't believe you were a 1960s flower-power child. If only you had listened to yourself, you would have realized that mentally ill people use drugs to normalize irrational emotions and fears. We—others I know, and me—resort to drugs as a way of dealing with the not-fitting-in experience, to cope with unexplainable behaviors, to rationalize the voices, and to place in context the hallucinations. Under the influence, our distorted reality makes sense. We don't have to explain it even to ourselves."

He was so right. If we live in denial, we don't have to think about it or see it. The more distant I am from Tito, the easier it is to dismiss him.

"Still, the family was not willing to accept this possibility," he said. "They readily believed that drugs were my problem because addiction was potentially treatable. Mental illness comes with more social stigma; it's a life sentence that could, at best, be medicated into passivity, but never cured. Addiction was preferable to you guys because I could potentially recover. But adolescent turmoil was only the beginning for me. More would be in store for us. With mental illness rearing its ugly head, we could no longer pretend that all was well with our family. Yet it took us a while to figure out that mental illness is also a family and social disease. It doesn't just belong to those of us who are mentally ill or those who treat it; it is also baggage for the loved ones.

"Soon after, I started acting out suicide attempts. Repeatedly, I tried to put end to the pain. Initial attempts barely yielded a couple of scratches. First I tried to carve the flesh in my wrist to get to the veins, then I jumped off of a building too short to really harm me. That effort left me with nothing more than humongous headaches, Momma, like that time I jumped off the San Lorenzo River Bridge. Got home all bruised up and limping, but the effort didn't kill me, only mangled me a bit. But these efforts opened a new way to manipulate you guys—my family. But the time came for you. You finally considered schizophrenia. In between reaching that conclusion and your prayers that it was all drug induced, you lived under the pretense that all my problems were just growing pains."

Tito paused. "Gotta go. I'm tired. I have to rest. I'll see you next time. We can talk some more when you come and see me next time."

Rather than just up and leaving, Tito warned me this time. Still, I have learned not to take his leaving personally. Even when my sister and mother visit, Tito marks the pace of our stay. It's the same when we tell him we're coming to visit—he times us. If we say we will be there in ten minutes, then it means ten minutes—no more, no less.

Drugging It to Normal

Teens with early onset schizophrenia often self-medicate. . . . Substance is a good match for the underlying disorder. It relieves negative "feeling states" like anxiety, frustration, anger and rage—allowing the teen to feel normal.

—Aspen Education Group, *Dual Diagnosis Teens*

"Guess what, Momma?" Tito asked me "You get to hear about the drugs. After all these years you'll learn about the part they played in my illness. Do you want to hear it? Can you handle it?"

On my second visit of that long weekend, I went to see Tito as I had promised. He desperately needed to talk. He greeted me with these questions and drew me in with an explanation of his reliance on self-medication. "Yeah, drugs brought me over the edge," he said. "It was an overdose of crank—that's when the shit finally hit the fan. My world ended as I knew it. July, 'member? It was around the Fourth of July 1991, although I don't recall a single thing. Only thing I know is that I was refusing to eat or drink—thought they were trying to poison me or that I was being fed the flesh of their enemies. Didn't trust anyone, not even my family. That's all I can tell you. It was after I left the safety of your mother's house because I couldn't cope with the rules. Moved in with my girlfriend. Stayed with her at her mother's house with other siblings who qualified the family for aid—their cover for illicit dealings. They ran a drug house on the side—dependency as public charges was a con for their drug business."

I was overwhelmed with sadness. I wanted to interrupt him, to say I understood, but I kept my words to myself.

"By that time, Momma, I was almost twenty-one—just about to be an adult—but instead of becoming one, an overdose gave me a one-way ticket to perdition. It was then that I entered that place where disposable loonies walk the streets of the living dead—mental illness hell. Dad, you, everyone was devastated. Still, steeped in denial, you all held onto the notion that my problem was dope. You readily accepted addiction as the reason for my behavior, believing that it gave me an option mental illness would not have. But you weren't alone; even the experts couldn't agree on the diagnosis."

Seemingly sorting things out, Tito stopped to listen. He was stretched to the left as if trying to catch something that was coming from far away in that direction. Then, verbalizing his thoughts, he began to utter words that appeared irrelevant to our conversation.

HOMEBOY: "Homey, I need a cigarette. Boy, can you talk, or what?"

DRUGGIE: "Let's get the heck outta here. Look at how she looks at you."

ANGRY MAN: "Thinks you're a piece of work."

HOMEBOY: "Chale, homey. Let's jam."

ADORING FEMALE: "That's it. That's it. You said too much."

DRUGGIE: "Need a cigarette. Gotta go."

"See you next time, Momma," Tito said in his own voice, "visiting hours are over."

Tito was barely able to endure a one-hour visit from me, and when I left, he appeared more agitated than when I'd arrived. My son left muttering under his breath and probably went for a smoke to get calm. There would be other talks for us.

Tito's current facility is the one in which he has stayed the longest, and there were no plans for me to leave San Antonio any time soon. The way it looked, neither of us was going anywhere soon. "We have to do the best we can with what we have," I said to myself as I walked toward my car.

Board-and-Care Warehousing

It's an injustice. . . . They take advantage of the mentally ill. At the cost of over $1,000 to share a room, we live in squalid conditions. The rooms in those homes are dirty. . . . Meds are often not given as the doctor prescribes them. If you don't take them the way they say, you don't get them. They say you are refusing them and don't give them at a later time. When they feed us, we're lucky if we get a peanut butter and jelly sandwich. They discourage visitors, so they don't witness the conditions of the homes, which are usually rodent and cockroach infested.

—Tito

Realizing I was returning to Texas the next day, on my next visit Tito took me back to the story of the onset. The urgency of his narrative kept me glued to his demeanor and thoughts, my aim being to discern what might be going on with him. "Momma, do you remember that drive to Santa Cruz, when you came to pick me up at Mary's—my girlfriend's mother's—house after the overdose?" he asked. "Well, as smart as you are, and despite your education, you tried to get me to describe 'my reality.' Asked me what color the trees were. Can't believe you did that. Guess, you wanted to know if I saw things the same way you did."

"What did you expect?" I said to my son. "After all, I'm a social worker. You know they teach us just enough psychology to get by."

"Maybe you were trying to, as you say in the field, triage me," Tito replied, speaking to himself more than to me. "I'm so tired of hearing that damned word. You might've been trying to understand, to place yourself in my shoes. I can see why you would say that—yeah, you were just trying to figure the shifts in my mind. Yeah. Sure, Momma. I get it."

Tito continued recalling the onset of schizophrenia—the beginning of mental illness for him and all those around him.

"When I think of that first break," he began, "I can only recall the weirdness. Things became more bizarre with every day that passed. Believing I had killed someone, I talked to you about eating human flesh in the pizza. Apprehensive of anything that I placed in my mouth—everything tasted like blood to me—I refused to eat. As I have done other times, I'd rather starve than eat. Didn't trust the food, even yours, Momma. I was like Velcro attached to you, hovering over you, invading your space. 'Member? You couldn't go anywhere. Couldn't leave me alone in the house. Feared what I may do to myself or someone around me."

If there ever was a time that was difficult, it was this time, when I finally accepted that I could not tend to my son. The memory brought tears to my eyes.

"Momma, it wasn't long before you finally realized that you couldn't help me. Started searching for assistance. Called your friends. Tried to get me to help. But none of them would give you a hand. At your wit's end, after having tried everything, having called everyone you knew, and seeking help everywhere you could think of, acting on the idea that this could be a drug-induced problem, you took me to Victory Outreach, a church-based program that finally agreed to accept me at the East Palo Alto facility. Despite the almost fifty-mile distance, you drove me there from Santa Cruz, just so I could get the help I needed. Guess you finally realized that you were not the best person to help me.

"You were and always have been busy. Had things to do—your work, school, and activism. But Momma, you still made me a priority. Can't charge you with dismissing or ignoring me. You always came through. Sometimes you even go against your better judgment in order to help me, like when you buy me cigarettes. The only reason I agreed to go was because of the program's religious affiliation. It appealed to me somehow. It helped to keep the demons that were starting to come out at bay. Those ugly specters I had to contend with, like the ones I had read about in *Tales from the Crypt*. So hideous, I can't even begin to describe them to you—but they were real and always coming after me."

As Tito described our visit to an organization that worked with drug addicts, images of religious associations dealing with mental illness, both positive and negative, emerged in a silent conversation that remains in my mind. "When you and I got to Victory Outreach, I could tell that those recovering addicts really wanted to help us. They must've felt sorry for you, Momma. Tried to give you a hand in any way they could. You completed the paper work. They went over the rules with us, convincing me to stay because I would be safe under their care, to give you some distance and let you deal with the changes we were facing. They, too, thought it was drugs that had me in the state that I found myself. But it wasn't too long that I stayed there. As soon as I could, I ran. No sooner had you left the facility than I began to walk back all the way to East San José—where my relatives lived.

"So I made my way to Highway 101, going south, and from there I walked as far as I could until the California Highway Patrol arrested me for walking against the traffic. As soon you got home, a CHP officer from Palo Alto called you. Immediately you came to take me home. Initially, the officer was going to give you a half hour to get there, but upon learning that you lived in Santa Cruz, he agreed to take me to Uncle Tomás's house, where he and his girlfriend had agreed to receive me. So two cops dropped me off in front of their house. I waited there until you arrived. All the while, my mind continued to become filled with psychotic ideas that became more intense and frightening, even to me."

The constant worry and anxiety I live with resurfaced as Tito narrated that walk on the freeway going south on Highway 101. "Can't believe all I've put you and my family through. You must've felt horrible, but not as bad as I did. You guys have no clue. You don't understand. Lived in at least thirty-five to forty board-and-care homes and residential facilities—Blocks, Loves, Heaven's Gate, Julian Street Inn, Casa Olga, and other anonymous residential and unlicensed facilities. The illness is a major burden; I have kept running from myself, and without really intending to, I've made you pay the price. Can't believe I did that to you. It's cost you tens of thousands of dollars."

Looking directly at me, he said, "See how much you love me?" He didn't expect a response. "All my relatives didn't know how to deal with me. Think I scared them. Having exhausted all resources and feeling unable to help me in the way that I needed, once again you called the Community Exchange, a mental health referral service. You described my behaviors and what Uncle Tomás and his companion Celia had experienced with me. They told you to call the police, to commit me, an option I would later use when I needed help. Only the police could take me in for observation at a psychiatric facility because of potential harm to self or others. It was the only way they could help me."

It was not easy to convince Tito to voluntarily commit himself to a psychiatric ward, I thought as he continued to talk. But it would have been more traumatic for him to have been taken there by the police.

"Rather than do that," Tito continued, "you decided to take me and have me voluntarily go on a seventy-two-hour hold. You thought this would be sufficient for an evaluation. But try as you might, you could not persuade me. Don't know how or why, but my Uncle Tomás and my brother, Corky, finally talked me into it. Thanks to them, I didn't have to be taken by the cops to the psych ward. Instead, all of you took me so that I could be voluntarily admitted. By this time, my behavior was so obviously out of the ordinary that the hospital had no choice. They admitted me. It wasn't easy, for you, though. Even though your tears were not showing, I could see them inside you. Your social work knowledge became very handy, as you begged them to accept me, asking them to keep me beyond the initial twenty-four hours so that I could get diagnosed. Used all the expressed behavioral information you had collected on me since the break to convince them I needed help. Now I know you did it because you wanted to help me. It was through your efforts that staff at the psychiatric ward finally admitted me. You were doing the right thing, Momma. So I agreed to a hold—what they call the time I would spend there. They finally accepted me for observation."

At the time, despite my professional preparation and my continuous research on schizophrenia, images of snake pits, demons, and madness had filled my mind. How could I not have helped you? I thought.

"For you, it didn't stop there, Momma," Tito went on. "You continued advocating for me. After much effort on your part, my seventy-two-hour hold, the period of observation under mental health guidelines, was extended to fourteen days. However, my girlfriend got the hospital to release me, under the pretense of wanting to help me. She must've been afraid of what I would tell. Convinced me that all would go back to normal once I was clean. She made me believe it was the drugs. So I went home with her before a complete assessment of my condition was made by the resident psychiatrists."

Tito, I wanted to say, I remember. It was difficult to convince you that more needed to be done and that drugs had to be ruled out as the problem. But you were not listening to my concerns about your state of mind. Instead, you returned to the drug world that unleashed your onset.

"Yeah!" he went on. "I was too frightened to listen; I could barely hear myself. So it was inside that first delusional stupor that I went to Lake Tahoe. Married my girlfriend, Vicki Herdez. Believed that if I was one of them, I would be safe around her family. Gave me the false sense of safety I needed, but it didn't help my mental health problems. On the advice of my mother-in-law, Mary, and Vicki, I stopped taking the medication. Managed to stay at their house, but only for a brief time. There, things did not become clearer for me and I went deeper into the paranoia. Every minute I could, I got on the telephone and called, asking you to take me home. Feared that a hit man would break in and kill me. That they would not protect me.

"Didn't feel safe at my in-laws' house. Was afraid that they were going to kill me for what I knew. This fear hasn't left me. After almost twenty years, it returns every time my delusional thinking comes back in that fictive gang community I carry inside. I still fear they will kill me. In my life of intrigue, every one of you—my immediate family members—was suspect. I remember calling you and telling you, as my delusions became more intricate: 'Momma, I'm sure they're going to kill me. Come get me. Please pick me up.'"

The people he had made his family were not palatable people. Tito, I wanted to tell him, they would have hurt you without giving it a second thought.

"The extreme fears were reality based—these delusional characters were just like my in-laws and their associates," Tito said. "Things went from bad to worse. It wasn't too long before gangbang delusions overtook the demons that had previously inhabited my reality. After this, drug pushers and hit men controlled my mind. Everywhere I went, Norteños and Sureños—the gangs who wore red or blue rags and identified with Northern or Southern California—controlled my existence. Made it so real I walked in fear, avoiding their gaze when we passed them by. Momma, you brought me home again. Didn't know what to do with me or for me. But you tried the best you could to make me feel safe. More for yourself than for me, you would tell me that you were trying to help me."

As if reacting to him, I heard myself saying during that difficult time, "Tito, I don't know what to do with you. I'm doing all I can."

"Again and again we walked the treadmill, made the rounds," he replied. "You appealed to mental health personnel you knew at two county mental health facilities, even calling head honchos from your past. But as much as they knew, they were no help to us. At best, they referred you to several drug programs—gave you what you already knew. Still, wanting to believe my problems were drug related instead of caused by mental illness, Momma, you accepted and pursued their referrals. The possibility of my problem being drugs gave you a clearer solution and a direction to follow. It was better than not knowing what to do.

"Like a *calzón de* you-know-what-but-I-can't-say-because-you'll-get-insulted—the coming and going—no one wanted to deal with me. Some of the workers would be as kind and honest as they could, like the drug counselors who told you that my problem was beyond their scope. But Momma, you refused to hear it, didn't listen. Deep in denial of my illness, you still clung to the hope of my recovery. Simulating the Santa Cruz Boardwalk carousel that went round and round, you aimed to achieve your goal in the end. I guess being a drug addict was better than remaining a mentally ill person for life. But you were fooling yourself. We were just repeating the cycle all over again. Still, determined to get me the assistance I needed, you followed every lead. When you exhausted these, you sought other options, giving me hope."

As often happened, Tito suddenly changed the subject. It was one of the ways he finished his conversations with me. At other times, he changed the topic to prioritize what was uppermost in his mind.

"See why despite the horrible food I remain here?" he said. "I have no one, not even you. Yeah. You come here and then go away, leaving me to stew in the madness. But what do you care?"

Then, as if refocusing on what we were talking about, he changed the subject once again, talking about his residential facility: "I recognized that Casa Olga has given me the longest time without a mental break. The food is horrible, and I wish they'd make more Mexican food, but I'm still surviving. The nurse takes care of me and listens to my health concerns, even if she doesn't like me. I know—she doesn't have to tell me, I can see it. The staff here does not ignore me and they tend to my mental and emotional needs. Here, I've learned to advocate for myself, not just for others. Momma, I'm not trying to be a superhero or anything. I'm fighting for us to have a better quality of life. Finally, I'm learning to see myself as worthy of living."

And then, reminding me that visiting hours were over, he said, "It's time for you to go." Of course, he expected me to return, because he knew that I would not return home until the next day.

"I may be crazy, but the trees are still green!"

Running Away to Mental Illness

[A] mentally ill Southern man with a history of schizophrenia and depression was unceremoniously dumped by the Nevada facility [and sent to Sacramento, California]. . . . The patient is but one of millions of mentally ill Americans—and especially those with housing insecurity—who find themselves falling through the cracks in the social safety net.

—Sy Mukherjee, "How Mentally Ill Americans Are Falling through the Cracks in the Social Safety Net"

Tito has lived in every type of facility there is for mentally ill men: shelters, independent living, group homes, and semilocked homes. I only know what my son copes with from the outside. While I am familiar with the conditions of the facilities in which he has lived and I make sure to know those who are in charge of and run those facilities, I cannot imagine what it's like to live in them or to deal with the residents.

"You really don't know what it's like to live my life, do you?" Tito said to me one day. "Seldom talked to you about the details of the revolving doors. All the board-and-care and group homes I've lived in, from 1993 until I got to Casa Olga. God, I'm so sorry for what I've put you all through. With names such as Love's Board and Care and Heaven's Gate, more like cults, not warehouses of broken-down men and a few women who could not or were not able to live at home—these

147

were but two of the places among many. You remember any of the people who have passed through my life? Most have moved on. Some are still around, going from one place to the next, and sometimes even sleeping in the park because there is no other place to stay."

Tito recited their names: "Jimmy. Tim. Juan. José. Lala. All these people were either newly ill or middle aged without a place to go, who ended up warehoused in those homes of oblivion. Their families could not or were not able to deal with their illnesses. You remember Jimmy?"

I nodded my response.

"Yeah, Jimmy—he was a Gulf War veteran—lived with images of war so horrible, some of us nut cases had to hold him down when he had flashbacks of burning flesh flying all over the place. His best buddy was blown to pieces in front of him. Acted like the bits of his buddy, who was a Chicano like me, were being slung at him. When Jimmy had these flashbacks, he got into kicking and flailing fits to avoid the imaginary flesh slung at him. I could always calm Jimmy; he listened to me. Except for those episodes, he was a walking dead—he never talked to anyone. Although he sometimes followed me to Taco Bell or to get cigarettes. At the board and care we shared, he went from here to there, from corner to corner of the reception room, and he always looked like he was waiting for someone who seldom came. Jimmy's father, serving in the Middle East, would sometimes pick him up."

Focused on Jimmy, Tito continued: "Took him horseback riding. Jimmy told me it was the only way he felt alive. Being from Texas, Jimmy believed he was a cowboy. Always slept with his boots and Lone Star belt buckle on—this made him a target for ridicule by his roommate, who often made fun of Jimmy to get a rise out of him. Didn't work. Jimmy didn't see anything wrong with sleeping buck naked in his lucky charms or 'amulets.' What he called his Lone Star buckle and his boots when he was clear of mind. You know what, Momma? He would always respond to me—must've reminded him of his buddy. How sad, huh? His friend—the one I told you about that he lost—was only nineteen when he died."

Moving on to the other people who had passed through his life, Tito said, "Tim was an artist. All his paintings hung at Love's Board and Care. Somber faces with flesh in colors of green, orange, and purples attracted those who visited. Found his work 'interesting though peculiar' as some of the do-gooders would say. Residents thought his work too weird for contemplation. They already carried enough creepiness in them, so they gave him no mind. Most stayed out of his way when he painted, 'cause he became irate and violent when we told him flesh was not the color of the tones he chose. Though there were times we went to bother him just to get some excitement going. Soon he would ignore us and go back to his painting.

"Remember Juan? He was originally from Tucson, Arizona. He came to Santa Clara when it was known as Santa Claus County, as some people around here still think of it because it was like a horn of plenty, a cornucopia to everyone who needed services. Here, Juan found a home, after roaming all the county's homeless shelters. In San José, he didn't have to roam anymore because there was a place for him. Waiting for those visits that never came, Juan lived hoping someone would take him away. At the board and care, his spot of choice was the porch. Juan would be the first one to spy you when you came to visit. He got me so you wouldn't have to wait. Other times, he opened the car door for me to get in when you picked me up. Remember, he really liked you and appreciated that you came to see me and brought me things."

Is that what happens to you when I wait too long to visit? I wanted to ask him. But he barely paused before going on.

"Often heard him tell those who came to visit that his parents were coming to see him, but he had no parents; they had died when he was nine years old. Other times he tried to impress the visitors by telling them his case manager, who neglected him, would be coming by to see him. He was like a little kid who still believed in Santa Claus and the Easter Bunny—it was only in those holidays that visits came and gifts arrived. Never told me who sent them, but he must've had someone who cared. To me, it seemed as if Juan would have to wait forever. Wait for something or other that never came. But you know what? Miracles do happen. One day, before I got kicked out for being a druggie and getting into arguments and fistfights with the residents, someone from Juan's mother's side of the family came and took him back to Arizona. The visitor Juan expected finally came. Took him away. And the mail Juan had waited for stopped coming when he left. Don't know what became of him.

"Momma, we are so disposable. Couldn't tell you where most of the people I shared space with ended up, except for Juan, who returned to Tucson, and Bill, whose family took him back to Boston. We move with the wind and become as transparent as it is because no one sees us, even when we're right in front of them. You know what I learned? According to the experts, in our later days schizophrenia becomes less severe. We are easier to deal with. So it must've been their time—both Juan and Bill were middle aged and pretty manageable. They had very few personal problems when both returned home. Or maybe they just learned to fade into the wall, not making any trouble or questioning their surroundings. Don't know what happened to Lala. One of the few women who lived among us—they were like fleeting ghosts in our lives, as most of us who lived in these institutions were men."

In an abrupt break of topic, he asked me, "Momma, you think that may happen to me? Do you think you'll take me home when I'm their age?"

"I don't know" was all I could say to my son. "We'll see. I guess it's possible."

But Tito didn't want a vague response from me. He interrupted me and continued talking, with the hope that he could return to our home. "With families who don't understand or cannot tend to us, we end up housed in these places eating day-old food or mush that takes our appetites away. We find ourselves saving every penny, conning each other or panhandling, to go to Taco Bell to buy fifty-nine-cent tacos—ease the hunger that permanently lives in our bellies."

As he continued talking about his life, Tito became more agitated. Our conversation turned into another one of his efforts to persuade me to bring him home—to San Antonio, where he has never lived. "Discards," he said. "That's what we are. Society's unwanted. There is no place for us. Why can't you see how hard it is for me? When I first got sick, I couldn't stay at your house, and not finding a facility that would take me, I ended up at Julian Street Inn in San José, a homeless shelter. I had two problems: schizophrenia and self-medication with drugs. Most places didn't want to deal with someone as messed up as I was. The facilities either housed the mentally ill or drug users, but not both. At that shelter, even in the depths of my illness, it was difficult for me to stay there. There's a pecking order for who sleeps where, who gets to stand in line first, who gets to shower, who gets to eat. Often got pushed around because I'm short. Made me afraid to stay there, so I bailed. Decided to be on my own."

Guilt engulfed me as Tito reminded me that I have pushed him out and sent him to places in which he might not have been treated well. It wasn't that I didn't want to take care of you, I thought. It was that I couldn't.

"Stuck in-between. Couldn't stay at your house. Wanted to, but I didn't want to be a burden to you and Dad and I wanted to do it my way, without any expectations from either of you. So I left and ended up in a state park in Aptos, California, near Santa Cruz. Since the weather wasn't that bad, I was able to hang. In the daytime, I could be found at the Metro Center, where all the buses start and end their routes. Fit in really well with all the unkempt hippies who littered the streets of the Pacific Garden Mall. Didn't even have to ask for help, people offered it to me, giving me a quarter here and a dime there. Things got better when I hit upon the idea of reselling bus transfers for hardly anything, to get money. Didn't want to panhandle, though. Then I got used to being sick and liked the easy access to illicit drugs. Those board-and-care homes were drug havens. They were really no help, except for pointing me in the direction of dope. There was the trafficking of drugs that went around—crank, marijuana, PCP, you name it—drugs were everywhere."

My intuition had told me this was so. I had protected him from that type of life, and here he was in the middle of it all. I hear you, Tito, I thought.

"At first, they offer drugs without expecting anything. Then, when they hook you, some of the people I lived with even went as far as selling themselves or stealing to buy their drugs. Didn't do that. Instead I begged, asked, and cajoled money from you, my aunts and uncles, and whoever came to see me, so that I could get my stash. With excuses of needing food 'cause the food was awful, I got a bit from some. Feigning to need shoes, I got some from others. With tales that my clothes had been ripped off by some of the residents, one story or another, most of the relatives provided the money I needed to score. And when I had no money, I just got it on credit. Later, I would bug you to help me pay my debts. Told you residents would beat me up if I didn't pay. If I got you fed up enough, I knew you would give me what I needed to shut me up, so I pushed you to the limit.

"Remember the time you brought Susie Q. López to visit with you? I remember her because we had our last name in common. That was the first time I got kicked out of Love's Board and Care. The dual diagnosis program person, my case manager, found me another place. But the program had no more money to pay for yet another first and last month's rent plus deposit for me to move into a new place. So I called you for a hand. It was the second-to-last place before I went to Casa Olga. Didn't think you would help me, though. Last time this happened, you had said, 'Enough.' But somehow you got the money. This was a place I would share with three other guys. It wasn't a licensed facility, it was a group home run by an expert at scamming the mentally ill out of their county or Social Security checks in exchange for a room and measly meals. Anyway, Susie Q. and you came and brought the rent money. And you left twenty dollars for my personal needs. What I didn't tell you was that Susie Q. gave me money on the sly. That night I got so high freebasing that I burned off my arm and face hairs. That scared me into quitting drugs. I've been clean and sober for almost fifteen years, except for the bundle of prescription drugs I take."

Without hinting that he was moving onto another topic, Tito started talking about the side effects of the medication he takes for his condition. He told me he was beginning to experience some.

"Now, it's not just the mental illness," he said. "It's the high blood pressure. The diabetes and whatever else is fermenting in my body from taking too many chemicals. I am a walking laboratory of one. For me it's 'better living through chemistry,' as my dad says, but not really. Things don't get much better, we just get numbed or somewhat silenced."

Helping me out of my chair, Tito said, "Time for you to go, visiting hours are over. Had enough. Didn't even feel like talking to you, anyway. Told you more than I care to. 'Bye."

Tito walked me to the garage area where he goes to chain-smoke—the only area that's not off-limits. It was hard to believe my son had so much to say. But I finally got to hear how he survived those early years of his illness. While he talked a lot and told me much, there were things he did not discuss with me—that he will never discuss, even when I ask him. Still, the one-way conversation about how Tito survived gave me insight.

Recently, a pattern has emerged. When Tito talks about his living arrangements, about when he first got sick, the issue of going at it alone, renting a room, moving out of institutional settings often comes up—and it feels like he is beginning to experience a break. Like the time he was going to move away with Carol Silverstein, one of the many pearls on the string of women he was going to marry, or when he was going to room with Bryan. It's his way of bailing out of institutional living. He will take anything but living in an institution, even if it's only make-believe. Often, relationship breakups predict an impending change in him, but Tito usually attempts to shield the emotions tied to his losses. However hard times are for him, he is forever searching to have a relationship that gives him the companionship he needs.

Telling Tito I would call him when I got home, I left the residence. When I got to San Antonio, I phoned him to let him know I had arrived. He said he had news for me. Sienna, a resident who is younger than Carol but still ten years older than he is, was his new girlfriend. Things had not worked out with Carol. They had broken up after Tito figured out that she only wanted him for the cigarettes and other gifts his family brought him. When no one visited or there was no money, Carol stayed away from Tito.

He was talking marriage again. He wanted a good life with someone—or with anyone who would take him. He warned me that he would be asking me for help to buy Sienna a wedding ring, but I advised him to put it on hold, not to rush into anything. I didn't want him to be disappointed yet again. He insisted that Sienna was the one, the one he had been waiting for all his life. Using a Mexican cultural practice, I told him to test out the relationship with a *plazo*—a period of waiting. That way they could get to know each other. Then, if they stayed together for a year, I would gladly support him and attend his marriage. I'd even help him buy the ring.

At first, when I suggested the idea, Tito fought it. So lonely and so desperate to have a family or someone to be physically there for him, he longed to get married. It was the solution for him. After some thought, he decided that a plazo was a good way to test their commitment to each other. "We will wait," he told me. "Both of us will work on our relationship. We will try to make it last so we can get married. Thanks, Momma."

I hung up the telephone, wondering if this relationship would end as the others had. Most of the time I'm with him, I pray that he finds someone to share his life with. Not so I can be released from the responsibility, but so he can have love and companionship. Oh, how I wish that for him.

Later, Tito called me again. He had more to share. The times we spent on the phone were never sufficient for him—and this time he wanted me to hear more about the last time he took a flight into health with our family's assistance. "Last time you came to visit and we talked, I didn't tell you everything, Momma," he said. "Forgot to tell you about what brought it to a head. Well, Love's Board and Care evicted me once again. I lost count, but it's somewhere around thirty."

Tito talked as if I had not been the one who made all of the arrangements for his last move: "My Uncle Ricardo turned me on to his former mother-in-law who lived in Hialeah, Florida. She runs a facility for people like me. That was when the idea of moving became like a light bulb attracting bugs. Obsessing on that place as the magic pill to my problems, I asked you to send me there. Then I started begging you, not leaving the issue out of our conversation until you finally gave into my demand. In my deluded mind, I thought this move would get me away from everything I experienced, and everyone that persecuted me. It made perfect sense to me—I was in the middle of one of those paranoid phases—that the distance would take me away from it all and make me less of a burden for you and our relatives. Thought I could run from all I feared, all that bothered me, away to that paradise I imagined Hialeah to be."

Taking me back to that flight into health, Tito said, "When the eviction came, I had finally convinced you to look into that place called Casa de Paz, or House of Peace, in Florida. Even its name called out to me. It turned out to be a legitimate business that checked out with everybody. It was licensed, and having Xiomara—not a Mexican but a

Cuban who ran the place and was a retired pharmacist who understood how to work with people like me—made it even sweeter for you. Remember? You made all the arrangements. You reserved a place for me with $1,500. Helped me transfer my case. Jenny Nolan, the case manager who tried to discourage me at first, also did all she could to help. But deep down inside, I suspected she wanted me out of her caseload. I really made her work for her money.

"Not convinced that this was the best thing for me and with reservations, Jenny transferred my Social Security to Florida. When all was finally arranged and payment reached them, a room was set aside. And Momma, whether you agreed with it or not, you bought me a one-way ticket, warning me that I had to deal with my new environment in the best way I could. But you didn't make it easy for me to leave. You tried to convince me that I was running away from myself. Told me schizophrenia would go with me and unless I left my mind behind—I laughed at your unintended humor—it would all go where I went."

I now better understand the fear that had pushed Tito away. I remembered. He didn't want to hear anyone tell him that all would come to naught. Away from all that was familiar, which he imagined as bad and harmful, Tito believed he was in a better place without acknowledging that he would find himself immersed in the fears that instigated his anxiety.

"In spite of everything, and against everyone's advice, I left the area. Failed to listen when you told me that if I were running away from gangs and drugs, I would likely find them in Florida. My mind was set. I had already decided to get away from it all, and the only viable solution for me became Florida. Only other option I would even contemplate was to live with my family—there was no other recourse. But I had burned all my bridges and no one wanted me in their places—I was trouble and all knew about my manipulative ways. I guess that's what a mentally-ill-in-training-of-twenty-something-years does when he has no explanation for what ails him. None of us had a clue, least of all me.

"So I took my one-way ticket ride. Went on the Greyhound. Still can't believe I did it, what with all the paranoia I carried. But I stayed to myself. Didn't talk to anyone. Just minded my own business. When I arrived in Florida. I tried to become part of the new place. But what I didn't count on was the way these people would feel about me, a Mexican cholo-identified retard. That's how I think the Latinos saw me. From the beginning, I had troubles with the caretakers—I think they were undocumented workers from Colombia or Panama. The only thing that saved me was my family-member status of sorts. My relationship to Uncle Ricardo protected me somewhat, but not with those who wanted to keep me in my Mexican place. This was when I learned that some Cubans and Central Americans are just as anti-Mexican as gringos.

"Soon I began burning the telephone wires with calls to you, every chance I had. I called, called, and called. Told you I thought I had made a mistake but I would try to stick it out. Two, three, four, and five weeks passed. It was hard not seeing my family, just like you had told me. If I had been afraid of being lonely with some of you around, I now felt completely isolated, with absolutely no one to visit. I truly was on my own. And here I was on the opposite side of the country, thousands of miles away. Wished I had listened to you and all who warned me."

Things did not get any better for Tito. He was more needy, and just as desperate for attention, but he took on a more acceptable demeanor.

"There, I made some appearance changes," he continued. "Shed my hard-guy, ese-vato-loco image. For fear of being harassed, one thing I did was drop the red rag. No more colors. No more Dickies. Gave up my Chinese slippers. I got rid of my cholo-ized way of dressing, fearing that gangs would soon find me, even in the remote corners of Florida. Dressed more in a preppy old-man style, with slacks, suit jackets, and a tie. Florida was good for me. I could mingle without being tagged as a mentally ill troublemaker. After two months, though, I realized that this was not the place for me. And as you and Jenny had warned, the things I was running away from never left me. Still, filled with ideas about what it means to be a man about it, I tried to make it work.

"One problem I had was with my roommate, who was more depressed than me. One time I found him trying to hang himself. Don't know how, but I talked him out of it. Kept him distracted. Told him about my situation so he would see he wasn't the only one. That he wasn't alone anymore. He listened and was fine for a while, but that only worked once. His pain must've been too great, greater than his fear of dying. He needed to get away. The day came when he killed himself. Good thing I wasn't in the room. But I found him. He succeeded in hanging himself from a beam in the bedroom we shared. Blue-black and lifeless, there was nothing anyone could do. The morgue came and took him."

I never imagined the horrors, but it was at your own insistence that we relocated you, I thought as I listened. You really believed things would change, and I wanted them to change for you.

"Frightened by what I had experienced and without a roommate to distract me," Tito went on, "I became fixated on my fears and started begging to come home. It was then that the urgency to return dominated my mind. Again, I began burning the telephone wires with my calls to you, Momma. The trip to Florida was a hard lesson learned, though. All of you had been right. No matter where I went, I couldn't get away from myself."

The Genius Within

A compensatory transferential improvement of symptoms seems to qualify as a recovery of emotional health because of the sudden (flight) disappearance of pathology.

—Henry Kellerman, *The Dictionary of Psychopathology*

Tito always wanted to continue telling me his story. This day, as on so many other occasions I'd visited, his story flowed out, the words almost tripping over each other. He wanted to talk before I even had a chance to ask how he was. He was anxious to tell me about being *conserved*, or "when the state takes care of your affairs and you are not even a man to yourself," as he explained.

"When I returned from that magical escape to Florida, I had a break, after arriving in California, soon after my roommate's suicide," Tito said. "I don't know how you managed to get me the money, but you did. Poor Momma, they should change the rules to give you credit for taking care of me, develop programs that help you deal with your burdens. I know when I'm psychotic, it affects you as much if not more than it does me, 'cause I'm often so out of it, I can't even tell what's going on. All the money you've spent and I can't even be your dependent. There you were again, in the seesaw of my disease. You didn't have any money, so I had to wait in Florida until you could figure out a way to get me back. Xiomara, not wanting the troubles that came with my presence, paid for the bus fare. I was the one resident who taught her that she couldn't help everyone. Regardless of cost, she wanted me

158

out of her hair so badly that she paid out of her own pocket to get me home. Of course, you paid her back."

Such things had happened many times, and I couldn't even begin to add up the expenses. It was never about paying anyone back, though. It was about finding a place that would make Tito feel safer and better able to deal with his environment. But that never worked.

"Florida was hard," Tito went on. "They changed my medications. The lack of contact with family members intensified my loneliness. After my roommate killed himself, my problems became severe. I was too afraid to stay anywhere by myself, and I didn't like anyone they paired me with. I did anything I could so they would send me home. My desire to get away from myself had come to an end. Greyhound brought me home, or whatever could pass for it. Home again in San José, where Jackie Moore, an African American woman who had taken kindly to me, accepted me in her facility. She wasn't licensed, but Santa Clara County looked the other way. She was a good Christian woman who wanted to help people of my ilk. None of us realized that I was fading into a psychotic break. They had sent me without medication for psychosis, giving me only the blood-pressure meds. Without the meds, the bus ride became a nightmare. I was plagued by intense fear, imagining that any of the passengers who rode with me could kill me at any time. Make me disappear and no one would know.

"Heard voices—it was the evil ones invading my mind. Tried to focus on the sane one—the dominant voice of the nerd inside who told me to talk to Dad about the right formula to invent cold fusion. We could do it right, Dad and me. We would be famous. Make a difference for the world to appreciate our worth and Dad could become rich. Before going to Jackie's, I stayed at your house for a couple of days, Momma. Dad was in San Francisco, doing a postdoc at the university. Glad he was not there to deal with me. He would have noticed I was going off the deep end. Dad could readily tell when something wasn't quite right. Without him there, it was easier to sweet-talk you, Momma, to fool you into believing everything was all right. Some of the old behaviors came back. Fawning over you, I just about got under your skin. Only felt safe near you, Momma."

You became my shadow, I thought. How could I forget?

"More psychotic by the minute, the evil voices grew so strong that I had to let the nerd voice come out and told you I wanted to talk to Dad. On the phone with him, I proposed that I had a better way to create cold fusion—you heard it, you were there when I was talking to him. 'Those guys did it all wrong,' I said to him when you handed me the phone. Told you guys about the ways it would work. I had plans. Momma, you seemed to believe me—knew I was smart—but you looked skeptical. You didn't let yourself believe it, but you must've suspected I was losing it. Asked me if I was taking my medicine. Didn't take my word for it, so I showed them to you—I had them. That's when you decided to call Jenny, my former case manager, for a list of my meds, to make sure I was taking the right ones. It was the way you found out that I had been sent without meds—the ones that numbed the schizophrenia. Only taking the medicine for high blood pressure and a fungal infection I had gotten on my toes. No wonder I was going off the deep end.

"When things went from bad to worse—things weren't improving for me—you had to take me to the psych ward. Still recall what I told you. It's funny the way some things stay in my mind and others disappear. I said, 'What? You think I'm having a break just because I'm smart enough to invent something that could make us filthy rich? See, you've never believed in me.' It had been almost two weeks since I had taken any meds, but I was still sane enough to read the fear in your face. Still tried to manipulate you. We had gone through this process many times before. Didn't blame you, but I tried to pretend that all was good with me. Made an Oscar-winning effort to suppress the voices. But they came at me stronger than ever, rushing out without my control. Finally, I gave in. Agreed to go to the hospital. By this time the devil had gotten in on the act. He was trying to make me hurt myself. Had me thinking that you were going to hurt me. Get rid of me because you didn't love me. *Chamuco*, the 'charred one,' teased me about my worth."

ANGRY MAN: "You're no good to anyone. You're mine. Can't get away from me."

"The evil one kept whispering in my ears," Tito said in his own voice. "Told me I was going straight to hell for all I had done. There was no doubt about it—he guaranteed it. This time at the psychiatric ward, I didn't have to wait. The doctor could see I was falling into the abyss. Took me in. Gave me a shot. And for the first time, they had to restrain me. I really wanted to kill myself, end it all. Things were so bad I even scared myself. That was the time I became conserved—had to have someone assigned to look after my affairs. Made me a ward of the state. There was no choice. I was an adult and you, Momma, had no right to make decisions for me. They would not let you. In my craziness, I believed that I was big and healthy enough to decide for myself. Didn't need anyone, least of all a stranger to make decisions for me. That's when Cathy Balanchine, my first conservator, came into my life. She found me this place—Casa Olga—and made sure I stayed in the hospital regardless of the cost. She knew I really needed help. Momma, no wonder you have nightmares about my illness and about the way I deal with it. You must be tired. There's not much you can do, just be there for me, OK?"

I nodded at Tito.

"Even when I'm at my best, there are times I still want to die," he continued. "Often wonder why I'm still alive. When I tell you that, you remind me, 'The world would not be the same without you.' Just as is the case with George and that Christmas movie I love so much, *It's a Wonderful Life*. And while my life may not be so wonderful, I'm still trying to appreciate that I'm alive for a reason. If I'm going to continue struggling with life as it is, I have to believe this."

Talking Wishes and Repressed Delusions

Our hopes and dreams are not delusions. Our hopes and dreams are what makes us human.

—Kim T. Mueser and Susan Gingerich,
The Complete Family Guide to Schizophrenia

"Momma, you know what? It really helps to have you visit and to talk to you," Tito said before even greeting me on the telephone. "Meds by themselves don't do the job. Since there are no social workers assigned to us for talk therapy, I feel OK about talking. You make me feel safer with this illness."

He quickly continued. "Last night when we talked, you scared me. I know it's not the first time—you live inside a sea of nightmares with my illness. I know it's hard for you to remember dreams, but you readily recall the nightmares that involve me. My life consumes you, although you make an effort to go on about your life. Like you said to me, I have permanent residence in the back of your head. The dream story you told me has me freaked out. The one about the community get-together. It's so scary I've engraved it in my mind almost as a memory tattoo that proves your love for me. Don't know why, but I have a need to tell it to you? Can I?"

Without waiting for a response, he began to relate my dream back to me. I listened as he told me the story from my own point of view.

162

"All my friends, relatives, Jorge, my professional colleagues, and our neighbors attended," Tito narrated. "You were visiting. Didn't know why but you were particularly jumpy and in an acting-out mood. Making every effort to push the envelope with family, you told someone that you were going to kill yourself. You drank alcohol and beer every chance you got. I worried because of the medication. Your behavior was offensive. Your resentment toward me was written all over your face. I became aware of your every move, even when you were not in my presence. I also tried to ignore you. Your hyper-vigilance dominated and constrained my interactions with the family. Then I lost sight of you. Couldn't find you. I asked Corky if he'd seen you and told your cousins to go find you, to go see what you were doing. But you never left. You stayed hovering above me. I chased you away, told you to get off and leave me alone.

"Something, I don't know what, took you out of my mind for an instant. I heard gunshots. In my heart, it was you. You had been shot. In my sleep, I could feel my pulse racing inside my veins. I had difficulty breathing. I saw myself running all over the house, trying to find you, but I couldn't. It was then that I came upon four policemen in their summer blues. Couldn't quite make up what was taking place. Someone approached me, crying, '¡Es Tito! It's Tito!' Over and over again I heard the words. But I couldn't figure out where they were coming from or who was speaking them. Running, in a daze, it took me forever to reach the crowd. But I finally found you. You were on an ambulance stretcher. Your dad was beside you, blood dripping all over the place. Both of you had been shot. Then I saw both of you move. Gave me hope."

These dreams of mine are constant but readily forgotten for my own protection. Sadly, because of that, it is difficult to remember the happy dreams about Tito in my life.

"Your dad, in a loving and caring way, tried to comfort you," Tito went on. "He stopped you from killing yourself with a gun and he got hurt in the process. Screaming, I awoke, saying, 'A gun? Where did he get it?' Someone calmed me. Told me it would be all right. You said nothing, but you seemed relieved at being alive. The ambulance took you both away. I stayed behind. The prince for attention that you are, I saw you wave to the crowd. You acted as if you were a celebrity in a television show. Feeling accomplished, victorious, you glimmered like a prizefighter who had just won his trophy. Soaked in my own tears, I woke, shaken by the inextinguishable hurt I always feel for us. I was unable to understand it."

The retelling of my dream over, Tito said to me, "What a horrible life you have Momma, it must be terrible for you. How sad that you have to live that way—inside a permanent nightmare. Like I've said to you before, I guess I'm your schizophrenia. I know what it's like to wake up drenched in sweat. Sometimes that happens to me, so I know how you feel. But this must be your way of coping with my mental illness. I live inside your mind just like the schizophrenia lives inside me. Thinking about me, even when you're not aware. I'm always there, living in your subconscious."

"M'ijo," I told Tito, "I think these nightmares are devices that help me to deal with your illness. It's just like the meds that help you with the delusions, paranoia, hallucinations, and other complications of your illness. This is my way of coping with everything that both you and I live with day to day."

"Maybe," Tito replied. "But there are times when I wish it had been different. Momma, it pains me to think that you blame yourself for my illness, and it is during those times I appreciate the physical distance. This is when I am able to understand that the geographical space spares both you and me from the disease. But that's not the way other family members see it. They want me to be a child for whom you would care, leaving everything aside. Tell them I'm not a child, Momma, just mentally ill. Don't get mad, Momma. I still can't help but to dream of living with both of you. You are the only ones I mostly feel safe with. I long for the nurturing and comfort that comes with living at home. It has become clear to me that living apart is in the best interest of all, but there are times I push the envelope, try to convince you and beg you to let me come back into what I perceive to be the safety of your home."

Just before he hung up the phone, he said, "You're a good mother. Momma, you have tried so hard to be fair. But my illness is a no-win situation for both of us. Thanks for listening, Momma, I have to go to group now. 'Bye."

Right Under Your Nose

Having strategies for coping with mental illness is extremely important. It's hard to enjoy your life if you are constantly having symptoms. However, believing in yourself, having hope that things will continue to get better, and looking forward to your future are also vital in overcoming mental illness.

—Kim T. Mueser and Susan Gingerich,
The Complete Family Guide to Schizophrenia

On the plane to San José to visit my son, I rehearsed the conversation I would have with him. Clearly, he was concerned about my welfare, so I wanted him to know that I appreciated it.

"The last time we talked, Tito," I began when I saw him, "you said you worry about the ways I cope with your illness. I know it's not easy for you, but you seem to be getting better every day. I'm proud of the way you have learned to cope with your environment, knowing your limitations and advocating for others' rights. It has been really good to see the way you've learned to advocate for yourself, to ask questions, and to seek help when you need it rather than pretend you're not plagued by schizophrenia. It's comforting to know you realize that your illness affects me in very deep ways, that you're not thinking only about yourself but also about all of us who are affected by your condition. I am really proud of you, m'ijo."

It was my intent to start out with an affirmation for all the hard work Tito had done to manage his mental illness. I validated the way he had taken ownership over it. Yet before I could begin to share with him what I had rehearsed in the six hours of flight time, he took control of the conversation.

"Momma, you've probably heard this before," he said. "And no doubt I sound like a broken record to you, but I have to say what I have to say. Since becoming ill, I've lived in more board-and-care or independent-living homes than I care to remember. During those moves, I've lost my clothes and had my stereo and television stolen, although in the past I admit to faking some of the robberies to get money from you. I am thankful that you have coped with and managed to get through all of these experiences."

He had an urgency to talk about what we have gone through, the facilities in which he had resided. They were still part of the story he wanted to discuss, and so he continued the thread of that conversation. "Momma, it's been the different facilities that have taught me new ways to survive *en mi mundo de locos*—in the madness of mental illness. In some of them, I just learned to get what I wanted, using your name as a threat. You monitored the facilities to make sure other residents and me are fed right. It's not above you to show up without calling during one of those meals to check out the fare."

Tito seemed bent on affirming my part in his life, talking about the ways in which I have been there for him, regardless of his condition.

"I've hinted, and I'm not sure I've said this to you before," he continued, "but the fear of drugs has kept me running. Haven't clearly said it because I am afraid that you would abandon me. Dread of using and easy drug access in these homes has kept me moving from one board-and-care facility to another. Yet many a time those changes of address were ruses to get myself out of debt situations when I've used drugs. Other times, it was plainly to scam you, like that time I called you to tell you that my recovering roommates were using dope in the house, which forced you to relocate me once again. The drug card always has worked, especially if I claimed to be serious about not using. You always came to my aid. It always worked.

"I'm so sorry, Momma. It was those times that you went about like a chicken without a head, desperately trying to find me another place. Maybe the fear of me living with you in your home pushed you to try

166

harder. Whatever it was, you worked off of the belief that I was better living among those lost souls that had become mentally ill. Regardless of motivation, you moved heaven and hell for me. Poor Momma, I'm sorry I've put you through all that. It was you and Mandy, one of my early case managers, who advocated in my favor, especially when you feared for my safety. Mandy partnered with you to find me another place, and another, and another, until there were no more to be found."

There were times I would have brought you home, I wanted to tell him. But it would have been for the wrong reasons.

"But this one time, in one of our countless housing quests," he said, "it came to two alternatives: live in an area known as a drug haven or move to a northern city of the county where drug access would not be as easy. Despite knowing that the first house, in East San José, was a drug-infested facility allegedly supervised by a known connection to crack, I chose to move there. You didn't discourage me. I wore you down. At first it was a great place. There I could self-medicate rather than take those pills that turned me into a zombie. Hated the side effects. Didn't want to look like those guys who shook like runny gelatin taken out of the mold too soon. Often faked taking the medication. No one knew. Made sure of it. That's why I opted for that street medicine to mask my mental illness; it was my preferred choice. That's how I ended back in East San José.

"Once there, it didn't take me long to connect. But my good fortune, if you can call it that, ended when Tía Felisa, who is savvy on the issue of drugs, paid me an unannounced visit. She told you about her suspicions. The surroundings, the manipulative caretaker whose red, runny nose and crackly breathing gave him away as a coke fiend, and the heavy foot traffic in and out of the house next door—all these clues gave Tía what she needed to warn you. For Tía, that home meant trouble, and it was reminiscent of a world of which she had intimate knowledge with her former husband."

Your tía always has our back, Tito, I wanted to say but didn't. I count on her for her wisdom.

"Soon after Tía's visit, you came to confront me. Didn't appreciate what I was putting you all through. You surprised me because I didn't expect you. When you showed up, Momma, I came to the door in a drug-induced voice that gave away my behavior. Didn't try to hide it. Instead, I was trying to con you out of a hundred dollars for new clothes, claiming that mine had been stolen from the home I'd just left. Using every device that had worked in the past, I really tried to make you believe it. No dummy, Momma, you quickly caught on to what I would do with the money. Told me you wouldn't provide me any more. Instead, you offered me a care package with used clothes and a pair of shoes.

"'Thanks, but no thanks. Is that all you think I'm worth—someone's discards?' I said to you. That wasn't what I wanted. It wasn't what I was looking for. Ignoring you while pretending to be angry, I told you that you were insensitive to my needs. Didn't want second-hand clothes—I needed to buy my own just like the ones you bought for my younger brother. Wasn't I as good as he was? Storming out of the house, I left you there and went to hang with the guys. Soon after, I returned to the visiting room and asked you to leave. Tried the silent treatment after that. Didn't call. Ignored you. Waited almost a week without letting you know how I was, not asking for a single thing from you. In my distorted mind, I thought I was punishing you. Was so self-consumed, I didn't even realize I was really giving you a break you richly deserved, although I imagine you must've been worried sick about me."

I was worn out. The manipulation, the demands—the abuses that come with our interactions had hurt the both of us and those around us. I wanted to scream but kept my thoughts to myself.

"By the second week, I called you," Tito said. "It was to tell you I had hit bottom. Had scored some dope with forty bucks I had gotten from Tía Felisa. Junk exploded in my face. It was worse than that first time, when I burned the hair on my face and scorched my arms free-basing crack. Terrified by the experience, I wanted out, to run away again. Asked for your help, Momma. This time, unlike other times I had asked you to take me home, I begged you to let me return to Heaven's Gate, another dual diagnosis facility. Wanted to return to the drug-free place I lived at before. Didn't have to try too hard to convince you. You wanted me out of the environment in which I had gotten myself. So you figured out a way to relocate me again.

"'This time I mean it' was all I could say, promising you that I wanted sobriety. Despite past history, you believed me and decided to help me. But I'm sure you doubted my newfound commitment. Maybe it was my fear speaking, as a result of the last accident with dope that convinced you, but you decided to help me once again. Deep down I think you doubted my resolve to quit, but with the hope that I would change, you got me out of there anyway. Three weeks later, I called you again. There was no one else I could rely on to understand me or put up with me. Needed your assistance again. 'Momma, I'm scared. I need your help.'"

Sometimes the easy way out is the only road I can see, I thought as I listened to my son. The regrets come later, but I push myself to be there and do all I can do at the time.

"Tired and hopeless about my situation, I had nowhere else to go," Tito said. "Momma, you had been there for me. Didn't believe you would give up on me now. You never had and you had come through every time I needed you. But this time it seemed different. You asked me what it was I thought you could do about whatever problem I was confronting again. After all, you were two thousand miles away in San Antonio. '¿Qué quieres que haga? What can I do, Robert?' I could hear the desperation in your voice, but it was then that I optimized opportunity to get you to do what I needed.

"Fed up with it all, I tried to convey the difficulty of things. Told you I wanted to die. I really was contemplating suicide. Called you to make everything OK. To have you say or do something that would get me out of that funk. You always seemed to be able to do that. But this time you were fed up with it all. I imagined thinking that if I killed myself we'd all be better off without me around. So I pressured you by emphasizing my dismal situation, hoping that you would understand that I meant it—to touch your soul so you could hear my desperation. 'I'm serious,' I said. 'I'm not making it up. They're after me.'"

I believe Tito's feelings were real at the time, and that he firmly thought someone was out to get him. Making every effort to help him control the psychosis, I nevertheless recognize now, as I recognized then, that I have no power over him.

"Those ugly feelings of persecution were back again," Tito continued. "Didn't know whether I was coming or going. The feelings of paranoia I confronted on a daily basis were drowning me. Thinking and feeling that I was unsafe even from myself. Submerged in the real or imagined fears of enemies inside my imagination, I couldn't take it anymore. You went silent for a while, as if catching your breath. For the first time you didn't know how to respond. Could just about feel your exhaustion. I might've even understood your disgust, because I was feeling it myself. Again I told you I was giving up. This time I really aimed to kill myself. Could imagine you thinking that this could be the best solution for all concerned. The thought that I might lose your support terrified me. But your silence didn't last long. As I expected, you came through. Tried to talk me out of my blues.

"It was that old game again, but in a good way—although it was a strange manner of testing your love for me, to see if there was enough left to reinvest in me. Hadn't you proven yourself yet? Still remember what you said, word by word. 'I don't want you dead, son. Other people have it more difficult than you do. Try to find the hope inside yourself. Tomorrow will be better. Don't forget it's one day at a time, m'ijo.' Although sappy, they were the words I needed to hear. You were telling me you believed in me and my capacity to survive. With that talk, you tried to get some clarity about my mental health status. You triaged me. Checked me out and assessed my situation, just like any good social worker would have done."

Tito's suicide threats were and are the most draining. I feel helpless and sometimes desensitized by them, and that frightens me.

"Realizing that my suicidal thoughts did not come with a plan or a weapon, Momma, you decided I would be all right, stating, 'You will survive this, m'ijo.' It made me feel better just hearing you. Believe it or not, your words gave me resolve. Talking to you about my plans to kill myself, I regrouped as soon as you listened to me. You did not forsake me. You realized things were bad for me, but you also believed I could cope with things and make them better. Although you sounded afraid that I would die, you agreed to pray so that I would be more patient and gain the wisdom I needed to continue dealing with my life. Thanks for being there, Momma. Since that day, you continue to get better at listening to me. I call you because you help silence the demons and the voices. Hope you never give up on me. I want to be able to get your comfort. Call you when I need your support. I think this is not the last time I call you for support, to hear me out. I think we have a long road ahead."

Keeping my thoughts inside, I told Tito, "You are not your illness and your illness is not you. Your family loves you just as you are. It's not always easy, but we do what we can for you. We consciously keep you in our lives rather than make you feel irrelevant or discarded, even though not everyone can physically be there for you. We love you."

Still Hoping for a Better Life

Family members look expectantly to the newest medication or the next treatment, hoping that this will be "the one" to bring about a cure; and they find their hopes bolstered when they see incremental improvements in their loves one's condition

—Larry Davidson and David Stayner,
"Loss, Loneliness, and the Desire for Love"

"Momma, the talk I had with you really took this time," Tito said, calling me to find out when my next visit would be. "Don't know why, but I stopped thinking about dying. Jesus! I've lost track of the times I've tried to kill myself." When the signal for the cellular telephone weakened, he called out, "Hello? Hello?" As I moved to the patio to find a better connection—here, the signal became vibrant—my son expressed concern about not knowing how to deal with the absence of the voices and the hallucinations that take over his mind.

"Momma, Momma," he said, making sure I was still there. "I don't know if I can deal with the silence. Can't help but think back to the chaos. My mind keeps pulling me to 1997. That year was particularly bad for you and me. Always kept you on edge. That year, from week to week, you lived in fear of my demise, hoping that my life wouldn't unfold into the horrible path over which neither of us had control. Your seesaw life with my illness didn't knock you off your path. You endured despite the complaints and guilt trips you got from some immediate family members and me. 'Member? Every time I called them for help, you would receive a call recriminating you for neglecting or abandoning me.

"I can hear their voices, 'cause they would do it right in front of me, as if I didn't know better or understand what they were doing to you. How sad. 'Tito is homeless, go pick him up' and 'Do something, Tito has threatened to kill himself.' Then, 'Damn it, take care of him. He's your son, be responsible for him. Can't you deal with the hand you've been dealt?' Regardless of how much they love you, Momma, despite knowing the type of mother you have been to me, they were quick to blame you for my illness. In their eyes it was your doing or something you failed to do. Their accusations hung in their voices, as they called you out on your inability to support me in a way that protected them from me, suggesting they would have done it differently had they been in charge."

My family members aren't the only ones who cast blame on me, I thought. Others have also commented that I should bring you to live with us. They have no clue how difficult that would be for both of us, my son.

"Some even questioned you choice of marriage partner—and my dad is so good to you and your children—also laying the blame on you for having married my biological father, Beto. Maybe he was the defective gene carrier. All these were irrelevant arguments, yet they were intended to absolve themselves from the dreaded disease. That's how little they knew. You didn't need them to remind you. To top it off, you lived with the fear of my imminent death; there was no relief for you. Why can't they leave you alone? You're better than the best of them—always there for me. We are connected to each other in ways that no one, unless they have experienced and survived what we have, can ever fathom. You are my mother for life, in a way that's different from anyone else. You're always trying to bolster my independence. You embrace me because my needs are great, and you understand me. Momma, I know it's not guilt. You have long disposed of that. That doesn't mean you didn't carry guilt during the initial years of my illness, and you often wondered how you contributed to it."

Posing a rhetorical question to which he didn't expect an answer, Tito said, "You questioned what you could have done differently, even to the point of retracing what you ate when you were pregnant with me, remember?" Then he continued to reflect on the ways the dreaded illness had affected us.

"It was awful to see that perplexed look in your face that even I could make out. To recognize your desire to have done things differently, to spare me—that still haunts you. If they only realized that mothering has never ended for you. That I'm the cross you bear. That you're on call twenty-four hours a day, seven days a week, attending to every impending crisis I may face. As if I were a toddler who cannot take care of his own needs, you tend to me and try to teach me self-reliance to no avail. You encourage me to help myself. Yet in your quest to not abandon me, you always come to my aid. I'm not sure it's always that helpful, but it feels good to have someone there who never lets you down.

"I witness you trying to explain that to our family, time and again, as you hold me accountable for my independence. Go figure. I've heard you talk to my aunts and uncles in your effort to free them of the guilt or responsibility they assume over me: 'Tito, my son, is mentally ill. His condition can be managed with medication. Tito has a mind of his own. He has a case manager and services at his disposal. He needs to be independent. He just needs clarity to learn how to cope with his illness. You don't have to help Tito if you don't want to. He has a support network. Send him there.'"

I'm tired of the judgments, I thought as I listened to him. We don't need their criticism or lack of support. It's easy to blame someone for circumstances for which you only have a partial understanding. I kept my thoughts to myself, but I knew Tito understood.

"Momma, I don't know why they don't understand. You said it to them so many times, I've lost count of the times I've heard it. But you're always there—your sense of responsibility is great. Then there are times you detach from me. I always think it's about me rather than assume that you are at the end of your rope. Still, you cannot keep away. It would be so easy for you, but you don't abandon me. All you would have to do is not answer the telephone, ignore my calls, and return them only when you have the time and patience to deal with me. But you can't even do that. You hear my condition in my voice. It is those times when you break your telephone agreement and call me to tell me I'm not alone. That you love me."

After telling me that, Tito hung up the phone without saying good-bye. I went about getting ready for my graduate class, but not before taking a break to reflect on his words. At times it's so hard for him to put one foot in front of the other, but that day I celebrated my son's insight and ability to deal with his life. Tomorrow would be another day.

Fears and Mental Illness

Findings suggest that efforts to improve medication usage among Mexican American individuals with schizophrenia should take into account social supportive factors such as instrumental or directive, hands-on assistance from family caregivers.

—Jorge I. Ramírez et al.,
"Family Support Predicts Psychiatric Medication Usage"

It was Wednesday. Robert called me, about three minutes after I came home from work, to talk about his relationship with the family. I had no idea what had happened to bring this on, but he wanted to inform me about what was going on in his life. The conversation was so clear and so focused, my son sounded like a university student rather than a mentally ill person. I happily extended my greetings.

"Hi, Momma!" Tito replied. "How's it going? Need to talk." With that, Tito launched into his story: "Remember that time that Uncle Juan called you to express concern about one of the many psychotic episodes I was experiencing? It was that time I told him that some guys were chasing me, wanting to kill me. The seriousness of the threats I heard inside my mind, and the bullying voices, drove me to ask my uncle for shelter. Reminded him I had no one else. Made him feel really bad about my situation while emphasizing how abandoned I felt. This tale, wrapped inside stories about gangbangers and weapons, made my uncle believe it was real and not just a delusional break. He freaked out and hesitantly let me in the house. For me, this was nothing new,

176

although I did not link the extreme fears to feelings associated with the paranoia that comes with the illness. Unaware as to how to deal with my issue and sensing the gravity of the situation, Uncle called you, Momma.

"In a terse voice, without even a hello, and casting blame on you for discarding me, Uncle told you that you could do better at mothering me. Reminded you that you, and not the family, were responsible for me. 'After all, regardless of his problems, he is your charge, he's your son. Help him, don't abandon him,' I remember he said to you. His words were soaked in judgment. And it's not beneath me to use them against you now and again, but it's not as easy to hook you with that anymore, right? Basking in the comfort of the plaid couch in his living room, listening to the one-sided conversation, expecting to get much juice out of the situation—I witnessed it. When Uncle was done talking to you, he handed me the telephone."

How dare he say that to me? I thought, remembering the incident. What gives him the right to condemn me?

"Momma, I'm sorry," Tito continued. "I could hear the sound of his words trapped inside your throat. You weren't able to say much. The tears were choking you. His judgmental ways had really gotten to you. Still, patiently and lovingly, setting your feelings aside, you instructed me to go see my case manager. Told me to have them regulate my medication, as you clarified that I was expressing schizophrenic symptoms and that I should explain that to my uncle. Then you calmly told me to hand the telephone to him so you could tell Uncle to send me to the Downtown Mental Health Clinic."

"That wasn't the only time you involved your uncle," I told Tito. "Somehow you must have felt protected by him, because you sought him out whenever you found yourself in the middle of conflict with other men in your community of treatment." This was an opportunity for him to repeat the story as if I had not heard it before. For some reason he needed to get it off his chest.

"Yeah, Momma, that was the time some goons were really trying to kill me," he continued. "Uncle didn't understand my illness. Didn't want to put his family in jeopardy. Momma, you put my uncle's call into perspective for me. Told me it was his way of showing concern. He didn't want to risk believing what I was telling him and he wanted to help all at the same time. Uncle didn't realize it was my mind, didn't understand it was all part of the disease. He was taking my words literally and I wasn't well enough to make him aware that I was delusional. He called you to tell you about that time, remember? 'Tito really believes someone is going to kill him. I don't feel safe with him here in my house.'

"Yeah, I'm sure, I thought to myself. Even in my confused mind, I couldn't believe he felt threatened by those imagined communities in my mind. I could see the way Uncle could have been caught up between fear of what I might do and his concern about listening to me. But I think he was more afraid of the harm he imagined would come to his wife and son. He wanted me away from their home because, as he saw it, I was placing Auntie and his son in harm's way. Although I couldn't hear your side of the conversation because you were on the telephone, by the way Uncle responded, in my mind I was hearing you say, 'Risk of what? That you will be assassinated by imaginary demons? He won't hurt you.' It wouldn't have been the first time you said that. But the only thing Uncle wanted was for you to come and pick me up. Take me away from his family. Didn't want me there. For that reason, he challenged your sense of motherhood."

Your story feels like manipulation, son, I thought. But it still hurts. What is it that you imagine for yourself? Unspoken words remained with me as Tito continued to talk.

"This time it felt more like badgering and a dare. 'He is your son, your responsibility. Don't you give a shit about him? Tito needs to be with you. Don't you give a damn about him? What kind of a mother are you?' It was beginning to make me mad. Didn't like the way he was talking to you, Momma, but I got what he meant to say. He wanted me out of his sight. His words and accusations made me want to cuss him out, but how could I? After all, he is my uncle. It wouldn't be the first time I had to read between the lines, but this time I was hearing it myself. In a way, I didn't blame him, because I was about as fed up with myself as he was with me. As if he were reading my mind, he said the words himself to you: 'I'm tired of dealing with your son. I don't know how to tell him to stop coming to me every time something is wrong. Get him out of our lives. I don't want the burdens that Tito brings.'

"In a way, I understood. It was his frustration speaking. To release him of the pressure, I agreed to get help, but he was still on the phone with you. By this time, you had convinced Uncle that I was having another episode. When he got off the phone, he seemed less angry. Calmly, he asked me if I had taken my medication. He was learning how to deal with me: 'How long has it been since you last took your meds? Your momma says for you to go see your case manager. When was the last time you saw her?' Reassured that it was the lack of medication that had me in that state, Uncle sent me to the Downtown Mental Health Clinic. As I was leaving, he offered me a ride to see the case manager. Despite all the drama, he helped to get my medications stabilized.

"While he seemed to come around, sooner or later all of you get tired of it. The next time I saw him it was as if nothing had taken place. To me, it was a sign of acceptance, especially when he invited me to a backyard party at his house. Sad to say, Momma, you and he talked a long time. Both of you refrained from sharing your resentment about the episode. Living in the moment, a strategy that you have learned to use, Uncle and you set aside the anger to get by. Later, in a new board-and-care home near Uncle's house, I lived close enough to ask him for help, but I also tried to stay away. Didn't want it to affect how you and he got along. So I refrained from frequently asking for help, except in those emergencies where I could not reach anyone else. He was and continues to be there for me. However, I learned to go to someone else before I ask him for help."

I'm proud of you, Tito, I thought. You are figuring out how to keep the family in your life. And when you make room, I will share how proud I am of you.

"Uncle finally has figured out that it is the way my mind works," he said. "Now and again, he includes me in his family. He's found a space for me. I take the train to San José, and Uncle and his wife pick me up. My favorite visits are the Fourth of July and their Halloween parties. As for me, I've learned it's hard for you guys to see me in a psychotic state of mind. So I share little of what's going on with me. Thinking I'm adult enough to deal with my own issues, I try to deal with things myself. Only seek my family's help when I'm desperate. You said it to me when I was trying to convince you that marrying Sienna was a good thing. Remember when you said mental illness does not forgive and age is irrelevant? I'm learning that lesson. I have to contend with those times when the inner workings of my mind fail me and my reality becomes unhinged from everyday life. It is those times I search for a supportive person to help me sort things out, and although none of you are mental health experts, you have been able to do that for me. Despite the impatience and complaints that sometimes come from the burden of living with a loved one who is mentally ill, I have your love."

With a long pause for reflection, Tito left a gap in his monologue to make space for me to comment on his story. Because he had just told me about those in my family who had given him a helping hand, I provided an affirmation.

"M'ijo, I'm impressed with the ways you've handled your illness, even when its effects are not so positive for all of us," I said. "While not every one of our relatives visits you or includes you in their lives, some of us have not abandoned you, particularly Tía Felisa and Grandma. They always find time to visit you, even when you harass them about cigarettes. They bring you tacos or burritos, diet soda, and a bit of spending money for your treats. You and I are very lucky to have them in our lives."

I tried to keep him engaged by asking questions, but Tito had had enough. He wanted to get off the phone, so he did not comment on my observation. He had done enough talking for the day. After saying goodbye, he hung up. It was one of those days. He could only say so much.

In the Onset

All Together Now

Higher family instrumental support predicted regular medication usage among Mexican Americans with schizophrenia.

—Jorge I. Ramírez et al.,
"Family Support Predicts Psychiatric Medication Usage"

Once again it was time for Tito to tell stories. This time, he returned to the onset story. He went back to the time I had no choice but to ask one of my friends for help. It was a terrible time, when Tito was in the depths of his first break. Showing off his gift for writing, he brought with him some poems he had written about the onset. Still, he seemed somewhat confused, as though he was both present and not present, and his concentration and ability to focus weren't there. I had to remind myself to patiently wait until he filtered the noise inside or found the gaps among the voices in his mind that would allow him to tell me what he wanted to reveal.

Unable to find someone who could help me, feeling completely hopeless, I finally called Lorelei Hammond for help. A clinical social worker, friend, and former student, Lorelei lived on a ranch that had been a facility that served mentally ill people and was now a private residence. Thank God for Lorelei.

Closing his eyes, as if to picture what he had lived, my son began to talk to me, telling me about that time. I listened attentively.

"Momma, I can't believe you were able to convince Lorelei about the urgency of getting on with your doctoral studies. Without thinking twice about it, she offered to take me in until you took your orals. It was the exams that would advance you to all-but-dumb candidacy. It had been a trying time for you, my dear momma. Boy, what a long journey it had been. I'm talking about August 1991. It had only been a month past the onset of my illness. Somewhat hesitant and with a load of guilt for asking, but knowing that Lorelei had expertise with mental illness and drug abuse and that she would help you, you reached an agreement with her. You needed to meet your educational obligations and I wasn't helping the situation. So you and Dad drove me to Philo, California. Spent the night there. As soon as we arrived, Lorelei began with the questions: 'This is not like Tito, Josie, what happened?'

"Lorelei, who had known me for about six years, asked you questions. I just listened. Shut my mouth. Felt tense and somewhat out of my skin. Yet wanting to impress them all with my control, I tried to keep it together. In denial about what I was experiencing, I did my best to suppress the paranoia, mask the confusion, and hide the agitation brewing beneath the surface. Best way to achieve that was by staying silent. Only one who seemed to notice how I felt was Dad. He kept reassuring me: 'Tito, you're far away from the people you fear. Listen to Lorelei.' His words made me feel more at ease.

"Still, when we all went to bed, I begged to sleep with the lights on. Locked myself in the room before going to sleep. The next morning, I could have won an acting award for my performance as I managed to convince all of you that I was feeling better. You guys went home. And I stayed behind in Philo. Soon enough, emotions—and fear, in particular—intensified between Lorelei and me. Must've called you, Momma, at least a dozen times a day, increasing in number with the length of my stay. Because I was around her, Lorelei had ample time to diagnose my condition. Having observed my behavior and my fragmented talk, I couldn't hide it from her. She soon determined it was not an overdose. The way she saw it, my symptoms pointed to mental illness: 'Tito's hearing things, seeing things, and is still extremely agitated. He fronts some rational sense of his surroundings, but he cannot cover his delusional thoughts, Josie.'"

The dreaded call finally came. Lorelei had triaged and deduced that Tito was mentally ill. She was frightened of having him around, and I heard it in her voice.

"As for me," Tito continued, "instead of easing up, things became emotionally tense. Sought a weapon to protect myself. In fear for our safety, Lorelei hid the cutlery and whatever sharp objects she had around. She became concerned about potential harm that could befall us. Having observed me for a while, her initial assessment was undeniable: I had a serious mental illness and I had to be treated. Lorelei took me to the hospital. But they didn't give me any medication. Because I lacked the necessary medical insurance, the hospital did not admit me. They gave Lorelei some pills to administer that would lessen my paranoia—Prolixin and Cogentin—from the free samples they had. Must've felt really sorry for her. Despite or because of these drugs, I remained confused and lethargic and was unable to follow instructions. The medication made me more manageable, less paranoid, and more cooperative, but my behavior became odder and weirder with each day that passed.

"Lorelei had to take me with her everywhere she went, just like you did when I first got sick. I did to her what I'd done to you in the past, when I was having a break. She didn't feel safe leaving me in the house by myself. So I went to work with her and she tried to find me a place to hang out, but I couldn't be too far from her. As had been the case with you, I became attached to Lorelei—went everywhere with her but to the bathroom. Because I had to go to work with her, my pacing and hovering became a problem. Her colleagues didn't understand the intensity of my attachment. As a solution, they tried to send me to the nearby park or to the library or the shelter facility where people who were experiencing what I was found themselves day in and day out. But I refused to budge. Didn't want to leave her side. The more they pushed me away, the more difficult I became. Insisted on being near Lorelei. Fear controlled my every thought and move. From there, things just got worse. Constantly on the phone, calling you, Momma. Wanted to go home."

Seeing that I was trying to stop the tears that were surging forth with his retelling of the story, Tito said, "Don't cry." But though he paused to note my emotions, he continued to talk about that time he went to stay with Lorelei.

"Momma, it was a very difficult period for all of us. Can't even begin to describe what we went through. Poor Lorelei. Put her through hell. And she wasn't even related by blood. After I had been on the medication for one week, Lorelei finally told me to leave. By now, I was unable to follow directions. Failed to help around the house—not because I didn't want to but because I lacked the concentration to do the tasks she assigned. But I couldn't even explain that to her. Rebellious and contentious, our friendship wasn't enough reason for her to put up with my shit. Even in my insanity I could tell that much. It was as if I wanted her to kick me out.

"When she had done all she could and after having helped you get through your qualifying exams, Lorelei called you. Told you she was going to send me away: 'Josie, I told Tito he could no longer stay. I asked him where he wanted to go. He said he wants to go to Modesto to be with his Aunt Mague. So I bought him a Greyhound ticket.' On my bus ride there, I fell asleep and ended up in Sacramento. From there, I took a ride from a drunk driver. Ended up in an accident. From a Lodi Hospital, I called you, Momma. It was in the wee hours of the morning. 'Mom, I've been in an accident. Please come pick me up.' Didn't know what else to do. All alone, I found myself in need of help. But you refused to drive the two hundred–plus miles to pick me up. Didn't blame you, but this was not the time to set limits."

The distance. The money. The needs. However long, expensive, and intense these are, they appear simple and possible to Tito when he imposes demands on me. Setting limits is the only thing that saves us. I want the journey to be his lesson.

"Somehow, I arrived at my Aunt Mague's house. Spent the night. The next morning Aunt Mague called you to tell you that she didn't know what to do with me. 'Josie, Tito has been dropped off at my doorstep. You need to come and get him, please.' Afraid of me and at a loss for what to do with me, she had her husband, Angel, take me to my Uncle Juan's in San José. As soon as we arrived, Uncle called you to ask what to do with me. Not feeling satisfied with your response, Uncle had me talk to you. In that conversation, you convinced me to return to Ukiah, where Lorelei worked. She had already agreed to find me emergency housing in a homeless shelter. Connect me with a mental health and homeless advocate so that I could begin the process of applying for General Assistance and medical insurance. That was the plan. Since it was the only option I had, I agreed.

"Uncle took me to the bus station and bought me a Greyhound ticket. That's how I returned to Mendocino County, with the intent of establishing residency, so that I could begin to get treatment. Next to Santa Clara County, Mendocino was a good place for people like me—they had a good mental health system to tend to my treatment. Once in Mendocino, I was unable to complete my application for assistance, a necessary step for obtaining help from Social Security. Then, when I finally got around to applying, I found out I had to meet a thirty-day residency requirement. Wanting things to be done on my terms and when I needed them, I couldn't deal with the delay. Afraid and at a loss for what to do, I became frantic because my housing arrangements ran out two weeks before I met the eligibility requirements. Instead of asking for assistance or figuring things out, I once again called to plead with you to let me return home. 'Momma, please! I only feel safe at your house. Please! Let me come live with you.'

"You refused my plea, and, as in other situations when I didn't get my way, I thought you were a selfish bitch who didn't want anything to do with me. Stuck inside the illness, I heard you explain that I needed more help than you could give me, but I just heard it as a refusal to help. You told me that living at home was not an option. The teeter-totter of mental illness, the back and forth, was not helping any of us. There were services for me if I would only follow the steps to get them. All were things I'd heard before—sounded like excuses or added to my perception of your rejection. You kept reassuring me. Told me again, 'We need you to get help. The social services you have received in Mendocino have been the most humane and receptive to your needs. Stay there. At least you know what you have to do to get help. Lorelei says that services for someone in your condition are excellent in that county. M'ijo, wait it out.'"

Tito's response at this time wasn't even a smooth retort. His desperation cut to the quick, and I fell for it once again.

"Rather than comfort me, your words felt like knives through my chest," he continued. "All I heard was rejection. You didn't want me to come live with you. You were too selfish to help. Didn't matter to you. Felt you were pawning me off onto somebody else. Weren't you aware of your obligations to me? You were my mother, after all. Shouldn't you jump when I ask? On the brink of ending up on the streets, and terrified by that prospect, I continued to call you until I wore you down. Soon enough, I returned home, but only under the condition that I would let you find me a shelter or mental health program. Told me I would not be able to live with you and Dad. I had no choice but to agree.

"So Tim, Lorelei's husband, drove me to Valley Medical Center—Santa Clara County's hospital—where you met me at the parking lot. Your heart was breaking, I could see it on your face, but for me that became the incentive to pressure and push you to let me return home. It was the only place I felt safe. But instead, you took me to Julian Street Inn, where I stayed for about three weeks. It was not until early 1992, and through your intervention, that I entered an experimental dual diagnosis program. It was a program for those who have mental illness and drug problems. It was their staff that placed me in my first board-and-care facility. This finally allowed me to establish a routine. It was then that you and the family began to understand my condition. Thank goodness you guys made an effort to include me in your lives and make me part of the family gatherings. I attended birthday parties and was occasionally invited to dinners and taken to the movies or sporting events.

"After six long years, even though I was still angry and upset about my diagnosis, I learned to accept I was schizophrenic. You and my family have tried to support me as best you can, even though most don't fully understand my condition. But you guys made an effort to deal with my illness. You, Dad, and my brother have created a space for me in your lives. You visited me. Picked me up to spend weekends. I've had to do it on your terms, although I have taken those visits as my opportunity to beg to come back and live with you. When I've visited, I've not been allowed to sit idly. Dad finds things for me to do, to earn money for those cigarettes I could not give up. He's not the type to just hand me anything without expecting me to make an effort. So even mowing the lawn or raking leaves around the house, chores I hated to do when I lived there, were activities that became welcome sources of money for me."

During those visits, especially when Tito's dad was present, all worked beautifully. All the pieces of the puzzle fit perfectly—until I had to take Tito back to where he lived.

"But it wasn't easy for me to do those things," Tito said. "It's been very difficult to deal with responsibilities and my social surroundings, with the exception of relating to you guys, my family. Even then I had problems. It had become uncomfortable being around large groups of people, despite being intimately connected. Felt unsafe. Often found myself wanting to run away. Only way to deal with the discomfort was by sleeping, and I did a lot of that. I told you, 'Momma, I'm not lazy. Don't dislike working. I try. Believe me, Momma, I try.'

"Yet despite my best efforts, I have a hard time following complex instructions. I'm unable to do anything that takes more than two steps. It has been very frustrating and disabling. You and Dad raised me to understand the value of work by helping around the house and being responsible for my own cleaning and grooming needs. You taught me to wash, fold, and put away clothes; to clean house; to cook and iron; to maintain the yard and wash the car; and to clean the garage. Can't even do that now. What was familiar is now sometimes beyond my comprehension. It has become difficult for me to do simple chores I could do before the illness. In the best of times, I can cook some things and I can wash clothes, but that's about it."

It is difficult for you to concentrate, I thought as he spoke. You are unable to do complex tasks. But your feelings and emotions are intact—you easily cry and get hurt.

"Despite schizophrenia, I'd like to think that I am a caring, considerate, and respectful person who is very honest. My tendency to please other people often drives me to tell you guys what you want to hear instead of what I think, and I can be easily conned. Good at pretending things are better for me than they are, I talk about going back to school and becoming a teacher or a social worker, but I lack the necessary concentration to read even the simplest book. I've tried several times and failed in the attempt. You have no idea how horrible it is, Momma. Before schizophrenia, it was not unusual for me to read books and novels. Now, I can't even keep my attention on the comics in the newspaper. Can't even watch formerly loved cartoons because I'm unable to focus longer than five minutes. So talk about becoming self-sufficient and going to work only comes from the self-reliance I learned from our family. Deep down inside, given the limits on what I can do, I don't believe I will ever be able to hold even a menial job."

Tito paused. "I fear what's in store for me," he said after a moment. "When depression renders me unable to support and care for myself, my hygiene becomes poor. Don't brush my teeth, I fail to take showers and my nails become extremely long, and I don't change my clothes, living in them for days. Throughout the length of my battle with schizophrenia, anxiety and depression have had a roller-coaster effect on me. Yet I have come to learn that the disease is forever—there is no cure. They call me a functioning schizophrenic because I've learned to accept my illness and religiously take my medication. Momma, you make it a point to say, 'It's to your credit,' but I think it has more to do with the emotional support and acceptance I receive from you and my family, even though sometimes I don't think it's enough. While I appear to be articulate, I find myself having to sort out my thoughts before speaking. Having difficulty concentrating, I become upset. But I try to make some sense of the reality around me and make an effort to do the best I can under the circumstances.

"Due to your advocacy and some family support, especially from Tía Felisa, Uncle Ern, and Grandma, I no longer have to wonder what could happen to me without medical and financial support, because I have them and my benefits. Unless seduced by a flight into health that makes me believe all is well with me, I'm trying not to become another mentally ill person who lives in the streets. While I may not have all the coping skills necessary to survive, with all your help, I'll continue to do my part to stay healthy and alive."

I thought about my son's strength. Despite his clinical depression and ever-present suicidal thoughts, he makes every effort to go on about his day. I attempted to convey my message with my eyes, rather than through words, for Tito felt compelled to continue his story.

"Momma, you know what has really helped me along the way? People like you who treat me like a human being. The first one to do that was Sandy, or SSW—Sandy Social Worker—what I called her in the code language they used. We were dual diagnosis clients, or DDCs, to them. Sandy was a staff member in that dual diagnosis program that first took me in as a patient, and she was the first one to help me start understanding mental illness and substance abuse problems. But I'll talk to you later. I'm tired. Have to go."

My son had had enough of retelling his story. Exhausted, he suddenly wanted to stop. Before he left to hang out and smoke, I gave him a bear hug and said my until-next-times. I had to catch a plane in three hours, and getting there early would give me chance to catch up on my grading.

Drugs Only Masked It

Compared with other schizophrenic patients, those with a dual diagnosis were found to show more positive symptoms, and have a greater risk of psychotic relapse and noncompliance with drug treatment.

—Michael Soyka, "Dual Diagnosis in Patients with Schizophrenia"

My visits and Tito's conversations about the disease have synchronized. I don't even have to ask him what's going on. A pattern has emerged: Tito starts with some story or another. Sometimes there is a chronological sense to them, and at other times he speaks about what is urgent to him at that moment. On this visit, I was ready to continue listening. I hoped he wouldn't be spent and we would have time to eat at Wings, the Chinese restaurant down the street that Tito loves so.

"Momma," he began, "did I ever tell you how good Sandy became at knowing when I was trying to scam her, even though I had just met her? Same as you, she has a lot of guts to be working with people like me. She wasn't afraid of us. She wasn't afraid of me or of anyone else, like others were."

He stopped talking and quickly turned to his right, as if to warn someone to cease. "Shh!" he said as he disengaged from talking to me.

HOMEBOY: "That's what you thought, ese? You ever see the looks she gave you?"

ANGRY MAN: "Quit your bitching. You know that doesn't work here."

"Momma," Tito went on, "I don't know if you remember, but it had been two years since I had gotten sick; that was sometime in 1993, and Social Security was still playing the pendejo game with my application—it was lost, no one knew where it was, it was sent to another department and such—but the only pendejo dummy was me. They were taking me for a ride. They made you go through all types of red tape to prove my illness was real, going against the hope that my illness could have been something treatable. But come to think of it, Momma, you were forced to dig up what led to my illness, you had to write letters to fight and advocate for my benefits, finally made you accept the fact that I was really sick. There was no denying it."

Whispering, leaning in to just about my ear, he said, "But the burrocrats denied my benefits twice because I lacked two actual hospitalizations. Made me wait until I had a second relapse. It was then they reexamined my claim."

Now, no longer whispering, he said, "Momma, even though you're familiar with the mental health system as a professional, you never diagnosed me or treated me as if I were mentally ill. However, at that crucial point in my life, your knowledge and skills served to document, analyze, and name the sets of behaviors I confronted with my illness. When they denied my claim, you did not sit idly by and accept that I was ineligible for benefits because some sane person perceived me able to perform unskilled work. You fought for me. Did all you could to have their decision overturned. How could a person such as me, who was confused and disorganized, who had lost contact with his surroundings, work to support himself?"

Sadly, those who make decisions do not understand the difficulties someone with a mental illness must navigate. It's not laziness or the lack of desire to work—Tito would rather work than receive Social Security supplemental payments; it's that most employers do not even give him a second thought. Too often I have witnessed his broken heart when he doesn't even get hired for a dishwashing job.

"They kept telling me I was employable," Tito said. "That I could work in fast-food chains. But even I, who wasn't all there, couldn't figure out how those fat cats came to the conclusion that I could work. There was no way I could do what I used to; the only job I had ever held was working at a fast-food restaurant selling hot dogs. But the way I was, I wouldn't even be able to keep track of the food items people ordered. You know that deep in my heart, I wanted to work. Didn't want to depend on no one else. Yet however well intentioned I was, and no matter how much I fronted for others, my paranoia and anxiety about being around people, and the claustrophobia that had become part of my emotional makeup, severely narrowed any job possibilities for me, keeping me on edge. The state's conclusion that I was employable, however unskilled the job was, did not take into account my recent social history or whatever difficulties I had dealing with daily life."

I know, I wanted to tell him. You were only hired to do security and fast-food jobs. But Tito, with your lack of attention, level of anxiety, and inability to follow through, how do they deem you to be employable?

"It has been hard coming to terms with this dreaded illness, but after going through a grieving process, I have come to accept it," he went on. "There are still times, like my family did in the beginning of my illness, that I wanted drugs to be the source of my problem, because it would have been something explainable and potentially terminable. If it had been drugs, I could've kicked them and lived the life of a recovering twelve-stepper—but a real one, not a pretend one. In spite of my denial, I recognized that drugs were a cover for my illness. Might've even realized that these affected how the medication worked. But I didn't let on. I just wanted to hide the horrible way my mind worked. The drugs made it seem normal to think about and see the world the way I did.

"It's sad to say, but all of us mental health zombies were easy marks for the pushers. They had no trouble getting whatever money we had on us for a joint that was laced with I don't know what. Got good at self-medicating. Learned just what buttons to push to get money from you and other family members. Every chance I had, I tapped into your guilt. The drugs served to normalize the voices and the presence of demons inside. Under the influence, at least I had a reason for hearing the voices or fearing the monsters that controlled me. Still, even in my confused mental state, I tried to help myself by going to Narcotics Anonymous, seriously believing they would help me get a grip on life. Thought they'd help me understand my need to self-medicate or explain it away."

192

As had become his habit, Tito simply stopped talking. I waited longer than usual for him to regroup. Then I reassured my son that everything would be all right: "Tito, you're doing well. The way you have kept away from drugs and the influence of those who could talk you into using is admirable. Some normal dudes, as you call them, should be as good as you are at that. I know it's difficult for you. What a hard life you've led. It's great that you have promised your grandmother that you would stop using drugs. You should be proud of yourself."

Even though the story had been that my son stopped using drugs for Grandma, Tito shared the real reason he stopped: "Because I am doing it for myself. It's what's best for me."

Friends and Family
Kept Me Afloat

The effect of familiarity was somewhat pervasive: respondents who reported to be familiar with mental illness expressed a less strong desire for social distance.

—Matthias C. Angermeyer, Herbert Matschinger, and Patrick W. Corrigan, "Familiarity with Mental Illness and Social Distance from People with Schizophrenia and Major Depression"

As Tito entered the visiting lounge one day, he said, "Momma, I been thinking about you and my family. The way you've had my back throughout this illness." Always self-reflective, he was trying to figure things out for himself.

"Such a pain in the ass I've been," he continued. "Don't even know how you guys put up with me. In each of your respective ways, each one of you has tried to help me. And while it's hard for you and Dad because I can be a drain on your emotional and financial resources, Momma, you guys still try to support me however you can. At least you haven't abandoned me, forgotten me like many of the discards that live in the same environment I do. Though I complain that you're not there for me, I'm not sure I'd be doing as well if I didn't have your support. You're there for me when I need it most. Even when I *demand* help from you, you still assist me."

"Yeah, Tito, you are very lucky," I told my son, affirming the appreciation he has for our assistance. "You are very fortunate. There is no other resident who gets as many visitors or receives as much support and love as you get."

"I know," he replied. "You all love me. Show it through visits. My Aunt Felisa and Grandma also bring me homemade burritos, and money at least every other week. Can't forget the generous allowance you and Dad send every week so I can buy cigarettes. Then there are Gilbert and Belinda, Elisa, Michael, Lorena, and other family members and friends who drop in on me. I am lucky. Both sides of the family remember my birthday. Those who live nearby invite me to parties, get-togethers like the Fourth of July, Halloween, Thanksgiving, and Christmas. Just like I told you before. Feel like a broken record sometimes, but I have to tell you so I can remember. Only thing that keeps me away from the family is my fear of crowds. If it weren't for the paranoia, the delusions, and the fear of people and their judgments, I would try to be around them more. Remember when I volunteered at the United Nations store? To allay the fears, I had to go out and smoke every few minutes. Got me fired, even though my labor was free. Things could be so much better, Momma."

You are so conflicted, I thought as I looked at my son's handsome face. How sad that the illness sets up such limitations for you.

"What a crybaby," he said. "That's how I feel sometimes, you know. People don't always understand. Don't know much about the illness. Some even thought that I would've hurt them or their kids. Could see it in their eyes. Some even told you of that possibility, asking you to get help for me or to tell me to leave their premises. Didn't take it personally, though. They didn't understand what it was like to deal with someone like me. Now, I know they love me and accept me regardless. They don't blame you, Momma, as they have done in the past. And you know what? They can't even begin to imagine what you've gone through. You lost me—your genius boy. The one who was going to be an attorney but lost his mind instead. You know, even though I manipulate or guilt-trip you, you still deal with me from a place of love. You don't let me get away with stuff. Set limits for me."

It was deeply sad to hear how lonely he was. I wondered if we needed more contact time, and although I wanted to ask him that, I refrained from interrupting.

"Don't you think we've developed a good pace, Momma? Talk to each other twice a week. Sometimes, I test our agreement, calling you above and beyond. But you know when I'm crying wolf. You can tell when I really need you. And for the most part, you're there for me. There are times you answer. Other times you let me figure things out on my own. Honor the boundaries you've set with me and I really, really try to keep the agreement we've made, but it's not always easy for me, especially when I feel lonely and despondent. Even though it's long distance, you seldom fail to answer and you call me. You've even set up an 800 number for me to call so you and Dad can pay for the charges. Can always reach you if I need it. If I'm not able to, I rely on Grandma Aleja to call you when I need to speak to you.

"Only condition Grandma gives me is that she'll try to call you after 7:00 p.m., because her calls are free then. However, most recently, because I have abused her support, Grandma is now screening my calls. She asks questions, wants to know why I'm looking for you. Tells me to be kind to you and 'stop calling just to call you.' Reminds me that you work with your mind, that you need me out of your hair to get the work done—research, teaching, and writing. Momma, you're so smart."

To get a word in edgewise, I thanked him. Tito hadn't stopped talking. He had an urgency to tell me about his life that I'd never felt before.

"At first I thought you and Dad, and the family, were ashamed of me," he went on, "but that was my own fear. It was my own sense of rejection making me feel that way. Mi familia makes me part of their lives. I've attended weddings, graduations, baptisms, and other types of celebrations. It's me that can't hang. Afraid of interacting in crowds, I usually ask someone—you, if you're there, or Aunt Felisa because she's like a second mom to me—to take me home. Can't deal with all the noise, all the chatter. Sometimes I try to stretch my time around them, so I can get used to it, but I just continue to bug until someone takes me home.

"There have been times I got really paranoid, thinking the family is talking about me behind my back. It's nothing they do or say. Sometimes I catch them looking at me weird. They have pity in their eyes. They don't have to speak to make me feel bad. During those times, I try to focus on their love for me. Try not to get hooked by the ugly feelings that trick me into hiding, that make me leave their get-togethers. Sometimes I can do it. Other times, one of you gives in and just takes me home—don't even complain anymore. Although I've gotten better at staying more than an hour, I still ask to leave because I feel more comfortable in the environment to which I've become accustomed. Once back in whatever place I call home, I feel calm. It feels safe to go back to the routine. I appreciate that you guys have not discarded or left me. I know even those who might've dismissed me from their lives are happy to see me when I show up."

"I know, Tito," I said. "Our immediate and extended family is trying to understand the illness, so they can learn to cope with it. Your aunt Felisa is particularly good at distinguishing between your depression and sadness. She knows just how to talk to you. She counsels you as someone who understands. Reassures you and tells you that she loves you. Aunt Felisa makes you feel valued. I'm so glad she is there for you. It gives me the freedom to continue doing the work I do. We are so fortunate to have her in our lives. She is an invested and loving aunt, your almost-second mom. She has been that and more for you. You have to agree that most of our family, while they may not have a thorough grasp of the disease, have made an effort to understand it. Making room for you in their lives, they continue to love and support you."

There was nothing else to say. Tito has always had a good sense of the support he receives, although he wants more of what he gets. After I spoke, Tito did not say a thing. He just nodded and left, as had become his habit. I departed with the promise that I would return the next day.

Detachment and Fear Run My Life

Patients and relatives describe a great variety of stigma and discrimination experiences in all areas of life, including health care. Isolation and avoidance are common reactions to those experiences. Publicizing these . . . experiences could help to reduce stigmatizing attitudes in society and result in healthier reactions from patients, favoring a better course of the illness.

—Miguel Angeles González-Torres et al., "Stigma and Discrimination towards People with Schizophrenia and Their Family Members"

Tito has learned to understand the stigma attached to schizophrenia. He attempts to explain the illness to those who are brave enough to ask. He does this without shame and in an effort to educate. He wants those around him—family members and strangers—to understand that he is mentally ill but still very much a human being. He is a good person whose only aim in life is to do the best he can with his life as it has been given to him.

"Yesterday, when we were talking about the family," he said on our next visit, "I realized that I do have some regrets. The younger ones are afraid of me. With few exceptions—my cousin Miliano and my niece Janaé—I don't have much of a relationship with those I grew up with or the ones that came after. I don't know if they realize that I miss them or that I would have liked for them to become part of my life. Then I think,

198

What use would they have for a moron like me? When I see them at family gatherings, I often wish that they would make an extra effort to approach me—it always has to be me and I feel like I'm imposing on them. But what do I expect? I probably would have done the same thing, if I were in their place."

As he often did, Tito spoke about the need to be close to family. "You know, I understand, but I don't like the isolation and the lack of attention I get from them. When I was younger, the only thing that mattered was what interested me at a given moment. Don't remember being concerned with much of anything else, only that which had urgency to me. Now that I find myself in this situation, I wish they would just come and have a brief conversation with me beyond the 'Hi!' or 'How are you?' they dispense my way. It feels like pity. Don't want any, if that's all they have to give me. Shit! Sometimes, I wonder if they are afraid to catch what I have. Maybe they're afraid to see themselves in my shoes.

"As the firstborn and the oldest child in your family, Momma, they had high expectations for me. Sadly, I've not measured up. Hope they forgive me for not becoming who they thought I could be. Often pray that no one else in my family develops this dreaded disease. Our Lady of Guadalupe, whose medallion I wear, listens to my prayers. She hears me, makes me feel that all will be all right. You know, Momma, I wouldn't want them to go through what I've experienced. Don't wish that on my worst enemy. Yeah. Some make an effort, but I wish all my family members were part of my life. That's what I miss most of all in this sentence of a life I've received. Wish they were part of my daily existence, like you and Tía Felisa."

I have never met anyone who longs to have his relatives around as much as my son does. There are times Tito has expressed regret over having decided not to have children, though he reassures me that he made the right decision. He is afraid they will inherit his illness and has made up his mind that the only children he should have around him are those who come to visit with the relatives who are not afraid to bring them. For the moment, his dream for children is on hold, but it's always something to which he returns.

Behind the Smoke Curtain

There is considerable empirical support for the idea that smoking in schizophrenia may represent an attempt to self-medicate some of the cognitive deficits of this disorder.

—Veena Kumary and Peggy Postma, "Nicotine Use in Schizophrenia"

Tito had been calling me nonstop. He called and called and called. And called again. Because he wouldn't tell me what was going on, all I could do was hazard a guess. Judging by the messages he left—twenty-two, but only because the tape ran out on the recorder—he needed cigarettes. They are the only thing that gives Tito peace of mind, rest from the anxiety that crawls on his skin. According to him, the smoke muffles the voices and quiets the nameless faces that live inside.

As soon as I got home and entered the house, the telephone was at it again. *Ring! Ring! Ring!* It had been a difficult day and I wasn't in the mood to answer the telephone, but the message Tito left this time got me really agitated. There's something going on with Tito, I thought as I called him back.

With very little compassion and patience for my son, all I could do was tell him how I felt. "Tito, don't you realize how annoying it is? Clearly, you call because you need to talk to me. I know talking to me makes you feel better. But you're driving me nuts with your calls for more of those damned cancer sticks."

He tried to explain, telling me that the cigarettes quiet the madness. He doesn't want to bother me, but he has no one else.

"M'ijo, I tell you, it's insane," I said. "I don't understand. How can cigarettes help you?"

The pay phone must have run out of money, because I heard a click and Tito was gone. Then it rang again. I contemplated answering it but let it ring instead. I wasn't in the mood to continue talking. It was about the cigarettes—Tito had confirmed as much to me—so what else was there to say?

But the telephone continued to ring. I tried my best to ignore it, letting it ring until it stopped. I wondered why I didn't turn off the ringer. That would have made it easier. What could I do? I had already set limits, and he continued to ignore them (it was one of the reasons we discontinued the toll-free number for his calls). The telephone was his link to sanity, but for me it was a connection to his illness. He was driving me insane.

It rang again. I'm not answering, I thought. I've had enough! It was maddening to hear the rings over and over again, but I knew that answering the phone was the only way I could put an end to the ringing. I began to talk to myself, observing that the last round of ringing made it thirty times he had called.

Then, being so resourceful, Tito had the long-distance operator humanize his desperation. "Collect call," the operator said. "Mark one for yes, two for no. Collect call." I sat in the living room, trying to sort out what else could be going on with my Tito besides his need for cigarettes or money. I listened to his voice over the recorder, gauging his intonation, and he didn't sound good. My arm, acting as if it had a mind of its own, reached out to pick up the telephone, finally stopping the incessant noise.

Tito was more persistent than me, and I gave in. I didn't know what else to do. I could have unplugged the phone, but it wasn't in me to shut him off completely. I had to find out what the urgency was about. When he answered the phone, instead of listening, I let my frustration out.

"Stick to your agreement," I heard myself say. "Don't be calling so much! I've already told you that I would send you cigarettes—you convinced me to send them overnight with twenty dollars to spend. I have. Now what else do you want?"

How horribly I spoke to my son. He had worn me out, stripping me of all my defenses. I attempted to regroup and talk to him with the love and compassion I know I have for him: "Tito, m'ijo, there are times I don't answer. More often than I care to admit to you, I answer just to stop the ringing. The other times I screen the incoming calls, especially if I am not in the best of moods, to protect you from my response. Then there are those times I don't listen to myself and I answer, only to become resentful when I give in to whatever request you have just so I can stop your calls. I don't want you smoking. But I still buy you those dreaded cancer sticks that slowly take you to your death. I mail them with enough time, so that you won't have to beg or borrow."

I knew I could stop the calls. It would have been easy enough to put a block on them, but it hurt me to think that he might need something or may be confronting difficult times. But give me a break! I thought to myself. So many messages. It's unbearable. "God, m'ijo," I told him, "I recognize that cigarettes serve as a badge of worth to you, that they are a symbol of wealth among the mentally ill. I've heard they make you valuable and important in the eyes of those who long for the smoke that calms them. But isn't there something else you can do? Can you get medicine to stop smoking? Get a patch?"

There was no response. It was as if I was talking to myself and this time he was the one not answering the telephone. Still, I continued trying to convince Tito that he could do something about his habit, because he has stopped smoking when he's been held in medium-care facilities or at the psychiatric hospital, where they don't allow smoking.

"Sorry, m'ijo," I said. "Why would I want you to take more pills? You're already taking enough. This is not easy for me, either. I get angry with myself for all the wrong reasons. I'm in a no-win situation. I get mad because I buy them for you, because I feed your addiction, because you dare to call, because you know I will give you whatever you want—and not always for the right reasons. That damned nicotine. I get mad at myself for refusing your request. Then I tell myself that it's only cigarettes and they give you the comfort you need in the mental prison you inhabit. Even though those damned sticks compromise your life, they soothe you, lessen your anxiety. God, I know this."

"Momma, they make me feel important," Tito said. "I'm a big man about town when I have cigarettes to dispense or money to lend. Cigarettes make me count to those around me. Give me value."

Tito paused, but rather than say something to him, I kept my thoughts buried, although I tried to explore ways to let him know I didn't mind helping. There were other things, besides sending cigarettes, that I could do to help him, but rather than following that line of thought, I continued giving him what I considered a rational argument for my decisions.

"Tito, it would be so much easier to respond to other needs, to advocate for you or to support another demand for your rights, to be of help to you," I began. "The calls would then have more meaning for me. It's when you call to ask for money or cigarettes that I'm most bothered, but regardless of what you call about, my mother's heart generally rules. I give in. The phone calls tax my patience, especially when you exhaust the tape on the machine with calls that trip over one another. I've lost count of your calls for help, especially those times you call over and over again, hoping to wear me out. And you do. I want the calls to stop."

The struggles we have because of smoking are the ones I most detest. I provide Tito cigarettes because they help him and make his life more bearable. They even give him some status among his community. Yet I dislike that I am providing him with the cancer sticks that damage his body, one already replete with countless harmful drugs.

"When it comes to your cigarettes, Tito," I told him, "you forget your honed sense of time. Time, to which you are so attuned, ceases to have meaning. It becomes everything and nothing all at the same time. It reminds me of your love for onions; you're like them to the core. You hide your feelings amid layers of protection that keep you detached from your illness, from the hurt, from the insults. That's when, depressed, you recoil inside yourself. You know that I have no choice but to answer. I feel like an emotional placenta—or attached to you at the hip like conjoined twins. Your efforts to make contact reach the marrow of my bones. We are so connected that I always seem to know when you need to talk. I feel the depression you're experiencing. I sense the rejection. It is then that I walk side by side with your emotions. I call you, despite my better thinking. It hurts to see you in that condition. I don't know what to do. I feel helpless."

"Momma," Tito replied, "I can almost touch the desperation in your voice as it breaks. Sounds like you're crying, but you continue talking over the emotions. I listen to your story to give you the break you seek. Even though I'm the crazy one, I listen to you, because your story is my story. Sorry, Momma. I'm trying not to cry."

He paused, then told me, "Excuse me a minute." After another pause, he said, "It's times like this when all the emotions intensify in me, when I realize that my illness lives inside you too. You get depressed just like I do. I feel it. Ache for you. Can't do much about my illness, even when I know these emotions are inside me. You don't live my life. That's why I try to express empathy to you. Even though you don't know what it feels like for me, Momma, I know what you have to deal with from my side of the fence."

I had just returned from work—I'm not very good at listening when I'm tired. And consumed with his need for cigarettes, Tito didn't hear me. I tried to reestablish our limits, capping his call to five minutes for him to share his concerns. I told myself that it was his illness surging forth. Full of self-pity, Tito talked about the way others treat him. Was it manipulation? Possibly. It wasn't unusual for him to use it.

"Momma, today some guy asked me where I live," my son said. "Told him at Casa Olga. Then I see it in his eyes. He doesn't speak. Vacant stares tell me what I've heard before: the nuthouse? They think I'm crazy. They confuse mental illness for madness, don't even show pity or veil their disgust for me. Filth. Disgust. I sense it. It brands me. Can't you help me, Momma?"

I didn't know what to say. I was irritated with him and more confused than ever. It was par for the course.

Cigarette Wealth

The Excessive rate of smoking and increased nicotine intake noted in schizophrenic patients serve as a form of self-medication, as well as upholding a possible role for nicotinic agonist treatment in schizophrenia.

—Veena Kumary and Peggy Postma, "Nicotine Use in Schizophrenia"

My sister Felisa told me about the most recent time she took cigarettes, the dreaded cancer sticks, to my son. "When I take cigarettes to Tito, the residents who live with him gather around him as if he were a honey bee," she explained. "With my mere presence, the residents are drawn to him, as if pulled by a magnet in slow motion. Before the last time I took him cigarettes, I'd never stayed to see what happens, but this last time I sat and waited for things to unfold. What I saw was your son, who appeared to stand taller than he is, dispensing individual cigarettes from packs I had taken him. No wonder he constantly needs them. I didn't see him exchange money or anything in return. I guess cigarettes are more than smoke for him, and when he gets cigarettes, they all get them."

Now more than ever Tito refuses to quit, making us believe that he is extremely addicted to cigarettes and cannot live without them. But Felisa and his county payee—an employee who is assigned the responsibility of managing Tito's financial resources—confirmed that cigarettes have become a cash commodity that provides Tito with status and gives him the social support he would not otherwise have among his fellow residents. It has taken me over twenty years to figure out that cigarettes are his economic base and help form his social support network. And my extended family members and I supply the coveted material. With cigarettes, Tito has developed a complex bartering structure whereby he satisfies his need for the nicotine that lessens his anxiety and gains access to social relationships and other amenities, such as gift cards for coffee and fast food.

It's difficult for us to be sympathetic to his addiction, given the cost of cigarettes. With the exception of Felisa's husband, who is a chain-smoker, no one in my son's cigarette support network smokes. Still, with amazing care and compassion, family and friends participate in this slow-death ritual—that's how all of us who take him cigarettes see his smoking. Because Tito claims smoking helps him to cope, we continue to buy and take him those dreaded cigarettes.

Until recently, Tito was able to access cigarettes from anyone in the family. He persistently made urgent phone calls and sometimes resorted to talk of suicide as a form of blackmail, and inside the guilt of sympathy for his situation, any of our relatives would come through for him and deliver several packs of cigarettes to his residence of the time; in the past year, his smoking needs intensified as he attempted, ultimately unsuccessfully, to survive in an independent living situation. After three medical emergencies with diabetes—his sugar count rose to over 500—he moved to a transition facility, then to a medium-care group-living home environment, which put him at four residences in the span of a year.

With his migratory movement from place to place, we have come to understand the massive amount of cigarettes he consumes. Felisa and I have devised a way to continue giving him access to cigarettes, but not in the amount he expects. We made this decision after Felisa witnessed several cigarette-exchange transactions. In addition, I was told by his payee that Tito relies on cigarettes as an economic system to secure sex, friendship, and other benefits. Granted, we want to help Tito, but at five to eight dollars a pack, it's not always feasible to buy him as many cigarettes as he would wish.

It's not the money, however, that concerns us the most. It is the impact smoking has on Tito's health. He doesn't need to add to his physiological burdens—the side effects of his medication are taking their toll on him. But for him, the only respite to his condition lies in those dreaded cigarettes. When Tito smokes he becomes another person—calm, self-assured, and confident.

I have often wished that pharmaceutical companies would go into the business of making nicotine pills. But I realize that this ritual of self-medicating and comfort is not just about lighting, puffing, and inhaling smoke. Cigarettes in his community, one primarily of men, make Tito feel like he has worth and value, especially among those who are more destitute and lack the support of a family.

But with the intensity of his demands and expectations, he may lose our support. My family and friends do not want to reject him, but Tito's needy demand for cigarettes makes people less willing to help. Until then, Felisa and I are his only source of support. And we will continue to provide him three packs every three days; that's our limit. For any additional smokes, Tito will have to figure it out.

Clean and Sober

His Reality

Acceptance appears to be the only thing that allows the person to hold onto, or regain, the basic sense of being a human being that most of us carry within.

—Larry Davidson, *Living Outside Mental Illness*

It was time for my monthly visit. Tito seemed to be in a really good mood this time. He was happy to see me and had not asked for anything, although I came armed with a carne asada burrito and a huge Diet Coke from the Super Taquería on Tenth Street in San José. He ran to greet me, hugged me, and I almost dropped the soda, but he caught it midair without losing a single drop.

"Momma, you know what?" he asked. "I just had my ninth anniversary. Been straight and sober for nine years. Yeah. Can you believe it? Stopped cold turkey once I figured out drugs interfered with the medication I took for my illness. But really it was mostly because my grandma asked me to stop. Did not want to give her more worries than she carries. But you know, it wasn't that difficult. I just stopped. Just like that. Wish I could do that with cigarettes, but I can't seem to shake them. Sometimes cigarettes are the only comfort I have. It is the one addiction I hang on to."

Oh, no, I thought, I didn't bring cigarettes. It was wishful thinking on my part that Tito no longer needed them. But instead of asking for cigarettes, Tito began to tell me about his life. He was very focused, and in his best storytelling mode he filled in the details of his life. This time there were no games. No manipulation. He really wanted me to hear his side of the story. He wanted to help himself. And he had learned that he could not impress me or disappoint me—I always accepted him just as he was. So he just talked.

"Momma, I know it was a difficult time for all of us," he began. "The teeter-totter of a life had become harder to figure out as the days and years passed. You continued trying to help me, and we both desperately wanted to believe that my problem could be fixed. Your efforts had no limit. With every rejection of the services we both desperately needed, you finally pursued the drug route, approaching two rehabilitation clinics for help. I know you know the story, but this is what's coming out today; I have to tell it. So I'm going to continue. I'm sure you'll figure out what to do with this story or maybe it will tell you something new."

Are you contemplating doing drugs or are you already doing them? I wondered as he spoke. It's sad to be so suspicious, but he and I have already walked this road. I remained silent for fear Tito would feel accused or judged.

"When you took me to the first drug treatment center, I was extremely agitated," Tito continued. "In a psychotic state, every car I saw carried someone who persecuted and wanted to kill me. I attempted to take everything in, shifting my eyes and head in all directions, and I was extremely frightened. At the first site, I refused to get out of the car. Wouldn't go into the facility because to me, the workers were devil worshipers who wanted to kill me or convert me to Satanism. In my mind, each person who passed had a pact with 'those people who want to hurt me.' Finally, I got out of the car, and with my agreement, you left me there to get help. But since most facilities were voluntary and unlocked, you would soon have to come and retrieve me, 'cause I raised hell with the workers and they didn't want to deal with me. Couldn't even remember how many times you did that with me or how you felt every time you returned to get me. Finding out you had no choice, you took me back again and again.

"But you continued trying anyway. Always put forth your best effort. Every facility we went to, the staff rejected me because they perceived that my problem was beyond their ability to help. Expressing regret for not being able to do something, they would send us on our way: 'His problem is not drugs. He's not acting or behaving like any other person we've helped before. He has other problems to deal with and we're not equipped to treat him.' Passing the buck back to you, you had to start the process over again. You tried Community Companions, a community-based program for the mentally ill. Although we were begging for help, I was not accepted into the program because of the drug overdose. Sending us from one agency to the next, my mental illness was diagnosed as drug related and they didn't work with addicts. Since Community Companions only worked with patients who were mentally ill and I had a dual diagnosis, my only option became the streets, where I lived for a while."

You memory is amazing, Tito, I thought. You do not forget anything you have dealt with.

"It was a horrible time in our lives, Momma. Couldn't live with you and I found myself living in the woods at Sea Cliff Beach, in California, with the homeless and social discards. This was the most grueling and painful experience I've ever had. Not sure I was that aware of the ways my condition affected you guys. Each and every member of my family lived in fear. Not understanding where to go next and hopelessly lost and without the help we needed to deal with my illness, you tried to find a place for me. Then there came the times when we lost our way or did not know how to approach things. This was especially when I was having an episode, when everyone and anyone became an enemy to me—even you."

It seemed to me that Tito was feeling better—it was so easy for him to speak about his feelings.

"Extremely paranoid, I saw and talked about devils," he went on. "Accused Uncle Tomás, your youngest brother, of having a pact with the evil one. Told my relatives that he had a contract out to kill me. Accused him of being associated with those thugs I had run with in the drug business—thought Uncle Tomás was one of Mary's goons. Even my younger brother wasn't free of my suspicion. I accused him of having an affair with my girlfriend, Vicki. Can you imagine that? How crazy is that? I remember telling you about it. 'Don't mess with me,

Momma. I know Corky is seeing my girlfriend. He is in it with them and wants to kill me.' I blamed you guys, my own family, for putting me in harm's way. Resented you all for plotting against me.

"But that was in the beginning. Since then, I've come to understand that my family loves me. That none of you would ever do anything to harm me. And you know what? None of you have cast me away. Sure, my neediness keeps everyone at a distance. As hard as it is I've learned to recognize that each one of you has a life. Although it's difficult to accept that I am not the center of your world, you have to go about being normal. I appreciate those who choose to be in my life, but wish more came to see me, visit me."

Why is it that so-called normal people do not have the ability to speak with the insight Tito shows? Despite his illness, my son is in touch with his emotions and feelings, to the extent that one would think there is nothing wrong with him. But I have also seen my son lose it. I've witnessed the ravages of his disease. Without therapy and the medication that keeps his chemistry regulated, I am not sure any of us could cope, least of all Tito. Still, there are times I wonder whether the meds are hurting or helping. I do not know. Sadly, that realm belongs to the psychiatrists, not to me, his mother.

Depression and All the Not-So-Positives

Recognition of depression in schizophrenia is important not only because of the morbidity of the disorder and the fact that it may represent a treatable aspect of the patient's condition, but also because mortality may be associated with depression as well.

—Samuel G. Siris, "Depression in Schizophrenia"

It is most difficult to visit Tito when he is depressed, especially when he becomes nostalgic and wants to talk about all the ways he failed his family, focusing on that second chance we gave him to turn things around. On one visit, blaming himself for not having tried harder, Tito started to tell me about the way he moved into a world of illicit drugs, as both a user and a bag boy or runner. Although I was not ready to hear the story, I was committed to listening mindfully. Obviously, Tito had something to convey that I may not have listened to in the past. In a conference room because he did not want to visit in the common area, he told me about his relocation to the Herdez family's home, where he got a job delivering drugs for his mother-in-law.

"As you already know," he began, "after failing to keep my agreement with Grandma and Uncle Ernest when I went to live with them in San José—I did not graduate from high school or keep a job—I moved in with my girlfriend, Vicki Herdez, at her mother's house. I haven't told you this, but they made their living from drugs. Opting for a lifestyle that was not of my family's liking, I got deep into the crazy life of drugs and gangbanging. Soon I became estranged from my family, easily folding into Vicki's extended family, turning into one of them in all ways possible—in the worst ways.

"With dealings in the illegal drug trade, their home became my haven. I became wrapped in their business, cutting off my relationships with my biological family. As bad as it sounds, once I moved into their home, my family only existed for me when I needed something from you, especially money. And when I couldn't get it, I asked some to buy groceries or requested others to help with my living expenses. 'Momma, I need money for groceries. The children haven't eaten. We have nothing to eat in the house.' Or 'Grandma, lend me some money, I'll pay you back' and 'Tía Felisa, do you have some money you could lend me? I need to contribute, and I'm out of work. Can you help me?'"

As difficult as it was for me, I continued to listen carefully to Tito's story.

"All of you tried to help me with money when I asked. But you soon got tired. It became difficult for me to dupe anyone out of cash or to get any other type of support. Soon the time came when none of you guys answered the telephone. Avoided me. And if I was lucky enough to reach you, you'd ask what Mary was doing with all the money she made on the side. You said, 'Tito, she gets welfare for those kids. What the hell does she do with her money? That's it! They're not my responsibility. Don't ask me for any more money.' After those rejections, I stayed away for months at a time. But soon enough, I shamelessly sought you guys out again. When I needed something, I went to visit, because it was more difficult for you to say no when I went in person. Using whatever approach I could devise, I continued to seek your financial support.

"Then, sometime in July 1991, you got a call from Mary, my girlfriend's mother. I had taken an overdose of drugs, as you know. 'Robert is tweaking.' Don't think you even understood what Mary meant by that term, but I could hear Mary telling you, using my formal name and not identifying herself. Momma, I know you had no clue as to what Mary was talking about, even though you had worked in and around families and youth who used drugs. I could only guess as to your response, but I could hear Mary telling you about my situation: 'He took an overdose of crank.

The only thing I know that will bring him down is a shot of heroin. I'm going to give him a shot.' Couldn't even imagine how you responded. ¡Pobrecita de usted!"

It was deranged for her to offer such a solution to deal with an overdose, I thought. How could she compromise your welfare like that? Tito continued with his story.

"'That's the only thing that works.' Mary repeated, as if to talk you into the only solution she had. As I expected, Momma, you refused to accept heroin as a remedy to my situation. Later, she laughingly told me what you had said: 'No! Don't you dare! He needs to ride it out. Give him plenty of fluids: orange and cranberry juice, and water. Make sure he eats. I don't want a *tecato*, drug addict, for a son. How can you even suggest that?' Mary, imitating your voice, agitated me more with her representation of you. 'Geez, your mother is real sonsa. What a fucking mensa.' Laughing in my face, Mary repeated her comments over and over again, telling me that you were so educated, yet so stupid. She then moved on to tease me about my middle-class upbringing, making fun of me for not knowing what it took to live in their world.

"Momma, I was glad that you didn't disappoint me. You rushed to Mary's house to get me. Although I was out of my head, you jetted through those topsy-turvy winding roads over the Santa Cruz Mountains to pick me up. You were there in record time. When you entered the house, I ran toward you, throwing myself at you like a magnet, tripping over my own words because my tongue and my mind were going every which way. Racing in warp speed, I tried to get to you before anyone else said anything because I wanted to tell you my side of the story. Still dazed and confused about my surroundings, I only felt safe in your presence. Still out of my wits, I blurted out the first thing that came to me: 'Momma, I tried to kill myself. I'm tired. Can't deal with what's going on inside my mind.' Told you with a conviction that frightened even me."

There have been only two times I really believed Tito was going to harm himself, and this was one of those times.

"Didn't want to scare you, I just wanted to impress upon you how sad and lonely my life was. Felt worthless, less worthy than excrement; at least that had worth for the environment. Felt useless. Must have

214

been the reason I couldn't talk. That was the only clear thing that came out. Otherwise I mouthed incomprehensible words, attempting to make excuses for my behavior. Didn't want to embarrass you, though. Knowing that there was something not quite right about me, I made every effort to regain my composure. Still I sensed Mary's fear and anger over her potential exposure. Fearing repercussions for the overdose, Mary asked you to take me home. Must've been afraid to get busted. She had an urgency about getting me out of her sight.

"'¡Yo no quiero problemas!' she exclaimed. 'Take him out of here. I don't want any problems.' Repeating herself, Mary asked that you get me the hell out because she didn't want any problems. Wanted to make sure you understood the seriousness of the situation. Mary just wanted you to take me out of there because I brought her problems. That was all that mattered to her. Didn't want her ass busted. Remember?"

Quietly listening, I nodded in response.

"Mary didn't give a damn about me. Just cared about her little business on the side. After having used me without pay, I was now worthless to her. Wasn't sure why I was thinking about this, but I'm telling you because I knew you had not learned about those times I got high on Mary's dope with her daughter's encouragement. Thought I would be better able to sell it, knowing the quality and all. Momma, Mary liked me wasted; it gave her control over me. She found it easier to handle and manipulate me. And I let her. At your home, I started to regain my composure. More relaxed, I still could not shake the paranoia I carried. It became more intense with each day. Didn't want to be left alone. Having you near made me feel safe. However you cut it, that was a week of pure hell for both of us. Drove us crazy. Became more psychotic as time passed.

"Chasing you around, I was like a little puppy hanging on to your skirt. Like a tick on a dog, I latched on to you. Didn't let you out of my sight. If you went to the store, I wanted to go with you. About the only thing you could do on your own was to go to the bathroom. Again trying to get me help, you called many people. Contacted several agencies in two counties. We found out that most were filled to capacity, while others had long waiting lists. Then, when all our hope was about gone, you found that Christian agency, Victory Outreach. They agreed to see

215

me and were even willing to accept me into their program. Don't know how you talked me into it, but I consented and even allowed you to leave me there. Must've been the religious tones. Made me feel secure. It was a way to cancel out the demons. But soon, as with everywhere else, I felt unsafe. Became suspicious of everyone around me. So I bolted. Wanted to get outside my skin and run until no one knew me or could catch me. Night didn't help. It was then the delusional tapes inside my mind grew more bizarre. That was when I became an insomniac with a mission—wanted to stay awake at any cost, fearing that if I went to sleep I would die at my own hands or by the acts of those voices reigning inside."

Tito paused, and I took time to reflect on his situation. I couldn't even imagine how difficult this time must have been for my son. I just knew what it was like for me and those around me.

My son constantly has to make sense of his reality. He continually has to figure out if what he thinks, what he sees, and what he feels is real or imagined. He has to make sense of his life from as many perspectives as possible, to sort out what is going on inside. As if that were not enough, he has to live with the stigma of mental illness, always enduring the stereotypes and expectations of normalcy imposed upon him, all the while fighting the sense of impending doom, of destruction or chaos—which he often reminds me is "mental illness and not craziness."

Wasting Away, and No One Noticed

People experiencing a schizophrenic break display outward symptoms like changes in self-care, unusual eating or sleeping patterns, changes in work or school performance, lack of energy, headaches, and behavior that seems confused or bizarre.

—Vanessa Taylor, "Schizophrenic Break"

I came to visit my son, but he was not at the facility. Somehow, because he is a mentally ill adult man, the workers at Casa Olga did not think to call and tell me that he had been hospitalized. If I hadn't come to visit him, I wouldn't have found out. After badgering those who work at the facility, I learned that Tito had been staying away from Casa Olga and that no one knew where he had gone. Thinking that she was helping me understand the situation, a nurse informed me that Tito had become more detached from his physical self, to the point of telling her that his body had its own mind separate from his brain. She added that Tito went about feeling disconnected from his body, only listening to the voices inside. In addition, his hygiene, which previously had only been a concern for those offended by his appearance, had deteriorated. The manager told me that Tito wasn't dressing up and that he couldn't have cared less how he looked, much less how others saw him. Helplessly, all I could say was, "Why didn't you call me?" As if my son was

217

irrelevant to me, the only response I got was, "We called the social worker and his conservator."

On hearing that I had been inquiring about Tito, Bryan, one of the residents, took me aside and told me, "Your son, he wasn't being taken care of. All he takes in is Coca-Cola and cigarettes—the brands are irrelevant. The puffs of smoke seem to be the only thing that connects him to himself. We all know that cigarettes are dear to us and that they make life easier, but he's told me that a cigarette, stuck between his pointing finger and the one he was known to use to give attitude to those who stare at him, makes him feel alive."

I was thankful that Bryan, who was not getting along with Tito, told me that his former friend was killing himself on Cokes and cigarettes. I did not expect him to tell me more, but he continued: "Most days Tito is dead broke. The money SSI gives him barely covers his room and board, so he pilfers cigarette butts on the sidewalk—something Tito had previously thought beneath him, unlike those of us who have no shame." He laughed, as if to normalize how low the residents get. I could imagine Tito resorting to that. Smoking was the only thing that gave him comfort from the anxiety that had overtaken his life, especially when his mental and emotional state was depleted.

After much looking and innumerable telephone calls, I found out that my son was in the hospital's psychiatric ward, but he was not allowed to have visitors. I had no choice but to return to San Antonio. Work and other responsibilities were waiting for me. A month later, I found out that Tito's depression had deepened. I was concerned. The nurse told me Tito had lost seventy-five pounds and they couldn't figure out what was going on with him. He hadn't even answered my calls because he refused to go to the pay phone. I decided to plan another visit.

Losing It
My Mind Is Not Right

After a century of studying schizophrenia, the cause of the disorder remains unknown. Treatments, especially pharmacological treatments, have been in wide use for nearly half a century, yet there is little evidence that these treatments have substantially improved outcomes for most people with schizophrenia.

—Thomas R. Insel, "Rethinking Schizophrenia"

I was finally able to visit Tito. He looked thin, but his mind seemed to be sharp and clear. He wanted to talk about the way Jorge had become an integral part of his care. According to my son, his dad is the most compassionate and loving person, and he is better able to listen to him than anyone else, including me.

"Momma, I'm really losing it," Tito said as if to normalize what was going on for him. "My mind's not right. Something is amiss. I'm obsessed with money. Got this madness going on. Obsessed like King Midas. Don't understand why. I've got none. Could it be that I'm not getting enough meds? Don't know if anyone has told you, but I'm trying to reduce my drug intake—the meds."

Tito explained this to make sure I didn't think he was back to self-medicating with street drugs. "With my psychiatrist's help, we are switching those that aren't as damaging as the ones I've been taking.

Did you know that some of them do more harm than good?" he asks without making space for me to respond.

He continued talking about his fixation with money. "I'm fixated on it. Money, I mean," he said, clarifying what it meant for him. "Did I tell you I'm part of a lawsuit?"

Asking me a question without intending to let me answer, as had become his habit, Tito continued telling me about the ways he was trying "to mine some bucks my way." And then he repeated the story about the lawsuit as if he had not just told me about it: "There are several class action suits going against some of those drug companies for the damage they're causing people like me."

He quickly changed the subject to his appearance, using it as evidence of the adverse effects the drugs have on him. "Have you noticed how skinny I am? Did anyone tell you that I'm losing weight too quickly? Been really losing weight so fast I can't even use any of the pants you bought me last month. Has anyone told you that weight loss is one of the side effects? Stomach problems are another. The social worker signed me up. Told me to join the suit. I want them to pay for their carelessness. They have no idea how they hurt us. Don't even test their medicine on humans, just animals," Tito said, repeating what he had heard from some of the health professionals who work with him.

The subject changed again as he returned to the topic of money and how much he will soon have. "Lately I've been feeling like I'll get a load of money. Been fantasizing about it. Just thinking that I'll be able to have money like never before. It's making me delusional. I'm not able to have control over what I eat. Overlook food. Remember that big fight I started with you, Momma? Accused you of wanting the money, of having received it and hiding it. Told you, 'You're hoarding it, keeping it from me, to use it for yourself. It's blood money. My kidneys and my liver are damaged. What does it matter? But you can keep the damned money.' You got really hurt. Had no idea that I was as bad to you as I was. You must've told Dad.

"Even though you are here visiting me, Dad called to check up on me and told me that you were beside yourself. He wanted to know what I had done to you. Didn't accuse me or anything, but Dad, in his matter-of-fact way, got around to telling me that I was being delusional about money. Told me there was none; it was imaginary. Dad told me that I was obsessed with it and that my illness was making me talk that way. He really listened, with his heart. Explained it to me in a way that I could understand. Took the time to hear me. Dad even outshone you in the way he dealt with me. Such love and compassion—how lucky I am to have Dad in my life. He's been there for you and me in ways that I can't even begin to explain. He's so good to us."

You and money are a bad combination, I thought as Tito spoke. This, along with gang and demon delusions, warn me that you are about to have a psychotic break. I hope you know that I'm glad we are talking about it—an ounce of prevention, you know.

"Not telling you to make you feel good, but people who know me get confused thinking he's my biological father. But I correct them. Tell them he's more than that, he's my dad by choice. I explain that we love each other because we've grown to respect one another despite our shortcomings, and he's taught me other lessons when I've hurt you so badly. Apparently, in my delusional rants I accused you of hoarding my money. Really believed that you were hiding or sitting on a settlement account. That you weren't letting go of that money I so desperately needed. Accused you of wanting to rip me off. Told you that you could keep it and bask in it—it was blood money anyway, and you could have it all. Can't believe I did all that to you. After all you do for me. But after my talk with Dad, I called you and apologized. Told you it wasn't your doing. That I shouldn't have screamed at you the way I did. You were so hurt by my insensitive words. Could see why Dad came to your support.

"Momma, after you returned to San Antonio a few days later, Dad, who seldom calls me, called back to check on me, to see if I was OK. Again he reassured me that neither of you would ever hurt me that way. Dad made me see that the money was all in my imagination. There was no settlement. He was right to do that. You were devastated by the way I treated you. Once again I called you and apologized. As you have in the past, you forgave me. Told me you were OK. In our family since 1976, by choice and despite all that I have put him and you through, Dad has stayed with us. He's the best thing that ever happened to us."

In a manner that made me feel all right about him returning to his institutional life, Tito said, "Time to go, Momma, visiting hours are over." I felt comfort in knowing that he was doing much better. He even changed the subject, away from hurts and money, to tell me that Belinda, a former student of mine from San Antonio, had brought Maribella, her infant, to meet him. He was elated about that.

Blarings and Glarings in My Mind

Schizophrenia can often produce hallucinations—hearing voices or seeing things that don't exist; delusions—having ideas that are obviously false and cannot be corrected by reason, such as that one has a special relationship with a famous person or a special role to play in an important event, or that one can read others' minds or that other people can read or 'transmit' thought into one's mind; and delusions of perception—such as that one is being spoken to directly through a radio or television, that random events all relate in a direct way to oneself or the belief that a common remark has a secret meaning.

—A Companion Educational Booklet for Schizophrenia

Back at the residential facility, Tito was desperate to talk. The noises in his mind were exploding. I didn't even have a chance to say hello before he began to tell me what it was like inside his mind. I've asked him many times, but he's never told me. This time Tito was ready to explain.

"Momma, I'm trying to make sense of my mind," he began. "It's like carrying eight television monitors turned on all at the same time, and with no option to turn them off—that's what it's like to live with schizophrenia. Those damned movies are always playing with my mind. Different programs running simultaneously, with various levels of sound disrupting my daily life, and yet it seems like these noises are the only excitement I have in my dreary existence. Do not always have control over the illness. But I'm trying to deal with it as best I can."

Tito had reassured me about this many times before. He had learned to monitor the symptoms and to tell the workers about it before things got out of control. "That's the way I went about my life, Momma."

He continued to tell me about the ways these symptoms emerged for him: "The images and sounds would have controlled me, but for my effort at concentrating. My very sense of self depends on the way I stay connected to the life I lived before the channels turned on inside—that time before I turned twenty-one, when the meltdown happened with that overdose of crank on that Fourth of July 1991. See, Momma, now you know why the stories are so important to me. They give me a normal life. Get to live life like everyone, even if in my imagination. It seems like such a long time ago when it all began. Eons ago."

Stories have value in Tito's life; they soothe him. Recently, on National Public Radio, storytelling was touted as therapeutic for people with divergent types of dementia, and while my son does not have dementia, he uses stories to call to mind his life before the disease. The storytelling treatment approach, as developed in Wisconsin, encourages the patient to make up a story, without having to remember facts or worry about being wrong. This therapy makes people more engaged, alert, and happier in general, as reported by Joanne Silberner (2012).

"Twenty-four hours a day, seven days a week, this had become my life," Tito said. "Could not decide on or change the images, voices, or stories running inside, but with my stories I have some control over what I saw and said. Listened with all my soul. I tried to separate every sound so as not to get lost in the confusion. The disease gives me a faraway look, as if I'm always somewhere but in the present. People could almost see the worlds I carry, when I get that look as I repeatedly try to sort things out. I hope now you can understand why I'm so anxious. See why concentrating is often so difficult."

As he had done in the past, and only in the safety of his interactions with me, Tito spoke the voices he carries.

ANGRY MAN: "You're worthless. Why are you even alive?"

HOMEBOY: "You're the scum of the earth. You only deserve to die."

ANGRY MAN: "We'd all be better off without you."

DRUGGIE: "The cord around your neck should've taken care of that."

"So tired, Momma," Tito said, returning to his own voice. "Can't take it anymore. The voices invade and consume me. They make me go inside myself. The worst one is the wimpy boy with a hunched back, buckteeth, and an overbite. This comic book–like character with a defeated attitude comes to remind me that I have not lived up to the genius expectations of my parents. That self-loathing weakling is the one who often goads me, when I am the loneliest and the most lost. Dares me to hurt myself. This one has put me in the psych ward—wasn't going to listen. It's been one of the voices I've learned to suppress, the one I've often tried to stifle. This voice is lethal. It is the one that could drive me to hurt myself. He's been telling me not to eat. Says they're poisoning me with the food. After a bout with this one, the only consolation that remains for me is that none of the demons thrive on hurting others. Sadly, most deride and devalue me. I'm their primary target."

ANGRY MAN: "The nurse's station has weapons you could use. If only you weren't such a momma's boy. What are you waiting for?"

DRUGGIE: "It would be so easy just to make a couple of little cuts with the scissors. Better yet, the pills are plentiful. They wouldn't know who did it. Look at all the nut cases running around. It could be any of them. What are you waiting for?"

"God, Momma, it's bad enough that I had to battle the demons," Tito continued. "Live with the worry of death at my own hands, and I have to squelch the desire to do myself in—suicide. I don't believe in it; it's a sin. This one was evil. Only good thoughts could drive him away. But after all this time, Momma, I have learned to do just that. Shut him out."

SYRUPY GIRL: "No. Don't do that."

ADORING FEMALE: "You were meant to be here. You're a good person. There's a reason why you came into the world."

ELDERLY MALE: "Don't listen to that voice. It doesn't have your best interest in mind."

ADORING FEMALE: "What would your family do without you? You're their conscience. You're their connection to themselves."

ELDERLY MALE: "Because of you they get to practice their patience, their compassion, unconditional love. If for that reason, stay alive. Don't listen. Your family loves you."

"The nerd and Goody Two-shoes stunted-altar-boy adolescent always comes to the rescue," Tito said. "Helps me to listen to the voices that would not harm me. He and a younger version of that elderly male in the image were the only ones who could get me to listen. This is the boy who had dreams of becoming a lawyer and did all he could to please his parents. He was the only bridge to myself."

HOMEBOY: "Let's scram, ese. They got you locked up in here because you let them. Jesus, homey. You should be running the streets with us, looking good, flying your colors. Instead, you let them pump you full of pills that make you dopey. Hey, that would a good name for you. If you jump this canton, we could give you that as a new *placazo*— el dopey."

DRUGGIE: "Homey, things are good out there for us. With times being so bad, more people are looking for dope. You should leave this joint full of *vejestorios* and *momias* with their life sucked out of them. We need you in the East Side, ese. *Las cosas* aren't the same without you, Lil' Man. In the streets you're a man. Here, I'm not sure what you've become. *Pura escoria*—just shit!"

"The dude inside that stood slanted like a slash to the left," Tito went on, "giving me attitude, calling me to action. He was a piss-ass Peter Pan cholo who never seemed to age. Wore khaki-colored pants with a 49ers jacket—the way I sometimes liked to dress, to be respected by the Norteños who hung around the places where I lived. Hung a red rag on his right-side pant pocket like the flag of a nation at war. Always ready to throw blows, giving attitude as big as the Grand Canyon. Interestingly, this voice gave me legitimacy as a Chicano, goading me to take my place in the world as one who had been wronged by anyone and everyone. Ready to throw at any time. Didn't even need a reason."

As he slanted his head to the right, as if listening to someone whispering in his ear, Tito said, "Momma, I have no control over the channels. Just make do. Try to make sense of the voices."

ANGRY MAN: "They don't love you. They keep you locked up in here because your younger brother is the favorite one. Don't you see it?

That's the way they planned it all along. Warehousing you is what they always had in mind."

DRUGGIE: "You're not really schizophrenic. Your family has convinced you of that to store you away in this dungeon of lunatics. Keep you from the family."

ANGRY MAN: "If they really cared for you, they would be taking care of you and loving you in their own homes. But no. Here you are in this medication-smelling, shit-stinking, closed-in Cracker Jack of an eight-story building in the middle of Anglolandia, where the only *raza* you see are janitors and maids. If your mother really loved you, like she claims to, she would come and take you away. Give up her job and make you the center of all she does."

DRUGGIE: "She's all talk. Call her. Ask her. Make her prove it to you. That's the least she could do. After all, she brought you into this world. You didn't ask to be born."

HOMEBOY: "Thanks to her, you're in hell. But she's sitting pretty, living the life in Texas. Couldn't get far enough from you, eh?"

Once again in his own voice, Tito said, "The druggie victim who drove me to become my paranoid self—he was the one who couldn't even get it together to ask for help. He's so chicken he gets lost in the crevices of my mind, only to surface as an option when I need an excuse or a reason for my illness. He was the fall guy for my addictive personality. The one who could never say no to any mind-altering substance but came apart at the seams while attempting to pretend he was powerful. He was the one I feared most. Thought he would be the one to drive me outside of myself, into despair or death. Only thing I had to fight this one with was the promise I made to my grandmother that I would stay away from dope. Today, my own voice is getting lost in the garble. Tried to quiet them down, but I can't. It's hard to make sense of what's going on inside."

ANGRY MAN: "All of you shut up! Shut your fuckin' trap!"

SYRUPY GIRL: "I'm a good person and my mother loves me. Am not going to listen. I won't hurt myself—it doesn't help me—tried and failed at it too many times."

HOMEBOY: "And you, fuckin' ese, I'm not gonna listen to you. It was you guys that drove me here in the first place."

"I tell you," Tito said, "the only things that help me are the cigarettes. They distract me from the voices. Smoke keeps me in the present and away from them. Can't you see that's why I beg you for cigarettes?"

"Tito, Diosito, I had no idea," I said to him. "Telling me what's on your mind is very helpful. Thank you for trusting me, m'ijo. I'm pretty insightful, but I'm not a magician. I can only imagine how you were doing. Unless you tell me what's going on, I am at a loss as to what to do. In the past, you've tried to hide the voices, even though you often tell me you don't like the food they serve: 'I hate chicken and I don't like fish.' Unless you tell me that you're not eating right or you can't eat, there's nothing I can do. You know I'm here for you. Sort out the voices, don't listen to them. What will listening to the negative messages give you? Have you eaten? Come on, I'll treat you to Chinese down the street. I know you like their food. Do you want something to drink?"

"Momma, you don't get it, do you?" Tito answered. "The voices are so real. It feels like someone is speaking to me. Often think they've come to warn me, to ask for help. That's why I call you. It feels like they're all turning against me. Thank God, the old-man-on-the-hill voice, the one I associate with Monsignor Sheen, whom I've known since I was about four years old, took over the evil voice. His voice gives me comfort. Serves me as a guide. Soothes the madness of the illness. Makes me happy when it comes to the surface. Makes me feel good. I feel like I have value. Those ugly thoughts about what I thought or looked like don't matter. Make me seek help to feel better. But there are other voices I could not suppress."

SYRUPY GIRL: "Just want to sleep. Leave me alone. I'm depressed."

"The hurt little girl voice inside makes me retreat from the world," Tito said. "She was the one who had to be prodded out of my mind. If I had listened to her, she would have turned me into sleeping beauty. This one controlled my activity. All she ever wanted to do was sleep."

ADORING FEMALE: "Cold fusion is possible. The guys that tried it didn't do it right. Talk to your dad about it. I'm sure he will see that the way you're thinking about it would work. They always told you that you were smart. There's no reason why they won't believe you."

"Momma, that's the mad scientist activist, who happens to be a girl," Tito explained. "She emerged when I returned from Florida, remember? She was the reason I let this beard grow. The scientist who lives inside my mind influenced me to see that having a beard gave me more respectability. It was also that image and voice that could sometimes let me reclaim my love for reading. None of the others allowed me to look at a book, but when I focused on the mad scientist, I could pick up a book and read it. The other voices are always disruptive. The scientist helps me appreciate the rainbow of pills. Saw them as regulators of my body chemistry. Pills were the only things that could muffle the voices and blur the images. I know they hurt me as much as they helped me, but what choice did I have? Yet there were times I almost didn't take those damned pills. Made me sick to my stomach. Didn't get me any better. Still don't know if they're helping or hurting me."

Tito paused for a moment. "Do you think I need to see the doctor? Momma, ask him about it. Will he be honest and tell me what they really do to me? What do you think?"

"Well, it wouldn't hurt to ask about the meds," I replied. "Maybe there is one that they have not given you that may help. Since you're concerned about the excessive weight loss as much as I am, I'll make you an appointment for you to see him. But before we do that let's go eat Chinese at Wings. OK?"

Gustos y Disgustos
Gustatory Delusions

Suggestions exist that AN [anorexia nervosa] symptoms appear as a prodrome of schizophrenia or disguise an earlier onset psychosis. . . . Recent investigations have emphasized distorted body perception's sub-delusional to delusional qualities.

—Barton J. Blinder, Edward J. Cumella, and Visant A. Sanathara, "Psychiatric Comorbidities of Female Inpatients with Eating Disorders"

I came back to San José, where I got a consulting job to defray the travel costs to come and see Tito. There continued to be problems with his eating. The psychiatric social workers who called me seemed concerned about Tito's quality of life. I couldn't help but feel guilty. I felt an urgency to do something about the situation. I had looked in San Antonio for a place where he could live, but the state of Texas and Bexar County are still in the dark ages when it comes to mental health treatment. I couldn't move Tito just so I could feel good about having him around, without concern for his treatment, but it wasn't easy for me to leave him warehoused in a new and understaffed room-and-board facility.

It's not as if I planned it this way, I told myself. After all, I also have a life. Tito has to make the best of whatever life he has been given. Still, I didn't really believe my own words

I couldn't help but be concerned about my son's weight loss, which was why I found a consulting job in the area. Jorge, my husband, had been encouraging me to read books about the medicines Tito takes, and I decided I needed to do an inventory of them as well as check to see if he's on the newest designer drugs. I needed to know about the side effects. I'm not a medical doctor, but it seemed to me that the atypical and psychotropic drugs were affecting his body and mind. He was having reactions to the medicine. The meds didn't even seem to be muffling the voices. It looked like they were causing more harm than good. I had always inquired about his treatment when I visited, but this time I had more informed questions, guided by the research I had been doing.

"What is he taking?" I asked. "What are the doses? How is his speech? How is his appetite? Is he having problems with digestion? Has he experienced any rushed gains or losses of weight? How about the water in the brain? What has the neurologist said about that condition? Will it go away? Is he still losing gray matter? Are there any new tics? Is he developing that medicine shuffle?"

In addition, I told them I needed a list of the medications he takes, along with a report on any counteractive effects they might have found. The psychiatric nurse told me that no one had ever asked those questions and she had no answers to give me. I had to research the problem. While the drugs I asked about may help those who live with mental illness, I needed to support Tito in the best way I could. Although his meds helped him cope with his lot in life, they were not the only solution to his health issues.

Asking questions and speaking to Tito's service providers did not help me cope. I still felt guilty about his condition. I was in another one of those self-blaming phases that come and go. Second-guessing if I'm doing right by Tito, I asked if he was developing tardive dyskinesia, a side effect that makes him drool or creates catatonic pauses or jerky gestures in some parts of his body. In a matter-of-fact and detached way, the nurse offered, "I have not noticed anything new about his walk." That was all she could say to one of the many questions that gushed out like an overflowing river from my lips. She was at a loss for what else to tell me. But she reassured me, telling me I had done the best I could with my son. That the distance between us was for the best and he was in good hands, that I should not worry about him. "He knew how to take care of himself, having learned to recognize the signs," she added.

She then told me she would ask the psychiatrist at their next clinical meeting about Tito's meds. She jotted down the doctor's number, telling me to get an appointment with him before I went back to Texas. "I know you don't need my support to demand services for your son, but I share your concern for his well-being," she said. "Don't let them dissuade you. I urge you to continue asking questions about Tito's health."

I imagined that she knew something about his treatments that she couldn't tell me. I asked her why she'd said that, and she answered, "A parent who cares and involves herself in her son's treatment—this is a new experience for me. Most often what I have to deal with is finding those relatives who have long forgotten their loved ones, so they can visit them for their last breaths. I haven't had to do that with Tito's relatives. It is only when he is losing it or longing for your contact that I've become a go-between; in all these years I've only had to call you once. Tito has no problems contacting you or impressing upon you the urgency of his need to talk. If he does not find you, his momma, he can always reach Aunt Felisa or Grandmother Aleja to track you down."

All I could do was thank her. Yet I felt the need to continue to explain myself. "There are times I think he pushes the envelope a bit too hard," I told her. "He cannot help it. The illness and the isolation drive him to call, call, and call again until we respond. We are trying to be patient with him. Then there are times when, too tired to deal with him, any one of my relatives or even I put him off. That hurts him deeply, although it is not our intent to wound him. We never maintain the silence for more than a few days—but this is a sort of respite for us. We seldom stay out of touch with Tito for long periods of time. Still, I know he often expresses the need to hear from us more often than we call, and of course he'd like a daily visit if we could."

Lonely by Myself

Unified detachment may be linked to favorable schizophrenia out-comes . . . [and] recent studies suggest that moderation in the level of emotional engagement is also linked with favorable health outcomes.

—Marina Dorian et al., "Acceptance and Expressed Emotion in Mexican American Caregivers of Relatives with Schizophrenia"

The psychiatric social worker called to tell me that Tito had complained about our lack of contact with him. "They're not answering my calls again," he'd said. Without trying to seem like she was making excuses or taking sides, the social worker informed me she had told Tito, "Maybe they're busy. You know, they have much to deal with and be responsible for." Nevertheless, she let me know that Tito felt isolated, and before she hung up, she warned me, "Josie, I've urged him to call you. To express how he feels, so he might be calling you sometime later today."

As soon as I arrived home, the telephone rang. I picked up the receiver and was greeted by Tito. I was ready this time, and I was glad it had been a light day at work—otherwise I wouldn't have been prepared to listen to my son talk about his depression and isolation.

"No wonder I've pushed you guys away," Tito said as soon as I lifted the telephone. "Through my talks with the staff I've been reminded of all I've put you and my family through. It's not just the countless num-ber of licensed and unlicensed homes I've lived in, it's the begging for money, for love, for attention. I can be so needy and demanding. I'm sorry, Momma. I don't know what else to do. I can't help it. I feel so alone. I appreciate that none of you push me away. If I can't find you, Momma, there is always someone from your family or one of your friends I can reach, but lately I can't find anyone to speak to me."

He paused. "Well, to be fair, recently Uncle came through for me, and he could have easily told me to scram. Instead, Tío and his family have found ways to include me in their lives. If anyone has a reason to keep me away, it's him. With the way he protects his only son, you'd think he'd want me gone. But that's not the way it is. Still, I feel alone. I guess I'm telling you about Uncle because he's the only one who has been able to make time for me. You haven't even come to visit me in some time. When are you coming, Momma?"

Without warning, Tito began to sob. His pain and loss seemed so deep. I waited for him to continue, giving him the space to stay in touch with his feelings—it is so easy to fall into a trap about what he feels or does not feel. So I just waited for him to talk. I didn't want him to think that I was ignoring him, but I wanted to give him the space to emote— even if it was through a phone call.

My son told me that the "diurnal nightmares"—what he'd learned to call his delusions—were engulfing him. Immediately, he changed the subject to his uncle, reminding me of the time he almost got killed because of him. "Should've listened to you, Momma, but thinking I was some big badass, I went against your wishes and moved in with two guys—a gringo and a black man—I barely knew at Heaven's Gate, that home I lived in that was only a haven for the dopers and hypes that hung around trying to sell their stuff to us."

He continued, telling me about one of the times I had to relocate him because of a wrong choice: "Anyway, this was before Cathy Balanchine was assigned as my conservator by the county. Couldn't stay on top of things, but I still received my own funds wherever I lived. It was before they became smart enough to figure out I couldn't take care of the money I got to support myself and pay my rent. Had been asked to leave by the manager, who was afraid I'd tattle on their business—I think he was in on it. Must've made money on the side, looking the other way. After all, we were only locos. What did we know? 'Better to live happy and high—that way, at least, we have something to look forward to.' He'd say that to me many a time. Was known for always being in a haze.

"Geez, Momma, I can't seem to get it together. My mind is all over the place. As I was saying, it had been less than a week since we had moved, and without someone to administer the medication, Gerald, who was really a mulatto instead of black, began to get really crazy on me—I even got scared. Without any money to eat, he began to sell our things, my television included. You see, he had paid $1,500 cash on the line, without a rental agreement, and we didn't have anything left. At least I had the family. I could drop in on them and they would feed me. But he had no one. Gerald came from New Orleans. He was completely alone."

That time, I really believed that Tito would lose his life. And the type of people with whom he associated did not remove my fears.

"Out of his mind, one day Gerald accused me of stealing his pop—that's what he called sodas," Tito went on. "Of course, it pissed me off. I don't steal. My family doesn't steal. So I told him to get off it and he went after me. All I could do was to run into the room and lock myself in. Scared out of my wits, I waited until it became silent. Called Uncle to come and help me. Told him Gerald was trying to kill me. As usual, I called at the most inconvenient time. But he believed me. Leaving dinner at the table, Uncle came to pick me up. And just as he was coming up the driveway, Gerald showed up. Cussing up a storm, he came toward me with a shovel that had been left by the workers who had been repairing the home. Tried to slam me with it. Uncle stepped right in, taking the shovel from him, knocking him to the ground. Told me to get inside the van. Uncle remained behind. Tried to calm Gerald, distracting him so he wouldn't go after me.

"To our surprise, Gerald went to his car. He opened the door and leaned over as if to get something from the glove compartment. By this time, Uncle and I had already gotten into his van and he had turned it on. Pointing a gun in our direction, Gerald yelled, 'I'll kill you. I'll fuckin' kill you!' Good thing he didn't have any ammo. The cops came. Someone must have called them. We were about a block away when the cops arrived. If we had stayed, we would have been taken in for disturbing the peace."

It wasn't clear to me what Tito wanted from me other than a good ear. So I continued to listen as he spoke about how badly he was feeling about his situation.

"Momma, I didn't know what to do with myself. Homeless again.

With no money for the remaining three weeks, I called you for help. Once again, you came and got the workers to find me another place. This time, Grandma lent you the money to pay for another month's rent. Told me to go see the social worker about transferring my housing costs. Did that. It was then that you suggested I needed someone to take care of my affairs. Since I couldn't do it on my own, the county had people to do that. That's why I'm sad. Wouldn't you be? Living the life I live and being such a burden on everyone. It's depressing."

With deep urgency, he changed the tone of his voice and warned me that Norteños were coming to kill him. With the speakerphone on, I sat on my hands so that I would not interrupt him as he told me what was happening.

"Momma, this time they're going to win," he said. "They have a spy—a housekeeper at Casa Olga who's one of them. He's giving me the sign that they're going to cut my throat. He flies the red rag—seen it hanging from the right pant pocket of his chinos. He's one of them."

I felt helpless, and all I could do was remind Tito how fortunate he was to have us—my family and me—and that we had not discarded him.

Although fears of abandonment will forever plague him, I acknowledged that life was not easy for any of us, least of all him. I spoke softly and reminded him that the illness is not just his; it belongs to his entire family. That we were there to help him when we could, but that we also have other responsibilities to tend to and he's not the center of our system: "Place your needs in context, m'ijo. You at least have a place to live and food to eat."

Whose Reality?

Schizophrenia is a complex mental disorder that causes disruption in thought processes, perceptions, and emotions. Olfactory processing is mediated by limbic structures implicated in the pathophysiology of schizophrenia.

—Paul J. Moberg and Bruce I. Turetsky, "Scent of a Disorder"

Tito entered the commons visiting area talking. "Geez. Hate to think that's the way I make you feel, Momma, but who am I to contest your sense of reality?" He laughed for effect, then he asked me to read the story I had mailed him so that he could get a sense of what it was like for me to carry his illness in the back of my mind. Called "Elevator Ride," it was one of the many stories I'd written to help me deal with Tito's condition.

"Here, this is the story you sent me," he said, handing it to me. "The one you wrote when you moved to San Antonio. Learned a lot from reading it. Didn't know you, too, had to deal with the disease in the way that I do. You told me before that it starts with a look, a medicated shuffle, a voice, or a smell that pulls you into my world. Momma, read me the story. I want to hear it in your voice."

I began to read: "Having learned to read mental illness with my senses, I had no choice but to experience it. But it was never so clear to me as that one time on the elevator at the university where I work. The elevator opened. Putrid, familiar smells—stale body odors mixed with the scent of medications—invaded my senses. Lost in my thoughts about the beginning of the semester, I didn't notice anyone inside the

237

elevator. Overwhelmed by the stench, my innards traveled to my throat, kick-starting my gag reflex. Then, in the corner of my eye, I saw him. I made every effort to melt into the metal walls of the elevator. As I lifted my face in his direction, the mentally ill homeless man became uncomfortable with my gaze. He quickly pressed the button to reopen the door. It was too late. We were on for the ride.

"Barely having left the first floor, my stomach lurched again as the elevator ascended. Now, in the left-hand corner of the elevator, wearing disheveled, soiled clothes and with a lost and petrified look on his face, the homeless man shook in discomfort. He continued to do his best to fade into the elevator walls, as if trying to walk into its structure. Seeing him, smelling him, and being in his space forced me to put my feelings into context. He had that look that penetrates and repulses all at the same time. I knew that look—my mind told my other senses. How frightened he must have been, but I was only thinking about myself. Eyes downcast, pretending to be invisible, he again pressed the button to get off at the second floor. As he got off the elevator, the combination of rancid smells, the curdled odors of turned milk, and the scent of dried feces turned my stomach, but I held it in. I did all I could to hold on to the breakfast taco I had eaten that morning. Reduced to tears by the combination of smells and the emotions his presence had stirred inside me, I imagined what it must be like for you, my son.

"Once outside the elevator, unable to see clearly from the tears, my senses began to regulate and my stomach settled down. Still, I ran as if trying to get away from the illness itself. Entering the nearest woman's bathroom, with the expectation of launching my stomach contents into the bowl, I couldn't throw up. Protected by the insulation of the stall, I sat and cried, and I remained there until I felt composed enough to continue my routine. My body had made me aware that it stored, like a silo, all the complications of your illness, making me conscious of the emotions that could emerge at any time. With your illness, I carried my emotions in my throat. You were never far from the back of my mind, except when you brought yourself to the front with your unceasing telephone calls.

"The experience with the elevator man brought up a surge of compassion and sadness, awakening memories of the life you and I have had to live. But what I have had to deal with, despite the shame and irritations, has been nothing compared to the complication you have faced in your daily life. You experience situations like the elevator man in your own skin every day. With your condition, you cannot get off the elevator. You cannot escape your lot."

"You know," I said after telling Tito the story, "this is not the first time I have had to confront feelings related to your illness. In many places and spaces, I have been reminded of the condition you live with and the life circumstances you must face. Understanding your loneliness and neediness, there are times I am thankful for the distance. I'm not always resentful about your desire to call me into your life. The life you live, despite being thousands of miles away in what I feel is a safe environment, makes my daily steps easier. Your physical distance tempers the reality and prepares me for the excursions I must take into the world of mental illness when I encounter other people with your condition. Even though they remind me of you, I'm protected by the distance.

"On the other hand, I am aware that you live with the desire to make contributions but remain restricted by the illness that produces your anxiety, your fear, and the agoraphobia that keeps you caged inside yourself. Unlike you, I am free to roam and live my life as best I can, until you call me again to check in or demand that I place your needs and concerns ahead of my responsibilities. Responding to your needs is second nature to me, but I know I have to keep myself sane. You see, m'ijo, the man inside the elevator, more than anything else, put it all in my face. I have the luxury of not living your life, but I also must live with your illness."

I reminded Tito of the times he had told me he was going to end it all: "How sad it is to live with the threat of death. Yet there were times I wished you would have ended it all, for all our sanity's sake. 'I'm tired of living in my skin, alone. I would be better off dead.' This was your call for help and attention. All at once, the tentativeness of your existence and the dried tears of a mother feeling threatened one too many times would give way to a calm voice once again, as I became the reality check for you. I store it all, but I make an effort to go on so I can be there for you. Being only human, there are times when the impatience becomes greater than the compassion. Indifference and detachment take hold—this is the only way I can survive until the next time you call. Our life is pretty challenging—don't you think? There are times I make a joke about charging you rent for living in the back of my head. You laugh and we go on about our lives. 'Your mother, who loves you with all her heart,' is how I signed the letter I sent you."

"Momma, why are you crying?" Tito asked. "It's pretty damned sad, don't you think? Imagine what it's like to be me."

Then he continued talking about what I had just read to him: "Knew it wasn't easy for you, Momma. It's been almost twenty years, and four of those must have been horrific for you. It's gotten better for both of us over time, though. Right? Age is mellowing both of us, don't you think? I'd only wish that damned disease would disappear with the years. I know it's all magical thinking—a way to be in denial about my health issues. But dreaming about that possibility gives me hope. I may be damned to this hell, but I'll try to manage as best I can. Thanks, Momma. I'm going to the fourth floor to hang out with the smokers. See you next time you come. Love you."

Can Trauma and Sexual Abuse Cause Schizophrenia?

Those who had suffered CSA [child sexual abuse] or CPA [child physical abuse] had significantly more positive schizophrenia symptoms (but slightly fewer negative symptoms) than those not abused.

—John Read et al., "Childhood Trauma, Psychosis and Schizophrenia"

"Momma, do you know if sexual abuse causes schizophrenia? Haven't shared all the skeletons in my closet." My son's question shocked me. I had just arrived for a visit, and all he wanted to do was talk about sexual molestation. I asked him to give me a chance to sit before he hit me with that. Hearing Tito pose his question that beautiful spring morning, I just about fell out of my chair. He had never wanted to speak about the subject.

"Didn't tell anyone, not even you," he said. "Until I became mentally ill. I've had a lot of time to think about it, and I've been wondering if sexual molestation caused or contributed to my mental illness. Are there any articles about this, Momma? Have you read about this as a possible link? Don't think it's easy to talk about it, but now—since I can't undo it or take it back—and now that I've told you about it, I've got nothing to lose by talking. It happened at my family day-care. No, it wasn't my day-care parents. I love them and they were very good to me, just like my parents. It was one of their daughters, her boyfriend, and their disturbed friend who molested me. Now that I think back, I couldn't tell you because of the threats, but I tried to show you I was scared to be in that house when

Sister—what I called her—was home. My excuse was fear of dogs, remember? The bunch of them had threatened me with dogs to force me to do what they wanted with me.

"How sick. Not yet teenagers, they got a big kick out of scaring me. Told me it was to teach me how to be a good husband in the future. That I had to pretend with Sister while the others watched to make sure I was doing it right. Even directing my child body to do what they said. Sometimes Fred, her boyfriend, would try to get in on the act. Didn't do anything to me, but he tried to get it on with Sister while she was messing with me. When they touched me and made my penis grow, mostly with masturbation, the fluids that oozed out scared me—I thought I was peeing in my pants. You know how that must've bothered me. Thought I was having an accident; I hated to pee on myself. They just laughed at me. Got a real kick out of hurting me."

Given my upbringing, I made every effort to find the best family day-care for Tito. An intact family with a stay-at-home mother who could take care of him. I wanted to give him the type of home environment I did not have. I regretted that I hadn't seen the signs.

"Almost talked to you about it, that one morning I got up with my chonis glued to my penis," Tito continued. "Crying, I went to tell you, Momma. You had taught me anatomically correct words for my body parts. Yeah, my underwear was glued to my penis. Thought it was never going to come unstuck. It really scared me. Afraid to tell you what was happening or that these fluids had come out of me before, I kept it to myself. Wish I had been able to tell you, but I couldn't. You explained it away as a wet dream. 'Something that happens to young ones when they dream about things that feel good to them,' you told me.

"Didn't tell you what it really was. Didn't want you to know that the dog phobia was linked to sexual abuse. Couldn't talk. The three of them often threatened that if I told, they were going to do something worse to me or hurt my baby brother. But I don't think anything ever happened to him. They left him alone. Momma, good thing you took us to another day care soon after. Didn't have a clue, though. You just wanted us to have a good social life with other children instead of hanging out with the old ladies going to church every morning of the week and shopping at the *segunda* or Macy's. Momma Sally and the

Guadalupanas, devotees of the Virgin of Guadalupe, were really busy tending to church affairs."

Still in shock because he wanted to talk about the abuse, I was at a loss for what to tell him. So I just listened to the story he needed to tell me.

"That's when you took us to Bella's Day Care, where I was able to just become a kid again. Buried the memories until I became mentally ill. It was then that all of it came back as if I was younger than five again. Maybe the molestation is tied to the schizophrenia. Do you think that might've had something to do with it? Momma, for the most part, I've made my peace with what happened. But there are times I find myself getting angry all over again, when I remember the way Sister hurt me. Should've told. But I was just a child who was easily controlled by fear. You trusted them with me. Had no reason to suspect her. What do think, Momma?"

Still not sure what to tell Tito, all I could say was, "I'm sorry I didn't suspect or see the clues. She had no right to do that to you. I'm so sorry, m'ijo. No one has the right to abuse you or to hurt you in any way." I told Tito that it was not his fault, and I informed him I would research the relationship between sexual abuse and mental illness, schizophrenia in particular. What else could I say?

As he had done many times before, soon after sharing that story, Tito left to have a smoke, but not before telling me to come back tomorrow. "Bring Tía and Grandma," he added, "and ask Grandma to make a couple of burritos for me."

When he left, he did not seem upset. In fact, relief was evident on his face. Yet he looked puzzled by it all. I was sure the reason he talked to me about it was not to make me feel guilty or to throw it in my face for not having seen it. Rather, Tito was trying to understand if that buried injury was connected to his condition.

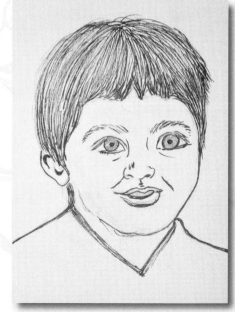

What Waits for Me?

Many older adults with schizophrenia successfully adapt to the illness, with increased use of positive coping techniques, enhanced self-esteem and increased social support. Although complete remission is uncommon, most individuals with schizophrenia experience significant improvement in their quality of well-being.

—Dilip V. Jeste, Owen M. Wolkowitz, and Barton W. Palmer, "Divergent Trajectories of Physical, Cognitive, and Psychosocial Aging in Schizophrenia"

More comfortable speaking to me about the disease that controls his life, Tito, as he had the last time we spoke, came in talking, as if he had been rehearsing what he was going to say. He seemed to be consumed with his thoughts—or at least that was how it seemed to me. He talked as if he were going away. It scared me to think that he wanted to take another flight into health, to move someplace else to leave the demons behind.

"Lately, I've been thinking that you're not going to be here all my life, or that I won't always be in yours for that matter," he began. "Can't expect you to see me through my illness. Momma, for a while there, I made myself believe you would always be in my life, but we are not getting any younger—either one of us. We will leave this planet, so I am trying to take care of myself. Workers come and go, and you are here, although far away from me. I have had to learn to deal with the illness and its consequences. Just have to take it one day at a time, as you often remind me After all, you and everybody else have your own things to deal with. And I have mine. Have I told you about Lydia? She's the new resident everybody is talking about. Did I tell you what she said to me? She has ESP! She's a seer and is also a card reader."

Wondering where this was going, I responded by asking, "Lydia reads cards? You've introduced me to her, just like you have every other person who comes into contact with me when I visit you. She has that clairvoyant air about her. I didn't know that. But it doesn't surprise me."

"Yeah," Tito said. "She read my cards." He said nothing more, adding a sort of mystery to our conversation, but then he continued to talk about Lydia. "You'll be happy to hear. Lydia told me. Said I soon wouldn't be mentally ill. She even thinks that I'll be able to hold a job. Can't wait for that to happen. But I am scared. Do not know if I'll be able to do it. Momma, I have had to make my world really small. It's just me and the residents and a girlfriend, if I have one. It's too noisy and confusing out there. Don't know what I would do with a job. Haven't been able to keep one since before my break with reality. It's interesting to see that there's something about the cards and my family. She doesn't know about Beto, but Lydia's reading linked me to my biological father and you. It's like that story you told me, 'member?"

As had become his habit, Tito repeated the story as though I had not been part of his father's life. Relishing the details, he talked about that time long ago, when our family broke apart: "Yeah, like that time when my father, Beto, was young and a card reader told him he wouldn't live to see twenty-one. Yeah, when he had the accident. That time they found Beto barely alive in that garlic field in Gilroy? The accident happened before Beto turned twenty-one, and he wasn't the same after that. He lost his life as it was, although he was lucky to have survived. Momma, who knows what was in the cards for Beto? Maybe he just got too careless thinking that he wouldn't be around beyond twenty-one, so he recklessly set about creating the conditions that led to the end of his life as he knew it. It was like a death, don't you think? It's like you learned about me. Momma, it was about my life change a few months before I had my break, when your freaky friend Laura Napoli threw the cards for you. That day when Laura and you had an opportunity to spend time together. Both of you had gone to visit Helen Michalowski, who was going through cancer treatment."

Narrating my story, Tito took me back in time. I was at a loss for words, so again I simply listened.

"Told me that when you returned from that visit, hanging around drinking tea, Laura mentioned to you that she read tarot cards," he said. "Didn't offer to read them for you, you made it a point to say it to me. I think you remembered it as just a comment to fill in the gap of time. It was a sort of overture for her to read the cards, so you asked Laura if she had her cards, suggesting that maybe she could throw them for you—that's how she got around to reading them. You emphasized that Laura didn't really want to read them to you, as if she had had a bad premonition. 'I've lost many friendships over the messages in those cards,' Laura said to you, and she wasn't ready to give up her friendship with you. So she tried to discourage you: 'Maybe another time. It's getting late.'

"But you insisted, reassuring Laura that you weren't that gullible. After all, it was all about chance: 'Throw them. Tell me what you see.' 'She wasn't all that hard to get,' you told me as you were narrating the story. You didn't have to beg or talk her into it, right? Believing you wouldn't take things to heart, Laura finally agreed to read the cards for you. At first, the reading was harmless enough. Messages came through about school, about moving out of the area within four years, about completing your degree. You would have another job somewhere out of California. You know, things that are bound to happen by chance, safe things that may come with life—it wasn't anything earth shattering or scandalous for you.

"Then Laura hit the black card, the ace of spades with all its ominous power," Tito said, "and she stopped with a sigh like someone had punched her right in the middle of the stomach. She hesitated. She didn't want to tell you what she saw. What she didn't know was that you also could read cards. In that ace of spades, you perceived something bad coming our way. Felt death staring you in the face. So you asked her to tell you what she saw. 'It's not death,' she explained. 'It's a major illness or disruption to your family. This card signifies a major change for you. Don't know in what way, but it will be major. Possibly a catastrophic illness. I can only tell you what I see with that card. But the changes will come by midsummer.'"

Tito reminded me: "It was 1991. Not knowing how to respond, Momma, you told Laura that you had had just about enough with this silly game. After this, Laura only hung around for a few minutes. Finished her tea and left, leaving your mind filled with worry. As you told me before, this had not been the first 'prognostication' that had walked into your path. You had heard my father, Beto, your former husband, ruminating many a time about not getting to age twenty-one because of that card reader who dared to curse him. But having other worries to tend to, you soon dismissed it, burying yourself in the books. You had to finish your field statements and were preparing for the qualifying exams, especially since Laura told you that you would finish your studies. Well, as we both know, Momma, this took place less than two months before things came to pass. It was the death of me as I was. The break of July 4, 1991."

Tito took a long pause. Then he began to ask me questions that I could not answer. They remained suspended in the wind. "Do you think my illness will go away?" he asked. "Has that happened to anyone? Maybe because of my age my brain will change. What do you think?"

An "I don't know" or "perhaps" was not sufficient for Tito, so he stopped asking questions and continued to talk about Lydia, providing whatever pedigrees she had as a way of giving her predictions some weight.

"Momma, you know, what? Lydia has a lot of degrees. She's like you, real educated and intuitive. Maybe what she sees in the cards will come true. It did for Beto, so why can't it come true for me? Pray that she's right, Momma. I'm so tired of being sick. I'd like a chance at having another way of living. Peace, without fear, and silence without voices controlling my mind. No sound. No distorted thinking. No strange smells. No breakdowns. That, for me, would be heaven on earth. It's so unbearable that there are those times I imagine it's not my illness but the medication that makes me the way I am. How do they say? It's a chicken and egg thing—I don't know which came first. One way to test it would be to give up the meds. Don't you think, Momma?"

It frightened me to hear him talk that way. As a way to let him know I heard him, I answered, "Well, Tito, there are those who believe that the meds help and hurt you at the same time." I didn't address his question; rather, I answered the one I carried inside my own mind.

In reply, he added his own take, linking Lydia the seer's words with his wish: "Maybe that's Lydia's message. Momma, can you help me ask the doc to reduce my doses? Will you go to the doctor with me, if he agrees?" That was the last conversation Tito had with me about the meds. After that, he was in and out of the hospital.

When I visit him, he still wants to talk about what was—the past as he recalls it. Repeating some old stories and creating new ones, he tries to calm himself, to ameliorate the ravages of the disease. The voices and hallucinations that at one time were numbed by the medicine no longer abate. He now tells me that he hears a voice of a child, crying for him and asking, "Why did you leave me, Dad?"

The visitors, while they still come, are not frequent enough for him, and I don't come often enough either. While he clearly feels alone and isolated, he's still trying to understand that this is yet another turn on the road to his recovery. "I need to learn to count on myself and to love myself, without relying on others to give me a reason to live," he told me most recently. "I'm tired of being alone and by myself."

In a few months, my son will turn forty-five. Presently, he is in a medium-care facility. Out of the psychiatric hospital but still locked up. I can only visit him with supervision. One nurse lets me into a visiting room that is padlocked while a second nurse goes to get Tito, then the nurse that opened the visiting room takes the northeast corner of the visiting area and stands as sentry, watching over us.

When I saw Tito at the facility, he was dressed in knee-high, light-green shorts and a woman's plaid shirt in pastel pink, blue, and yellow, which he had buttoned at the top—cholo style. He rushed in to give me a full bear hug and I stood to reciprocate. It was a loving and caring way of expressing his happiness. I was glad to be there to visit with him. When he sat, I asked him to unbutton his collar, a request to which he replied, "Didn't you notice? This is a woman's shirt and I'm not dressed in gang colors?"

He was right. Rather than notice he was decked out in colors that no self-respecting gangbanger would wear, I had gotten on his case. I apologized. He undid the button and we made an effort to converse.

Tito told me he was still hearing voices and hallucinating, even though his manner and appearance had improved 100 percent: he was clean-shaven and smelled shower-fresh.

Tito didn't seem comfortable having a nurse guarding our visit, so he spoke Spanish to me (the Filipina nurse didn't speak the language). Soon he forgot about covering up whatever it was he wanted to tell me and reverted to English. It was not about him or me.

"One, two, three, four . . . fifty-two weeks in a year, times twenty years," he said. "That equals one thousand forty times. That's how often she comes to see me. Wish all my relatives were like Tía Felisa. That's how many times she has visited me—once a week—all the time I have been sick. She loves me, Momma. Why can't the others be like her? My 'second momma,' that's what I call her. She has been there for me. Has bought me cigarettes, when no one else would. She has brought me food, when I called her to because they served things I can't eat. She has come to see me when I'm depressed. She calls me and answers my calls when I need her. Gives me a few dollars so I can buy sodas or get a snack. She brings me food that she or Grandma prepared. She's come to see me more than even you, Momma.

"But you know what? I'm worried about her. Did you know she might've had a minor stroke? I'm concerned. Can't call her so much. I'm going to give her a break. What with this new thing and the diabetes—stress is no help for her and I am her 'pain in the back of her neck,' like you've said about me. I'm going to try to give her a break, even though she has learned to put the break on me. At first, I didn't like that she was setting limits. But she has a life, too. I have to understand. She's been there for me. Gotta give her a break."

Tito doesn't want to impose on anyone; he just wants to keep his family around him. So he imagines ways to make that possible. And sometimes those possibilities happen.

"Momma, life would be much easier if I had family around," he continued. "If all your brothers, relatives, and friends came to visit me at least once a month, I would be less alone and Tía Felisa would get a break. Let me see. Juan, Ernesto, Tomás, Mague, Carlos, Sonia, Maria, Anthony, Vito, Yesenia, Michael, Patrick, Corky, Belinda, Grandma, Sue, Cliff, Anthony, Allan, Serena, Samantha, Ricardo, and others who may want to help us, like Marissa. That makes twenty-four people who can give a break to my Tía Felisa and a sense of peace to me. They wouldn't have to come every week, only two months a year. Wouldn't it be nice? Then I wouldn't be alone and the weight wouldn't fall on any one person. Can you make that suggestion to them? I need family and friends around me. Please, Momma, please."

Pills, Pills, and More Pills
And Now What?

Family members who perceived the patient as having control over the symptoms of schizophrenia tended to express greater negative emotions such as anger and annoyance toward the patient than did family members who viewed the symptoms as beyond the patient's personal control.

—Amy Weisman et al., "An Attributional Analysis of Expressed Emotion in Mexican-American Families with Schizophrenia"

On my most recent visit to see Tito, I confronted the trauma of schizophrenia and the ways in which it affected his day-to-day relationships with others. I questioned whether my presence was helpful to either one of us. He was extremely depressed, and my queries further aggravated him: he felt like he was under interrogation, increasing the paranoia that is overwhelmingly shrouding his ability to speak and communicate with me and anyone else around him. I wasn't afraid of him, but I felt helpless and unable to do anything for him except take him to purchase a pack of cigarettes to lessen his anxiety.

It was early Thursday evening when I went to pick him up. It was not a wise choice for me to go so late, but my concern and emotions over Tito's condition gave me a second wind. Despite having been awake since three o'clock in the morning, I went to pick him up, to remind him that he was not alone and that he mattered to me. Our visit turned out to be a disaster I wanted to put behind me—but my sister Felisa found a recording on her answering machine the following day.

It is still not clear how our conversation appeared on her machine. All I can figure out is that the connection from the last call Tito received on his cell phone from her landline remained open. However it happened, it gave me the opportunity to document the ways in which we communicate or fail to connect when he is deep inside the psychosis. The call was unwittingly recorded when we were at a gas station about two blocks from where he lives. At the end of an already strained visit, I confirmed that Tito was not taking his medication correctly: "I'm supposed to take twelve pills, but the way she gives them, she only gives me eleven in the morning. I know them by their shape. I only took eleven, instead of twelve."

Redundantly, Tito emphasized that he did not take the total number of pills he should have taken when he got up: "I only took eleven pills, but the way she gives it, though, she only gave me eleven in the morning, I don't know what they're for, but she's supposed to give me twelve—I only got eleven this morning. I don't know what they're for, but I recognize them by their shape, Mom. Mom. Mom, but she did not give me the meds right. I'm off one of my meds that I'm supposed to take this morning. So that's why I'm off one of my meds—that's why I'm so scared. So that's why I'm like I am. That's the crux. I freak out when it starts."

I made an effort to have him focus on one point. He ignored my request. All I could do was remind him that he had to go see his doctors: "Robert, I need you to get yourself to a physical doctor and a psychological doctor."

He interrupted, adding, "That's gonna happen on the thirteenth and fourteenth of this month."

"That's what I'm here for, m'ijo."

He interrupted again to let me know he had it under control: "That's going to happen on the thirteenth and fourteenth." He expressed his frustration in a loud voice that only escalated with his discomfort. An emotional intensity to emphasize his point.

"M'ijo, do you have to scream at me? I'm not screaming," I said to him, raising my voice as if to impose my authority. Speaking over him to assert myself seemed to work.

"Sorry, Mom. I'll just shut the fuck up," he answered in the peppered language he knows upsets me.

Rather than act toward him as the adult I know I am, one who is not experiencing a mental break, I fight with him, restating my point: "Is that what I asked? I said for you not to speak so loud. You know, I'm exhausted. I'm tired . . ."

Instead of remembering that I have come to see him because I am concerned about him, I chose words that agitated him that much more. Realizing this, I lowered my voice as I finished what I had to say. It seemed to work, and without asking any questions, Tito began to tell me about the condition in which he found himself. "Mom. Mom. Do you know what? I cut on myself. I burn myself."

With that information, I became agitated once again. I told him what he already knew, but he refused to connect to the break that he appeared to be entering. "Do you know that's a sign of active mental illness?" I said. "What are you doing?"

"No, it's not. That's about being depressed. I burn myself or cut on myself to escape from the way I feel about myself. I feel like a piece of shit."

In an attempt to disrupt the negativity, I called out his name: "Tito. Tito." I tried to interrupt, but he continued to tell me about the difficulties of his everyday life. He spoke about the staff in the board-and-care home as "they" and told me how he chastises them for the mistreatment that goes on in their facility. "I don't feel good because of the way they treat me," he declared. "I don't like the way they treat me. If they were treating you like that you'd feel like a piece of shit, too."

Rather than listen with empathy, I told him I know what it feels like to be discriminated against, not realizing that this was not about me but about my son, who was having a break. He interrupted me, letting me know I was off cue and not listening to him: "No. You don't. No. You don't!"

I still didn't get it. My ears and heart were disconnected from his pain. "You don't think they treat me that way?" I insisted, failing to see that I was not there to compare myself to my son but to try to understand what was going on with him. His voice rose in pitch. I hadn't been able to interrupt his monologue, but I'd done really well at failing to listen to him. "I'm just another Mexican to people around me," I said, without realizing I was undermining his feelings and reducing his emotions to insignificance.

He screamed in agony. I still did not hear him. "They call me 'the Mexican.' How would you feel if you did not have a name and every time you come in and every time you go somewhere, the Filipinos that run and work the place label you a Mexican?"

"Do you fucking live my life?" Frustrated and unforgivable words came out of my lips, and I finally realized that I wasn't making things better. I recalled my husband's caution: "You are not mentally ill; listen to him."

"Do you live *my* life?" Tito retorted. "No! You don't. It's really, really fucked up. My life is more fucked up than your life! How can you compare my life to yours?"

I tried to backpedal, saying, "I'm not comparing what anybody's life is like."

Tito spoke more calmly. "If I'm right and go back, I'm going to die. I really don't give a shit anymore. If that's going to hurt you, I'm sorry. But I don't give a shit anymore. I really don't."

My rationality didn't last long, and rather than empathize and de-escalate the situation, I brought up the psychiatric ward. "I'm going to take you to the Emergency Psychiatric Services [EPS]," I stupidly said. I knew that wasn't going to help, but I was afraid of what might happen to him.

"You don't know where EPS is," he answered sheepishly. "It's at Crestwood" (a locked facility he abhors with all his might).

"No, it's not."

"If you take me there, I'll never speak to you again. *Ever.*"

"But I would be happy to take you there, so they can regulate your meds."

"No! I would be dead because I will kill myself in Crestwood EPS like I tried to kill myself there before. I tied a belt around my neck and I hung myself for more than ten minutes at EPS."

He looked at his waist and offered, "Boy, I'm really stupid. I forgot to bring my belt."

I was at a loss for words. All I could do was say, "That you hurt yourself is very upsetting to me." I finally connected with the fear that he might hurt himself. And by this time my compassion had brought to a halt, for me, the tragic dialogue between me and my beloved son. But Tito continued. "If you take me there, I will be done with myself."

Feeling helpless, and not knowing where to go from there even though I had been there countless times before, all I could do was ask him another question. "Why do you fight with me? I just want to help you."

"I don't want to go to the hospital because I will kill myself," he answered. "If you take me to EPS, I will do away with myself."

Rather than connect with his fear, rather than use all the clinical training I had up my sleeve, I let another motherism come out of my lips. "Excuse me, am I forcing you to go to the hospital?"

"No. You're trying to."

I did not want to put him in the hospital. My aim was to have him understand that he needed to keep his appointments and medication regulated, so I told him, "No, I'm only suggesting it to you."

"You're not suggesting it when you start yelling it out."

"No, I suggested it to you."

He continued to speak, and I listened, really trying to hear him out.

"Not when you want to take me to the hospital," he continued. "It's neat that you and Dad are coming now and then, 'Oh, yeah we're going to be here for you,' and the minute I start asking for things you want to put me in the hospital. That's what you want to do now. I feel like shit."

Instead of taking myself out of the downward spiral I had entered, I retorted in frustration, saying, "Excuse me, it's time you work with fucking Momentum to find you another place. After all, that's what they are there for, to provide you services and help you manage your illness."

"This place [here he spoke under his breath and I was unable to catch what he said]. I'll get my own damn place myself."

He wanted his independence. He did not want to rely on anybody else for his care. Tito felt betrayed and let down by all those around him who collected a paycheck to provide him care, yet failed to do it. I began to get back in tune, but I once again put my foot in my mouth by bringing up the reality of his housing situation.

"Robert," I asked him, "do you understand what that means, for you to get your own place? First month, last month, and deposit with the rents around here?" Trying to be a sounding board for him, a reality check, I continued, unaware that I was not helping the situation. "With an average of $1,500 to $1,700 a month? So you're talking about $7,000 to move into a place?"

He answered dejectedly, "Yeah, I know."

At least he could dream. Have hope. "There are subsidized places I can try to get myself," he said. "There is one on First Street in downtown and there's another in J-Town in San José. There's another place that's just like, like, Casa Olga. It's on Winchester, it's just like Casa Olga."

At Casa Olga he did well, and somehow, his recollection of the place helped to calm us down. This time when I asked him to lower his voice, he did, adding, "I have a friend who lives there and he is going to help me get in. It's by Winchester. Near Santana Row, the upscale shopping center."

I told him to look into it and reminded him that his case manager should be helping him with it. But he spoke of his dissatisfaction with having to deal with the caregivers who are assigned to him. "She won't do it. She does what the owner of the house tells her to do. She doesn't work with me. She does what he says. She does what the owner tells her. What the manager tells her; she doesn't work for my best interest."

"M'ijo, it's gotta change."

"Well, it's gonna change," he agreed. "If she stops running her mouth, it would be better."

This statement, which I interpreted as disrespectful of women workers, got me hooked again and things re-escalated. I opined about the case manager and her efforts, saying, "She's not running her mouth. Listen, she says you are concerned about money. About profits from a book. It concerns me that you are fixating on money because that is a sign that you are spiraling down."

Defending himself and challenging her veracity, he said "No, I didn't tell her that. No. It was about my payee and the income that's coming my way."

I backtracked. "Maybe she got confused."

"Yeah. She got confused. Sure she did."

Accepting that things were not going to get any better, I informed my son that it was time to end out interaction. "Tito, I have to go. I'm tired. It's been a long day."

Without resolving the conflict but getting to a point of de-escalation, I left the gas station and drove to his residence, dropping him off at the driveway. Having the cigarettes on hand gave him a sense of calm, and he leaned over to give me a kiss on the cheek, thanking me for coming to see him, for taking him to dinner, and for buying him the cigarettes. We told each other "I love you" and said good night.

Not regretting having gone to see him, or taking him to eat a late breakfast for dinner at Denny's, I left knowing that tomorrow would be another day. As I drove away, I silently committed myself to giving Tito a good weekend. We had agreed to go to Santa Cruz the next morning to visit his brother and the niece and nephew he loves. The cycle of mental illness will continue, I told myself—but with the expectation that things would be better tomorrow.

My hope is that as we age, the travails that come with the illness will lessen as Tito continues to learn to deal with his disease. I pray that I too will be better able to deal with the consequences of his illness. I have to remind myself to remain supportive, empathic, and caring as I continue to practice the act of listening with a heart. My son needs that more than my desire to exercise my authority as his mother.

Tito 2014

Epilogue

Mental Illness or Mental Health?

Breaking boundaries and contesting taboos regarding mental illness, I wrote the story of Tito, my firstborn son. With this project, I am going against tradition. I sidestepped disciplinary technologies and professionalizing strategies in the academy, which call for us to live inside a culture that detaches and distances ourselves from the topic of study.

The lessons I have learned from having engaged Tito's voices and stories, and from my presence in the institutions that manage his condition, could not have been gleaned from any text. I have learned, firsthand, what it is like to live inside the culture of mental illness and what mental illness does to those who are afflicted by it and their families.

Feminists of color, like myself, who have learned to negotiate the world, cultivate our cultural and social knowledge and the various intelligences we use to carry out our work.* As the eldest child in my family, I learned many skills that would later become valuable in the academy. Also, I have had to engage multiple sociocultural expectations based on my gender, race/ethnicity, and class, as well as my position in the family, all of which have given me alternative epistemologies.

---

* Gloria Anzaldúa speaks about *facultad* as a process of coming to a self-knowledge and understanding. This process is reflexive and embedded in the social and cultural worlds we amble through as we come to *conocimiento*, or knowledge, of our surroundings and ourselves. It emphasizes the reciprocity of experience as a dialectical knowing embedded in emotional, cultural, social, and metaphysical engagements with the world around us. Who we are, what we do, and how we see the world shapes the ways we use the knowledge we amass in our social worlds. See Cherríe Moraga and Gloria Anzaldúa, eds., 1981, *This Bridge Called My Back* (Watertown, MA: Persephone Press), and Gloria Anzaldúa and AnaLouise Keating, eds., 2002, *This Bridge We Call Home* (New York: Routledge).

Moreover, learning to read myself in the world as a sexual abuse survivor has given me intuitive notions of power, and I have learned to develop divergent strategies to deal with inequalities in a variety of contexts. When you have lost and regained yourself, there is nothing to lose. One becomes reconstituted and reembodied.

This multiplicity of subjective spaces has become useful in my examination of those daily experiences I have confronted, as a survivor of incest and domestic violence, as a girl/woman in a patriarchal world, as a multi-situated subject who has had to contend with structures of inequality, including that of motherhood and the social work profession. These spaces have both given me insight and have painfully limited my dealings with a system of mental health that still carries vestiges of dehumanization when it comes to its patients, catering to the perception of clients as flawed, unfeeling, and unemotional human beings.

Not in My Family

Stigmatizing—the creation of spoiled identity—involves projecting onto an individual or group judgments as to what is inferior, repugnant, or disgraceful.

—Roy Porter, *Madness*

In this book, I wrote of my family's journey with Tito and mental illness, which first emerged for him two months and twelve days before his twenty-first birthday, on July 4, 1991. From the onset, it took almost three years to obtain medical assistance. Those years were hellish and dehumanizing for the two of us.* It was boot camp for what would come

---

* In modern times, stigma and spoiled identities kept those who suffered mental health problems institutionalized in cyclically changing systems of treatment, confining many to a destitute life of incarceration, while those who could afford treatment received the most innovative and humane service in privately paid getaway environments to protect their reputation (see Goffman 1961). Prior to institutional alternatives, families in Europe, Japan, and the United States assumed responsibility for their progeny and other relatives suffering from mental illness. Other means of treatment would evolve, depending on the philosophies and theories of madness that were emerging at the time.

later, as he and I came to terms with the identities he had assumed as a mentally ill person, and as one who had self-medicated with illicit drugs.

Similar to a shunned vagrant going from place to place, when I asked colleagues and strangers alike to help my son, no one heard my call for help. Rather than receiving support, I got mixed messages. Because of Tito's late onset and due to a history of drug use, I was told that he had to have two hospitalizations to be eligible for services— one psychiatric hospitalization was not sufficient.

Professionals and laypeople alike suggested that his condition was a consequence of drug abuse. Then, after two years of moving in and out of the professional worlds of treatment for drug addiction and treatment for mental illness, Tito finally had his second major break, which led to a second hospitalization, thus giving way to the official diagnosis of schizophrenia in 1993. Later his disease was diagnosed as the undifferentiated type because it coincides with clinical depression.

Cartography of Mental Illness

Our trajectory as a family—nuclear and extended—and what I have experienced in my life as a person, as a mother, and as a professional social worker and sociologist did not even begin to help me understand the changes in my son. As his mother, I found myself questioning how I had raised him, as well as how I might have contributed to the "living hell" he contended with on a daily basis. In desperation, I allowed myself to contemplate Freud's explanations, as I examined the ways I might have distorted or contributed to Tito's condition. All along I have tagged myself as the source of his imperfection, abnormality, or pathology, because I have been socialized to do just that, to take the blame for having produced a less-than-perfect child. These sentiments and thoughts still emerge, even though I do not subscribe to such thinking.

Since Tito's diagnosis, I have scrutinized what I did while he was in gestation, mulling over my diet as well as any suppressed or repressed emotions and how those might have affected his formation.

I have combed my health records to see if in the first trimester I had influenza, which has been connected with schizophrenia, and I have found nothing.*

Inwardly, I have examined how I might have contributed to my son's grim and lifelong condition. I have nitpicked and combed every possible explanation, simultaneously finding many and none. Blaming myself, and then finding a possible link in his father's side of the family, I searched for genetic and biological explanations.

Thus far I have no answers that satisfy me, but then I recall being in labor for almost seventeen hours, and I chastise myself for my choice of natural childbirth. This is especially true when I think of the trauma Tito endured as he was born with the umbilical cord wrapped around his neck. But this is a common birthing experience. With no demonstrated links between this event and schizophrenia and no evidence of mental illness on his biological father's side, I continue to search for a cause. I stopped looking to myself for the blame but started looking among my extended family for hints of trauma that Tito might have experienced. Intuitively, I looked for hidden injuries that might have contributed to the schizophrenia. I could always find something or another (for example, the sexual molestation he suffered), but nothing certain.

With the molestation, I had something for which to blame myself. Not wanting to repeat the sins of my parents in Tito's upbringing, I refrained from physical punishment, talked out conflict, found a loving Catholic family day-care, and used non-abusive disciplinary measures. Still, he experienced sexual abuse. What kind of mother was I to have let this slip by me?

Forgiving myself for not having seen this, I pondered other contributing factors. Was it the psychological and emotional trauma of the teasing and taunting games that are known to take place among relatives and siblings? That did not seem a likely source. But I did not end the quest there. I continued to ask questions. I asked Amá to tell me if there were any locos on Juan's or her side of the family, but she did not have an answer for me. Then I learned about my great-grandfather

---

* An August 13, 2004, Associated Press article reported that there is evidence to suggest that some women who get the flu while pregnant are at higher risk of having a child who later develops schizophrenia. For additional information, see Brown et al. (2004).

Sixto's epilepsy, and I linked the possibilities to my own paternal side of the family. It is an associated condition, after all.

For a minute, I took the blame again. But the epilepsy was not sufficient evidence to link Tito's illness to my demented and sociopathic father, Juan, who so ignobly betrayed his daughters. I then focused on Juan's antisocial behavior, enabled by a culture of violence that looks the other way when girl or boy children are violated, a possible link to the disease in my paternal line.

The self-interrogations, self-doubts, and blaming continue to this day, albeit in a more informed and less judgmental way. I am still trying to make sense of it. What did I do to contribute to his condition? How could I have prevented it? Did I do all I could have done? What do I do now? There is no end in sight to the questions. Did we do or have we done all that could have been done? What kind of mother am I that I do not give up my professional life to tend to him? Am I doing all that I can to support him? These and other questions often arise for me, as I deal with and support my son's struggle to deal with a condition he will likely always have.

Despite the years, and his shuffling in and out of dozens of public and private spaces that have provided him shelter, the questions remain unanswered. Mental health professionals, whether from psychiatric or psychological points of departure, still do not agree on the treatment or circumstances of his mental condition. We still do not have any answers. And the drugs he takes both help and hurt him. They muffle the voices, but they slowly kill his body and spirit, producing side effects like diabetes and physiological consequences that turn him into a "slobbery moron," as Tito has told me time and again.

With Tito's *historia*, sharing the paths we have taken to deal with his illness, it is my hope to illustrate our struggles with mental illness. Our strength is solid, but the ebbs and flows and the contradictions that surface complicate our life paths as we cope with aging and illnesses. Our extended family can only do what they can fit into their lives. As Tito struggles with the demons, the voices, and the imagined communities, so do we. His constant calls, his need for money, his loneliness and isolation—all varying in urgency depending on his mind-set—are part of our daily lives, whether or not we engage them.

Mental illness, my family and I have learned, can happen to anyone. No one is immune to it. Any of us can be stricken with it at any time—male or female, rich or poor.*

Perceptions of the Abnormal

Los locos y los niños dicen la verdad
(Crazy people and children speak the truth)

—Old Méndez family saying

Nowhere in my memory are there stored recollections or experiences with mentally ill people. Rather, the "strange" who were part of our family and our community were integral to our surroundings. For me, when I think of mental illness, my first memory is of our next-door neighbor's mother, who was locked up in a room in the back of their house. This woman, whom I passed on my way to school, spat and lunged at anyone who walked in front of the family house. She was a source of much curiosity for me, but I never got close enough for her to harm me. She was a lonely and isolated woman who was kept under lock and key for others' safety and for her own protection. In a way, that is what medication does for Tito—it controls him.

Then there was Consuelo, *la quemada*, the "burnt one," who lost her mind when her husband set her and her house on fire. Despite that tragedy, she could still feed and tend to her kids, even if she had to beg to do it. Geno, *la cieguita*, was blind but could still deal with the limitations of her life. And don Perfecto, who was not so perfect, had a big

---

* Erving Goffman witnessed the institutionalization of madness as a patient (1961) and elaborated on spoiled identities (1976); Michel Foucault (1967) examined power and how disciplinary technologies were used to control paupers and the insane; and others, such as Thomas S. Szasz (1961) exposed the "myth of mental illness." Roy Porter (2002), who has written several texts on the topic, provided various ways for understanding mental illness. Still, there is a dearth of material about the emotional pain and the experiences that families confront, unless presented in variable forms about how expressed emotions affect the mentally ill in their relationships with their families.

glob of dark-brown fat on his neck—maybe a tumor—but that was only a guess in my child's mind.

Stories of deviants—not my family's word but my own—such as a "funny" great-grandfather on the Rodríguez side and an epileptic grandfather on the Méndez side (all on my paternal line), and their respective quirks, were part of our family legacy.

Other "abnormal types" included a shy cousin whose name translated to "savior." He was known to scurry around the long way to anywhere rather than face and greet those who passed by him, strangers and relatives alike. He did not meet our gregarious social expectations. My left-handed relatives were also perceived as odd. As *zurdos*, they were thought to be "wronged-handed" and perceived as sinister; they were associated with evil. Although I never witnessed it, I heard about relatives who had their left hand tied to their waist with a rope so they would be forced to use their right hand. No one wanted them to be aligned with the dark side or have others judge them as weird.

My early experiences with those who deviated from the norm influenced me to see others as human beings with a variety of quirks. Yet when my son became ill, all the sociocultural biases about mental illness and our society's compulsion for normalcy framed our family's and my own perception of Tito's condition. Despite having worked with families and children who had experienced mental health crises, I learned that Tito's mental illness required more than the awareness and insight I had developed to deal with others who were confronting similar difficulties. Being on the other side—dealing with clients, in a clinical setting, who suffered from brief psychosis, anorexia, and bulimia—was indescribable, but it was all-consuming to be in the inside.

Even though I was equipped to triage others, when it came to my own son, I found myself in denial. I prayed that his problem was drug related because one can recover from that, but a serious mental illness is forever. I was willing to embrace a socially accepted diagnosis over an untreatable one. Still, being the inquisitive person that I am, I sought to learn all I could about Tito's condition. I read about the illness, reviewing the most recent publications of the American Psychiatric Association's *Diagnostic and Statistical Manual of Mental Disorders*

(DSM), the psychiatric bible.* And I continued to learn and question. It is not clear how much this helped Tito or me, but to this day, I still search for answers.

Is my son really mentally ill? I keep asking myself. Initially diagnosed as schizophrenic, he is now classified as paranoid schizophrenic, undifferentiated type. Why is he classified that? Although I know and accept the answer provided by the experts, I wonder if he is really sick, because at times he is so lucid. Why is talk treatment not always part of the services he receives? Is the diabetes he has developed an outcome of the treatment he has gotten for his illness rather than an inherited condition? Why do states such as Texas fail to make the mentally ill population a priority? If we treated them the same way we treat those suffering from cancer, we would improve the lot of mentally ill people, who currently are among the most oppressed classes. What makes us prioritize one kind of disease over another?

All these questions have provided me with some insight. I have concluded that in our normalizing culture, we brand anything that steps outside our expectations as invaluable. In our systems of classification, facilitated through the DSM, we reify ideologies of normalcy in order to exercise social control over those who live on the fringes of society. Gods and demons; witches and heretics; segmented bodies, minds, and spirits; and dated discourses still inform our perceptions about mental illness (Foucault 1967).

---

* According to Mayes and Horwitz (2005), psychiatry shifted its treatment approach when "the DSM-III imported a diagnostic model from medicine," making diagnosis the benchmark for "medical practice and clinical research" (250). In their historical examination of this manual, they outline several reasons for why the DSM-III was adopted, including professional conflicts, involvement in mental health by the federal government due to its research and policymaking interests, desire to show psychiatric treatment effectiveness, and marketing needs for pharmaceutical companies to treat specific diseases (249). They argue that the publication of the DSM-III changed our perception about the "psychological causes of mental illness," shifting our notions about its symptoms and its treatment with "psychopharmacology, the use of drugs to treat mental ills." With one fell swoop, the DSM-III universalized the ways we conceptualize mental illnesses by expanding its relevance to various professional communities, including insurance companies and managed-care organizations, which could now label and "categorize people as normal or disabled, healthy or sick." Moreover, the DSM-III is "the definitive manual for measuring and defining illness and disorders, [because] it operates as mental health care's official language for clinical research, financial reimbursement, and professional expertise" (266).

As society changes and finds new ways to theorize about mental illness, so do the discourses to explain, classify, and represent them.* In the past, vagrants, the unemployed, criminals, and the mentally ill were incarcerated in asylums, left to suffer until they could (theoretically) be disciplined into becoming productive members of society (Foucault 1967). Now, although we still criminalize some mentally ill people, because of deinstitutionalization and community living, they are left to live life as homeless and wrecked souls, becoming invisible and invaluable discards. It is still only those with privilege and material wealth and power who can hide their conditions. Dreyfus and Rabinow (1982) support the notion that the mentally ill, who have little or no power, are relegated to "liminal spaces"—"at the edge but not beyond" society—so we can control and pacify them (3).

Inasmuch as genetic and biological explanations continue to situate madness inside the brain, the condition still carries dated notions about sanity. It makes us feel comforted to know that there is a place and a site, even when we assign it to the individual bodies of those who are most likely to become society's refuse. Rather than perceive it as the social problem it is, we blame the victim for his or her insanity.

Mental illness of any type renders patients to liminal spaces of invisibility. Those who have the power to determine and diagnose what it looks like are medical doctors and pharmaceutical executives deeply invested in its maintenance as a profit-making illness. They stand to lose or gain much from the medicalization of mental illness. It will not be until society turns to an approach that humanizes those who stand outside the definition of normalcy that the mentally ill will have worth. Then we will see fit to develop the necessary treatments. While scientists' chemical creations have advanced enough to numb mental illnesses, they distort the humanity of those who are mentally ill, leaving them to stew in the paranoia of their delusional thinking and in their

---

* Robert Whitaker (2002) exposes the treatment of persons with schizophrenia, concluding that these mental health patients are treated worse than similar patients in the poorest countries of the world, and possibly worse than nineteenth-century patients. His social and medical history is truly an educational text about the social category we have termed "insanity."

physical, emotional, and spiritual pain.* Because it is not *our* bodies that those wonder drugs—of whatever generation—damage, we accept the rigidity of the treatments given to those who are mentally ill. Their bodies, uncontrolled receptacles of spastic gaits, become testaments of medical puppetry. As the mentally ill gain respite from one thing, they have to live with the consequences of their treatment.

Dehumanization and classification and control of human beings still pervade our dealings with those we consider mad. So long as they do not impact our lives, we believe we can live with the consequences. We leave the mad to the medical profession, and society colludes with our denial. We deride and dismiss them as damaged humans not worthy of investment, dehumanizing each other in the process. But it does not have to be this way. We can intervene by creating alternative treatments in a holistic approach that embraces the difference in those who think and act outside the so-called norm.

---

* With a discourse that discourages the use of psychiatric medications, Peter R. Breggin and David Cohen (1999) examine the dangers of these drugs. The authors examine the consequences of their use and their adverse effects, as well as what doctors communicate to the patients who take these drugs, and they argue against their use in a vacuum—that is, without the support of a mental health expert who can treat the whole person. As they see it, "Psychiatric drugs are much more dangerous than many consumers and even physicians realize. All of these drugs produce numerous serious and potentially fatal adverse reactions, and most are capable of causing withdrawal problems that are emotionally and physically distressing. Some produce powerful physical dependence and can cause life-threatening withdrawal problems" (ix).

Works Cited

Angermeyer, Matthias C., Herbert Matschinger, and Patrick W. Corrigan. 2004. "Familiarity with Mental Illness and Social Distance from People with Schizophrenia and Major Depression: Testing a Model Using Data from a Representative Population Survey." *Schizophrenia Research* 69 (2–3): 175–82.

Aspen Education Group. 2011. *Dual Diagnosis Teens: When Drinking and Drugging Is Really Something Else*. http://aspeneducation.crchealth.com/articles/article-dual-diagnosis/. Accessed October 17, 2011.

Birnbaum, Rebecca. 2010. "My Father's Advocacy for a Right to Treatment." *Journal of the American Academy of Psychiatry and the Law Online* 38:115–23.

Blinder, Barton J., Edward J. Cumella, and Visant A. Sanathara. 2006. "Psychiatric Comorbidities of Female Inpatients with Eating Disorders." *Psychometric Medicine* 68:454–62.

Breggin, Peter R., and David Cohen. 1999. *Your Drug May Be Your Problem: How and Why to Stop Taking Psychiatric Medications*. New York: Perseus Books.

Brown, Alan S., M. D. Begg, S. Gravenstein, C. A. Schaefer, R. J. Wyatt, M. Bresnahan, V. P. Babulas, and E. S. Susser. 2004. "Serologic Evidence of Prenatal Influenza in the Etiology of Schizophrenia." *Archive of General Psychiatry* 61:774–80.

A Companion Educational Booklet for Schizophrenia: Voices of an Illness. 1994. In *The Infinite Mind*, narrated by Jason Robards. Lichtenstein Creative Media, Inc.

Davidson, Larry. 1993. "Story Telling and Schizophrenia: Using Narrative Structure in Phenomenological Research." *Humanistic Psychologist* 21 (2): 200–220.

———. 2003. *Living Outside Mental Illness: Qualitative Studies of Recovery in Schizophrenia*. New York: New York University Press.

Davidson, Larry, and David Stayner. 1999. "Loss, Loneliness, and the Desire for Love: Perspectives on the Social Lives of People with Schizophrenia." In *The Psychological and Social Impact of Disability*, edited by Robert P. Marinelli and Arthur E. Dell Orto, 220–34. New York: Springer.

Dorian, Marina, Jorge I. Ramírez García, Steven R. López, and Brenda Hernández. 2008. "Acceptance and Expressed Emotion in Mexican American Caregivers of Relatives with Schizophrenia." *Family Process* 47:216–28.

Dreyfus, Hubert L., and Paul Rabinow. 1982. *Michel Foucault: Beyond Structuralism and Hermeneutics.* 2nd ed. Chicago, IL: University of Chicago Press.

Foucault, Michel. 1967. *Madness and Civilization: A History of Madness in the Age of Reason.* Translated by Richard Howard. New York: Mentor Books.

Frank, Arthur W. 2002. "Why Study People's Stories? The Dialogical Ethics of Narrative Analysis." *International Journal of Qualitative Methods* 1 (1): Article 6. http://www.ualberta.ca/~iiqm/backissues/1_1Final/pdf/frankeng.pdf. Accessed April 18, 2012.

Friedrich, Rose Marie, Sonya Lively, and Linda M. Rubenstein. 2008. "Siblings' Coping Strategies and Mental Health Services: A National Study of Siblings of Persons with Schizophrenia." *Psychiatric Services* 59 (3): 261–67. http://journal.psychiatryonline.org.aspx?articleid=99163.

Glynn, Shirley M., Amy N. Cohen, Lisa B. Dixon, and Noosha Niv. 2013. "The Potential Impact of the Recovery Movement on Family Interventions for Schizophrenia: Opportunities and Obstacles." *Schizophrenia Bulletin* 32 (3): 451–63.

Goffman, Erving. 1961. *Asylums: Essays on the Social Situation of Mental Patients and Other Inmates.* New York: Anchor Books.

———. 1967. *Stigma: Notes on the Management of Spoiled Identity.* Englewood Cliffs, NJ: Prentice Hall.

González-Torres, Miguel Angel, Rodrigo Oraa, Maialen Aristegui, Aranzazu Fernández-Rivas, and José Guimon. 2007. "Stigma and Discrimination towards People with Schizophrenia and Their Family Members: A Qualitative Study with Focus Groups." *Social Psychiatry and Psychiatric Epidemiology* 42:14–23.

Hayward, Mark, Jo van Os, Theresa Dorey, and Joanna Denney. 2009. "Relating Therapy for People Who Hear Voices: A Case Series." *Clinical Psychology and Psychotherapy* 16 (3): 216–27.

Hubl, Daniela, Thomas Koenig, Werner Strik, Andrea Federspiel, Roland Kreis, Chris Boesch, Stephan E. Maier, Gerhard Schroth, Karl Lovblad, and Thomas Dierks. 2004. "Pathways that Make Voices: White Matter Changes in Auditory Hallucinations." *Archives of General Psychiatry* 6 (7): 658–68.

Huey, Leighton Y., Harriet P. Lefley, David L. Shearn, and Cynthia A. Wainscott. 2007. "Families and Schizophrenia: The View from Advocacy." *Psychiatric Clinics of North America* 30 (3): 549–66.

Hyde, Thomas M., Amy Deep-Soboslay, Bianca Iglesias, Joseph H. Callicott, James M. Gold, Andreas Meyer-Lindenberg, Robyn A. Honea, Llewellyn B. Bigelow, Michael F. Egan, Esther M. Emsellem, and Daniel R. Weinberger. 2008. "Enuresis as a Premorbid Developmental Marker of Schizophrenia." *Brain* 131 (9): 2489–98.

Insel, Thomas R. 2010. "Rethinking Schizophrenia." *Nature* 468:187–93.

Jenkins, Janis, Marvin Karno, Aurora de la Selva, and Felipe Santana. 1986. "Expressed Emotion in Cross-Cultural Context: Familial Responses to Schizophrenic Illness among Mexican-Americans." In *Treatment of Schizophrenia: Family Assessment and Intervention*, edited by Michael Goldstein, Iver Hand, and Kurt Hahlweg, 35–49. New York: Springer.

Jeste, Dilip, Owen M. Wolkowitz, and Barton W. Palmer. 2011. "Diverse Trajectories of Physical, Cognitive, and Psychosocial Aging in Schizophrenia." *Schizophrenia Bulletin* 37 (3): 451–55.

Katschnig, Heinz. 2000. "Schizophrenia and Quality of Life." *Acta Psychiatrica Scandinavica* 102, Issue Supplement s407: 33–37.

Kellerman, Henry, ed. 2009. *The Dictionary of Psychopathology*. New York: Columbia University Press.

Kopelowicz, Alex, Robert Paul Liberman, and Donald Stolar. 2011. "Schizophrenia and Sexuality." *Armenian Medical Network*. http://www.health.am/psy/more/schizophrenia-and-sexuality. Accessed June 12, 2013.

Kruszelnicki, Karl S. 2012. "Can a Full Moon Affect Behaviours?" *Dr. Karl's Great Moments in Science*, March. http://www.abc.net.au/science/articles/2012/03/27/3464601.htm. Accessed October 19, 2012.

Kruzich, Jean M. 1985. "Community Integration of the Mentally Ill in Residential Facilities." *American Journal of Community Psychology* 13 (5): 553–64.

Kumary, Veena, and Peggy Postma. 2005. "Nicotine Use in Schizophrenia: The Self-Medication Hypotheses." *Neuroscience & Behavioral Review* 29 (6): 1021–34.

Lacan, Jacques. 1988. *The Seminar of Jacques Lacan*. Book 2, *The Ego in Freud's Theory and in the Technique of Psychoanalysis, 1945–1955*. Edited by Jacques-Alain Miller. Translated by Sylvana Tomaselli. Cambridge, UK: Cambridge University Press.

Macraven, Vincent. 2011. *Tales from the Mind of a Schizophrenic*. United States: Xlibris.

Mayes, Rick, and Allan Victor Horwitz. 2005. "DSM-III and the Revolution in the Classification of Mental Illness." *Journal of the History of the Behavioral Sciences* 41 (3): 249–67. Wiley Interscience. http://www.interscience.wiley.com.

Moberg, Paul J., and Bruce I. Turetsky. 2003. "Scent of a Disorder: Olfactory Functioning in Schizophrenia." *Current Psychiatry Reports* 5:311–19.

Mortimer, Ann M. 2013. "Another Triumph of Hope over Experience? Revisiting . . . Treatment of the Patient with Long-Term Schizophrenia." *Advances in Psychiatric Treatment*, July 2004. http://apt.rcpsych.org/content/14/4/277.

Mueser, Kim T., and Susan Gingerich. 2006. *The Complete Family Guide to Schizophrenia*. New York: Guildford Press.

Mukherjee, Sy. 2013. "How Mentally Ill Americans Are Falling through the Cracks in the Social Safety Net." http://thinkprogress.org/health/2013/04/08/1834261/mentally-ill-americans-medicaid/?mobile=nc. Accessed April 11, 2013.

Pies, Ronald. 1999. "How Families Can Cope with Schizophrenia." WebMD feature. http://www.webmd.com/schizophrenia/features/families-cope-schizophrenia. Accessed April 19, 2011.

Porter, Roy. 2002. *Madness: A Brief History*. New York: Oxford University Press.

Ramírez, Jorge I., Christina L. Chang, Joshua S. Young, Steven R. López, and Janis H. Jenkins. 2006. "Family Support Predicts Psychiatric Medication Usage among Mexican American Individuals with Schizophrenia." *Social Psychology and Psychiatric Epidemiology* 41:642–31.

Read, John, Jim van Os, Anthony P. Morrison, and Colin A. Ross. 2005. "Childhood Trauma, Psychosis and Schizophrenia: A Literature Review with Theoretical and Clinical Implications." *Acta Psychiatrica Scandinavica* 112 (5): 330–50.

Scharts, Bernard, and John V. Flowers. 2010. *How to Fail as a Therapist: 50+ Ways to Lose or Damage Your Patients*. Atascadero, CA: Impact Publishers.

Siris, Samuel G. 1995. "Depression in Schizophrenia." In *Contemporary Issues in the Treatment of Schizophrenia*, edited by Christian L. Shriqui and Henry A. Nasrallah, 155–56. Arlington, VA.: American Psychiatric Press.

Silberner, Joanne. 2012. "Alzheimer's Patients Turn to Stories Instead of Memories." http://www.npr.org/blogs/health/2012/05/14/152442084/alzheimers-patients-turn-to-stories-instead-of-memories. Accessed May 15, 2012.

Soyka, Michael. 1996. "Dual Diagnosis in Patients with Schizophrenia: Issues in Pharmacological Treatment." *CNS Drugs* 5 (6): 414–25.

Szasz, Thomas S. 1961. *The Myth of Mental Illness: Foundations of a Theory of Personal Conduct.* New York: Harper Books.

Taylor, Vanessa. 2011. "Schizophrenic Break." http://www.schizophrenic.com. Accessed April 18, 2011.

Weisman, Amy G., Steven R. López, Marvin Karno, and Janis Jenkins. 1993. "An Attributional Analysis of Expressed Emotion in Mexican-American Families with Schizophrenia." *Journal of Abnormal Psychology* 102 (4): 601–6.

Whitaker, Robert. 2002. *Mad in America: Bad Science, Bad Medicine, and the Enduring Mistreatment of the Mentally Ill.* New York: Perseus Publishing.